CHANGING VIEWS
OF THE HUMAN CONDITION

CHANGING VIEWS
OF THE HUMAN CONDITION

edited by

Paul W. Pruyser

MERCER

ISBN 0-86554-229-5

The paper used in this publication meets
the minimum requirements of American National Standard
for Information Sciences—Permanence of Paper
for Printed Library Materials, ANSI Z39.48-1984.

Library of Congress Cataloging-in-Publication Data
Changing views of the human condition.

Includes bibliographies and index.
1. Man (Christian theology)   2. Philosophical
anthropology.   3. Social   psychology.   I. Pruyser,
Paul W.
BT701.2.C42   1987   233   86-31067
ISBN 0-86554-229-5 (alk. paper)

CONTENTS

Grateful acknowledgment
is made to

LAWRENCE RACHUBA

for his financial support
of this publication

PREFACE

•●•

The sponsors of the enterprise that produced this book were two: the Institute for Ecumenical and Cultural Research and the Institute for Religion and Human Development, both located in Collegeville, Minnesota. These two institutes recognized their common quest for a dialogue between persons knowledgeable in the Christian tradition and those knowledgeable in the social sciences—persons who had been challenged to new understandings of what it is to be human because of their faith and their work as scholars, scientists, or practitioners. The participants in the dialogue came from different religious traditions. Most were from the Christian tradition, yet a spectrum of denominations was represented.

The Institute for Ecumenical and Cultural Research was established to study and promote the growth of ecumenical Christianity among the many churches. Its perspective is derived from understanding the relation of ecumenical Christianity to culture, society, and the individual. The institute was begun in 1967 by Father Kilian McDonnell, O.S.B., of Saint John's Abbey, and operates as an independent institution on the campus of St. John's. The Institute for Religion and Human Development, founded in 1954 as the Institute for Mental Health, has as its purpose the bringing together of psychiatrists (i.e., mental-health professionals) and clergy (i.e., pastors and ministers) to share concerns about the people in their care. Its goal is to articulate the relation of Christianity to psychiatry and the meaning of this relationship for both.

In gauging the hospitality of such institutes, one is naturally drawn to the Benedictine atmosphere of contemplation at Saint John's. Thomas Merton's words, written concerning the Institute for Mental Health but applicable to both institutes, states the matter well:

> Isolated in woodlands between two quiet lakes, Saint John's is a center of study, prayer, education and the liturgical apostolate. . . . One of the most interesting facets of the apostolate at Saint John's is made evident by the workshops on Pastoral Care and Psychotherapy carried on during the summer. Here Catholic priests from the secular clergy and the religious orders, together with ministers of various Protestant denominations, gather for instructive sessions conducted by outstanding psychiatrists and psychoanalysts from all parts of the country. So much active zeal and fruitful labor does nothing to alter the fundamentally Benedictine character of the life of our American abbeys. . . . The atmosphere remains that of a truly Benedictine community, knit together by

the charity of Christ and the spirit of humility and prayer which are essential to the Order.

The ecumenical experience of both institutes confirmed for the participants in the present enterprise the truism that in our present world questions concerning the human condition are universal. We found much value in drawing upon the knowledge and insight developed by any number of disciplines: history, philosophy, sociology, psychology, psychiatry, language, and theology. From these we sought to forge answers to our many questions, prompted by the dislocations in thought and culture we experience in our postmodern world. We present our thoughts here as individuals who have been challenged by the postmodern age and who have been chastened by an interdisciplinary discussion of the question: In the postmodern American world, what can perspectives gained from psychology, sociology, philosophy, and theology contribute toward understanding the human condition?

No one will be more satisfied than the authors when a further treatment of this same subject appears and supersedes the modest beginnings here made.

A. W. R. Sipe　　　　　　　　　　　　　　　　　　*Robert S. Bilheimer*
Baltimore, Maryland　　　　　　　　　　　　　*Collegeville, Minnesota*

CHAPTER ONE

A Transformational Understanding of Humanity

——————— • ● • ———————

PAUL W. PRUYSER

The deliberately ambiguous title of this book is meant to provoke questions. Does the title mean that views of the human condition are or have been changing and, if so, in what direction? Or does the title enjoin the readers to change their own and other people's views of the human condition—people for whom they may have some responsibility as pastors, educators, advisors, counselors, or supervisors? The answer is yes to both questions, and the book derives its content and format from both affirmations.

The book seeks to inform as well as challenge its readers no less than its writers were informed and challenged when, assembled as a task force by the two collaborating institutes at St. John's University, they were presented with a tersely worded question:

> Can what the Jewish and Christian traditions know about the human condition be put in genuinely reciprocal relation to basic dimensions of modern social-scientific knowledge of the human condition, for the enrichment of both?

Behind this question lie, of course, a number of observations or impressions. One of these is that views of the human condition have undergone drastic changes since the Enlightenment, most notably in the twentieth century. Another one is that Judeo-Christian lore and parlance about the human condition are still saturated with pre-Enlightenment ideas that put them at variance with modern notions derived from the sciences and humanities, including more recent theological reflections. Still another observation is that the various polarizations that beset the churches—such as liberalism versus conservatism, privatism versus social activism, modernism versus fundamentalism, clergy versus laity—have a bearing on views of the human condition. Each group sounds a different chord when it addresses such questions as "What is the human being?" and "What is God?" Reigning ideas and leading symbols that once seem to have unified Christian believers now seem to set them further apart. Each one's basic assumptions lead to different conjectures and produce strikingly different vocabularies. This in turn causes mutual disaffection, if not a Babel-like crisis.

A CRISIS CALLS FOR A FRESH LOOK

There can hardly be any doubt that within the Judeo-Christian tradition some long-simmering differences of opinion about human nature and the nature of God have today come to a boil. Among large segments of believers there is an awareness of being in a crisis. For many it is an intellectual crisis at least, and for some it is a crisis of faith as well. The crisis we seek to address in this book is not the conventionally alleged conflict between religion and science, but an altogether different crisis felt to exist *among* and *between* believers who are at odds with each other because they make dissimilar basic assumptions about humankind and God and seem increasingly unable to converse rationally with one another. In crisis situations people are prone to do unreasonable things, such as hardening their respective positions and becoming ever more suspicious of each other, which makes the crisis awareness more acute and dims any hope of resolution. Caught between awareness of crisis and the realization that no satisfying resolution is forthcoming, one is bound to react with a painfully mixed sense of urgency and impotence. An arduous, if not laborious, task lies ahead that will require information sharing among diverse experts as well as the overcoming of cognitive and emotional blockages.

Despite these difficulties, but with a sense of urgency, the subsequent chapters of this book seek to describe significant facets of the crisis situation in which believers find themselves and to contribute to its mitigation. What energizes and guides our efforts is the belief that such crises as the one we have defined should not be accepted as unwelcome, inevitable nuisances, but should be regarded as spurs by which the spirit—human and divine—incites people toward growth. The history of religion as well as the history of the sciences and humanities are full of such crises of understanding and faith, which have proven to be the harbingers of creative advances in people's appreciation of God, their knowledge of the universe, their enjoyment of beauty, their discernment in making moral decisions and, not least, their valuation of themselves as creatures who count in the destiny of the cosmos.

In the meantime something has been learned about intellectual crises that will stand us in good stead. In his work on the history of scientific revolutions, Kuhn (1970) introduces the terms *paradigm* and *paradigm shift* to describe what happens when a well-entrenched model of understanding becomes exhausted, meets with disenchantment, and is slowly (or more suddenly) being discarded, entailing a period of tension that will abate only when some inventive mind formulates an alternative model that can hold the fascination of theoreticians and researchers in some particular scientific domain. A paradigm is a prevailing vision to which workers in a field commonly subscribe if it has explanatory value and leads to fruitful hypotheses from which new knowledge can be gained. "Normal science," as Kuhn calls it, is conducted under the aegis of a prevailing paradigm. Science is periodically in a crisis situation, which occurs when an old paradigm fades and a new paradigm has yet to be introduced. For instance, a paradigm shift occurred when scientists moved, with considerable crisis awareness, from the particle theory to the wave theory of light. Another paradigm shift occurred in the neurosciences when the telephone switchboard model of the brain was replaced by a computer model and when awareness of the enormous role of unconscious data processing led to a diminished view of man's hitherto extolled rationality. But these shifts are commonly not as neat or sharp as these lines suggest. Frequently there are periods in which paradigms proliferate and cause prolonged confusion in which little progress is made.

Taking a cue from such descriptions of the scientific process, we propose that the commonly called Judeo-Christian "doctrine of man," along with its reciprocal doctrine of God (for the two always stand in a dialectical relation to each other), have been undergoing important paradigm shifts for some time, most significantly in our century. But many of the describable paradigm shifts have not met with a wide consensus; we must acknowledge that far from being involved in a lengthy period of "normal" unanimity about this doctrine, we have been in a protracted crisis period about it, with proposed new paradigms abounding though not producing a widely accepted paradigm *shift*. Only limited groups of believers have managed to make significant shifts in their constructions about the human condition, and even among them there are all kinds of selectivities, if not sharp disagreements.

Moreover, it stands to reason that such an encompassing idea as a "Christian doctrine of humanity" is bound to be skewed by national, ethnic, local, and sexist traditions. For instance, American churches share a predominantly white, anthropological vision charged with local ideas about human capacities, ideals, and destiny; this vision is heavily colored by pragmatic, utilitarian, and individualistic philosophies, and still bears conspicuous traces of the frontier experience. Over these ideas arched, from the earliest days in Christian terms and later in secular terms, a sense of destiny expressed at first in phrases such as "New Israel," then in "Manifest Destiny," and later in "Leader of the Free World," which were adopted by secular historians and church historians alike. To the extent that this traditional American anthropology functioned as a doctrine of humanity among American Christians, the latter were forced to live with unresolved and possibly irresolvable contradictions between their local vision and the image they found themselves celebrating in their Bible-based creeds and liturgies.

This American anthropology has begun to crumble in the last part of our century, much as its European counterparts came apart in the first half of the twentieth century. It could not withstand the onslaught of change, and the morality built upon it became powerless. Nor could this traditional image develop viable answers to man-made catastrophes with which our century has been afflicted and the even more dire nuclear holocaust that now threatens to be unleashed.

Given this situation, the two collaborating institutes at St. John's envisaged the possibility that a process of serious reflection and dialogue among scholars in the social sciences and in the theological disciplines and philosophy might lead to some clarification of what Christian anthropology is or should be, at least in its most basic dimensions. The institutes felt also that the moment for launching this endeavor was quite propitious since, despite growing constructive discourse between social scientists and religionists, and active organizational collaboration between social-science consultants and church leaders, no broad attempt to reexamine the current status of knowledge and conviction about the human condition had lately been undertaken. Moreover, as the question that launched this endeavor tacitly suggested, the members of the task force were supposed to use their respective forms of expertise without standing pat on its ultimate truth. They would seek to enrich one another's frameworks and allow themselves to be edified by the different perspectives of others. They were to undergo some growth experience themselves by moving from multidisciplinary discourse to interdisciplinary and, when needed, transdisciplinary thought.

A LESSON
FROM THE HELPING PROFESSIONS:
TRANSFORMATIONAL KNOWLEDGE

Given considerable freedom of operation, including the early exploration of what would eventually prove to be blind alleys, the members of the task force soon made some discoveries that had an impact on the strategies and content of their thought. For instance, it slowly became apparent that in the formal Christian tradition, theologians and philosophers had been preoccupied with describing *adult* personality or an *ideal mature* personality in their doctrines. Such ideas as transformation, metanoia, and conversion, and the distinctions between the Old Adam and the New Adam figure appear in traditional theological writings mostly at the adult level, with little if any consideration of the childhood that must have preceded the adult level being addressed. The so-called formative years of personality and selfhood are in no way prominent in classical writings about the human condition, except for pedagogical treatises advocating moralistic drill. On the other hand, modern psychologists and developmentalists have long been preoccupied with the early formation of personality and selfhood, often focusing on the possible pathology of selfhood (e.g., in autism, narcissism, hedonism, impulsivity) without paying equal attention to the growth processes that occur in the adult years. Only lately has the notion of aging been revised to allow for continuous maturational processes.

It was also discovered in dialogue that the psychodynamic theories of human development do not see the individual as an encapsulated entity as is often alleged, but rather as necessarily and naturally embedded in a social matrix. In fact, a long and deep trend in psychodynamic thought since Freud sees the individual as a microscopic, internalized "little society" in which various more-or-less personified psychic parties interact with each other. Our dreams and fantasies as well as the workings of conscience often proceed as if the mind were an internal stage on which people jostle and argue with each other.

It was found that sociology and social psychology mediate somewhat between the adult preoccupation of classical theology and the childhood preoccupation of developmental psychology by actually addressing the whole life span. They also mediate between conceptions of groups and conceptions of individuals; for instance, role theory describes not only the adaptations that people must make to their society, but also the formative influence that society exerts on personality and selfhood.

But one of the bigger discoveries made was that a great deal of theological and social-scientific work is focused on *understanding and bringing about change* (Pruyser, 1976, 1979). Both groups of disciplines have not only academic but eminently pedagogical aims that are in the service of promoting change in people—whether in individuals, families, small groups, large groups, masses, or combinations of all these.

It has always been the business of the religiotheological enterprise to *transform* people, not just to *know* what people are. The same holds true for psychiatry and a good portion of psychology and sociology, whose practitioners are always under pressure from urgent needs to make meliorative interventions—even when basic knowledge is shaky or lacking. The professional members of these disciplines—pastors, religious educators, psychiatrists, counselors, psychotherapists, social problem solvers and social policy makers—derive a great deal of their allegedly "basic science" knowledge not from impeccable theories but from practical engagements in which they often have to make innovative decisions, not infrequently by intuition. As practitioners, they are trained in or gifted with a special form of knowledge: it merits being called *transformational knowledge*. Transformational knowledge does not stem from pure, disinterested contemplation but is steeped in urgently needed meliorative—remedial, medicinal, salvational, rescuing—action.

Transformational knowledge is not based on the assumption that everything is malleable or fluid. There are limits to change, certainly over short time spans. Experience teaches us that nature, and thus also human nature, has structure and that there are in every complex entity or event both constant and variable factors. But it is today widely held in the social sciences as well as in the biological disciplines that structure and function influence each other and that the separation of these two is an artifact of our human thought processes. Unused structures succumb to atrophy; overused structures may become hypertrophic. Personality structures are heavily influenced and to some extent formed by personal experiences in early childhood, no matter how crystallized and constant they may appear to be during later years. One resolution to the old structure-versus-function and stability-versus-change dilemmas was offered by Rapaport, who said: "Structures are processes of a slow rate of change" (Gill 1967, 787). Though this formulation gives the edge to change, it is an important correction of older views that were too static. Given the prolonged preoccupation with constants in human nature, especially in classical theological writings, now is the time to pay equal attention to the variable factors and at least feel free to modify the "hard" versions of the human condition.

Our perception of this transformational knowledge base that operates in the helping professions[1] and in the disciplines represented on the task force led us to take stock of all knowledge and formulate some basic epistemological principles that could guide our discourse. We approximated a consensus on the following points:

1. Reality and its composition are better conceived as dynamic processes than as entities related by mechanical laws.

2. Each of the organized disciplines (sciences, humanities, theology, arts) can be taken as a systematized perspective on reality.

3. The mind of man is capable of freely assuming various perspectives; it is inherently pluralistic though of variable span.

4. All disciplines deal with reality—but on their own terms, by virtue of their unique conceptions, specific applications, acquired skills, and particular language games.

5. Nothing is anything in particular until it is placed in a particular perspective, subjected to particular operations, and caught up in a particular language game.

---

[1]The term *helping professions* is of fairly recent origin and refers broadly, maybe somewhat loosely, to disciplines whose practitioners are engaged in rendering personal services to people in need of special help, advice, counsel, or intervention. Typical instances are health and nursing care; legal advice; social support; counsel in preparing for marriage, or in dealing with divorce, bereavement, or child rearing; and the various forms of crisis intervention. Hence a considerable portion of pastoral work falls within this rubric. The various helping professions influence one another by mutual instruction in their basic theories and in their diverse techniques of helping, and frequently operate collaboratively.

6. All disciplines seek to transcend common sense; they are, in fact, critiques of common sense.
7. Many critical modern thinkers are weary of hierarchical models of the disciplines. They accept open-endedness (as an implication of perspectivalism), and enjoy the thrill of quest rather than find. Suggestions about "ultimate reality" are not in vogue, or are entertained only in a religiously modest spirit that leads to the position of letting God be God and accepting one's creaturely limitations.

The special point at which we arrived is that different disciplines have different tenors. The disciplines known today as the helping professions as well as those traditionally seen as the pedagogical (or even "agogical") professions stand apart from other disciplines by the *sense of urgency* evident in their pursuits. These disciplines or professions typically seek to understand and promote change—in persons or various social units—from an undesirable condition to one that is held to be superior. They address conditions considered "crises"or characterized by shortcoming, defect, insufficiency, primitivity, malady, sinfulness, captivity, oppression, etcetera, *seeking to transform these conditions* by making *interventions* that are aimed at their *improvement*. The praxis of these professions counts heavily in the vocational choice, motivation, and actual engagements of most of their members. The members of these professions typically preach, teach, heal, guide, counsel, organize movements, lead community efforts, influence the body politic, propose legislation, and so forth. In these activities they may lean on concepts and precepts from their various traditions, but more often than not they have to be inventive because much of their work is instigated by a sense of urgency. Something has to be done—now!—to relieve people in crisis.

We contend that the kind of knowledge that the transformational disciplines use in their efforts to intervene is a peculiar amalgam, different from the methodical knowledge used in the hypothetico-deductive, laboratory-based, "hard" sciences as well as from the "deep" or "pure" knowledge sought by the humanities in their academic and scholarly pursuits. Members of the transformational disciplines are always faced with the "messy" aspects of human life in which somebody is hurting or hurts others.

To put it synoptically, transformational knowledge or thought is characterized by the following:

1. Transformational knowledge is *in the service* of bringing about change, at any relevant level.
2. Transformational knowledge is derived in large part from, in some cases, centuries of interventions in a variety of untoward situations.
3. Transformational knowledge emerges from professional traditions that abound with intuitive and often ad hoc moves or interventions that later become stylized as transmissable skills.

4. All developed professional disciplines are complex "packages" of (a) basic science(s), (b) ancillary science(s), (c) applied science(s), (d) techniques or skills, and (e) a language game. Textbooks in most disciplines usually take the student from the basic science to the applied science and skill aspect, as if to suggest that knowledge trickles down from theories to applications. The peculiarity of transformational disciplines is that knowledge largely "trickles" upward from sometimes adventitious doings to the basic science level, at which the praxis becomes rationalized and legitimated. Outstanding examples are medicine, the cure of souls, pedagogy, and certain types of public policy making.

5. Transformational knowledge is inherently meliorative; it seeks betterment.

Theoretically, then, transformational knowledge speaks to processes of change from one condition to another, always entails a praxis, and takes the relations between any discipline's basic and applied science aspects and its techniques or skills as a dialectical one.

To illustrate, let us focus on a living and complex reality that increasingly holds the center stage in the attention of the helping professions and indeed in this book: the human self. Though it has proven to be exceedingly difficult to define the self to everyone's satisfaction, there is no dearth of selective partial knowledge about the self gained from distinct professional perspectives. Physicians know about any self's state of sickness or health; pastors and moral theologians know much about human vices and virtues. Indeed, much of the accumulated practical and theoretical knowledge about the self is couched in terms that bespeak a polarization between an undesirable and a desirable state, with the gap between these two bridged by the various ministrations that the helping professions have to offer.

A brief inventory of these polarities and the direction of desirable changes could be made as follows:

sickness	health
ignorance	knowledge
vice	virtue
sin	redemption
alienation	participation
symbiotic diffuseness	integration
damnation	salvation
nihilism	faith
callousness	concern
hate	love
fruitless compulsivity	creativity
slavery	liberty
stultification	spontaneity
selfishness	altruism

Precisely because the second condition (if reached) is grafted onto the first, the possibility of regression will remain; moreover, owing to the polarization of each dimension there always will be ambiguity.

One may ask whether any of the conceivable transformations partake of one or more overruling qualities of experience. Our hunch is that, in the example given, any move in any dimension has the effect of increasing an individual's or group's felt sense of freedom. If so, the list is also an inventory of the multiple parameters of freedom.

PROMISING MODELS FOR ADDRESSING CHANGE

So much for the general insights that members of the task force gained from earnestly listening to and conversing with one another. To gain such insights (often initiated by just one member of the group) typically entails also an informed judgment of the work still to be done. When insights lead to a fair degree of consensus, let alone enthusiastic affirmation, an intellectual camaraderie is engendered in which the technical expertise of each group member comes into its own and tends to achieve an acceptable form.

Traditional views of the human condition have tended to focus on its allegedly essential, if not substantive, features. Theological formulations that are grafted onto the biblical story of the Fall and the expulsion from paradise introduce the idea of transformation explicitly by stressing both the corruption and the need for regeneration of human beings. This idea implies transformability but subsequently opens up new questions about the agent that transforms: is it human or divine? However these questions are answered, the gist of liturgical and pastoral activity is to enhance desirable transformations, to help people move, always with a degree of urgency, from their fallen state to a renewed condition in closer harmony with the intentions of their Creator. Theology, then, takes the *need* for change as a constant factor in human nature.

In the following chapters of this book, the writers will selectively assume and define certain constants in the human condition without pretending that their suggestions constitute a tight package on whose contents everyone agrees. Some will stress "response-ability" to God's ethical demands, incompleteness, and the stamp of the *imago dei* as constant features of the human condition. Others will call attention to embodiment—the fact that one is either male or female. A degree of rationality and the capacity for self-questioning and ethical concern will be singled out. Still others will stress contingency as an earmark of the human condition. The presence of erotic and aggressive drives and built-in instruments for self-regulation will be noted, and much prominence will be given to human interrelatedness and social embeddedness. Nevertheless, these assumed invariable determinants of the human condition also will be shown to have diverse manifestations subject to spontaneous or assisted transformations.

From the many criticisms that have been leveled against the traditional substantive view of human nature, we are most impressed by those that derive from organismic thought, process thought, and dynamic thought. To put the basis of these criticisms and their alternatives all too briefly, organismic thinkers have convincingly argued that human beings are not stable entities with fixed characteristics, but rather are versatile, adaptive, and to a high degree self-regulating organisms equipped with a multitude of coping devices by which they can address various impinging external and internal changes and maintain individual integrity. The human being is not a machine, not even a very intricate one. People are materially not stable; their internal substances and the external substances of their environment are in a constant state of turnover. Process thinkers have maintained that becoming overrules being and that the essence of the whole universe is a process of transformations in which things as well as organisms are caught up. In principle, every happening anywhere in the cosmos affects all its constituent subprocesses ("parts," we ordinarily say), and conversely, the whole cosmos has to reckon with any change in its multitude of "members." Everything, including people, is in evolution. And God is an involved participant in that evolutionary process, if not its designer, fulfiller, and telos. Dynamic thought has attested that people are bundles of energy, constantly absorbing, transmitting, transforming, and giving off dynamic pulsations; and that the vital processes of life—from digestive, respiratory, and other vegetative functions, to perceptual and motoric process, and on to conceptual, imaginative, moral, aesthetic, and other symbolic functions—are better seen as plays of force and counterforce than as static structures.

In one way or another, the subsequent chapters in this book will tie in with these new paradigms about human nature. More than that, the diverse perspectives from which selective dimensions of human nature will be approached will actively foster the use of these organismic—process—dynamic visions, if only for the resulting heuristic richness of the arguments. One of our task-force members reminded us of the slogan of the World Futurist Congress in Toronto (1981-1982), which exhorted us to "think globally, act locally, and think newly."

REFERENCES

———————————— • ● • ————————————

Gill, M. M. 1967. *The Collected Papers of David Rapaport.* New York: Basic Books.

Kuhn, T. S. 1970. *The Structure of Scientific Revolutions.* 2d ed. International Encyclopedia of Unified Science, 2:2. Chicago: University of Chicago Press.

Pruyser, P. W. 1976. *The Minister as Diagnostician.* Philadelphia: Westminster Press.

_____. 1979. *The Psychological Examination.* New York: International Universities Press.

CHAPTER TWO

Kingdom, Creation, and Covenant: The Human Condition in Biblical and Theological Perspective

—————•●•—————

THEODORE RUNYON

Biblical anthropologies have traditionally emphasized the doctrine of creation and the doctrine of the Fall. Mankind was made in the image of God and then abruptly fell through the connivance of the serpent. These are two classical cornerstones of biblical thought about the nature and destiny of mankind. Theodore Runyon notes that several modern theological trends, including liberation theology, combine to form a paradigm shift in the Christian conception of humanity. The present emphasis is an eschatological one that singles out the motif of the kingdom of God—itself a further elaboration of the Hebrew idea of the covenant, which in turn was anticipated in the act of creation: "Let us make men. . . . "

Runyon's reassessment of the importance and relevance of classical biblical motifs entails a revised view of the human self in the divine plan. Former conceptions accentuated the saved individual (or soul) as the gospel's message; presently evolving conceptions stage a redeemed social order in which individuals gain grace by their participation in reconciled relationships. The biblical message is not elitist in the sense of holding out redemption of some few favored souls; it points to a future for all human beings in a transformed world. The human selves emerging in such a world will be different from those reared under conditions of selfishness, competitiveness, and oppression.

To attempt to identify *the* Christian theological understanding of human nature today is to focus on a moving target. Most traditional theological analyses drew their major inspiration from the biblical stories of origins, the stories of creation and fall. These motifs have for centuries provided rich thematic materials to describe doctrinally and artistically both the divine origins of the race and the ambiguity of the human creature, whose capacities for freedom and creativity on the one hand and evil and corruption on the other are evident.

Another motif closely linked with creation and fall is covenant. For the biblical writers, both the original calling of humankind in creation and the original sin of humanity in the Fall are to be viewed within the larger framework of the covenant relation to God. The motif of covenant sets forth the basic relationality in terms of what it means to be human. Without it none of the other categories can properly be understood.

However, two of the most influential theological movements today, the theology of hope and the Latin American theologies of liberation, propose a different starting point for analyzing the human condition. Taking their cue from the priority Jesus gives to the theme of the coming kingdom of God, they see this kingdom as the context within which everything else, including human nature and society, must be viewed.[1] Moreover, they understand that the kingdom Jesus anticipated was not interpreted by him as otherworldly but as a renewal of the earth. Divine justice and love will penetrate and transform this world until "the kingdoms of this world are become the kingdoms of our Lord and of his Christ; and he shall reign for ever and ever" (Rev. 11:15). How would our understanding of human nature be changed, ask the liberation theologians, if the fundamental angle from which we view humankind were not the past but the future, not what has been but what, by God's grace and the power of the Spirit, can be?[2]

---

[1]Cf. Jürgen Moltmann's now-classic *Theology of Hope* (New York: Harper, 1967) and Jon Sobrino's *Christology at the Crossroads* (Maryknoll NY: Orbis, 1978). In one sense eschatology is by no means a recent theological discovery. The kingdom of God played an important role as an ideal in post-World War I liberal theology, and H. Richard Niebuhr analyzed the historic significance of the doctrine in his *The Kingdom of God in America* and *Christ and Culture*. Yet for most Americans eschatology remained associated with otherworldliness and premillennialism. And the theme of the 1954 Evanston Assembly of the World Council of Churches, "Christ, the Hope of the World" (cf. the preparatory materials in *The Christian Hope and the Task of the Church* [New York: Harper, 1954]), seemed abstract and passive for Americans who were accustomed to the activist approach to all problems. The relevance of eschatology and hope therefore did not become apparent until the recalcitrance of both national and international problems had dissipated all natural and easy optimism.

[2]Cf. Jose Miguez Bonino, *Doing Theology in a Revolutionary Situation* (Philadelphia: Fortress Press, 1975) 132-53.

It seems obvious that any attempt to do justice to current theological understandings of human nature must take seriously the perspectives introduced by the theologies of hope and liberation. To fail to do so would be to continue to define humanity in provincial Western European and American terms. At the same time no theological interpretation can neglect the traditional themes of creation, Fall, and covenant, for this combination lends depth to and makes for a more comprehensive and convincing picture of the human condition.

Nevertheless, the methodological point of the liberationists is well taken. It does make a difference where one starts. If we begin where theology traditionally has begun, by tracing the dismal history of the race from its origins down through the ages (as does St. Paul in Rom. 1:18-3:18), we will doubtlessly be impressed not only by the persistence of human sinfulness but by the impossibility of doing anything about it and the unlikelihood of any improvement in the future.[3] Such an analysis unfortunately lends itself to use by conservative forces in society as a theological argument against any change. The motivation for change is undermined by the solemn reminder that every reform, every alternative form of human organization, will be subject to the same original sin that infests the present order. "Better be content with the evils we know," counsels the voice of realism, "rather than risk the new evils that would be introduced by change." Such a reading, however, turns a theological analysis all too readily into an ideology to reinforce and support the status quo, and in so doing robs the future of its promise.

THE TURN TOWARD THE FUTURE

If we begin instead with "the kingdom of God and his righteousness" and make this the starting point for our interpretation of human nature, the results may be quite different. If, rather than focusing on origin and first cause, we turn our attention to the final cause and the power of the "absolute future" to change the present—as does Catholic theologian Karl Rahner—the results may be quite different. This is not to deny the continued conditioning and even determinism exercised by the past. The effects of genetic makeup, social environment, and past experience never can be denied. Yet a doctrine that takes seriously the power of the kingdom will see persons and society not simply as the result of past conditioning but as in process, subject to the freeing effect of future possibilities. The future can also "condition," and does so in such a way as to break open otherwise rigidly determined situations. The philosopher Ernst Bloch calls this "the ontology of the not yet," the power of that which does not yet exist to transform present things. From a Christian standpoint this is an analogy to the creativity of the God who

---

[3]Cf. Karl Barth's commentary on this section of the epistle in *The Epistle to the Romans* (New York: Oxford University Press, 1933) 42-91.

"summons things that are not yet in existence as if they already were" (Rom. 4:16, NEB). Therefore, "hope alone is to be called 'realistic,' " writes Protestant theologian Jürgen Moltmann, "because it alone takes seriously the possibilities with which all reality is fraught. It does not take things as they happen to stand or to lie, but as progressing, moving things with possibilities of change."[4]

In similar fashion the Latin American theologians of liberation turn to the future, to the kingdom of God, as their starting point. Where did the Christian faith itself begin? they ask. Did it begin with a discussion of creation and original sin, or with the announcement that a new creation was at hand, that a transformed existence had become available to those whose lives were directed toward God's new order, which was marked by the intercession of Jesus Christ? Early Christians asserted that the forces of evil and death had been decisively defeated through the cross and resurrection and that a new age was dawning. Evident as it was to them that the kingdom had not yet arrived in its fullness, it was nevertheless possible to participate in the first fruits of the age to come through faith, hope, and the power of the Spirit. We confront this same theme in Jesus' own ministry and message. Is there any phrase more central to his preaching than the repeated call to "seek first the kingdom of God and his righteousness"? To turn to the kingdom of God as the locus from which to derive an understanding of human existence is for these Latin Americans not an escape. If the kingdom of justice and peace is God's intention for human flesh, it is the ultimate reality and truth toward which this world must tend if it is finally to be sustained. Moreover, awareness of this truth heightens consciousness of the discrepancies between God's intended order and this present order. It robs the rulers of this world of the kind of legitimacy that religion traditionally has lent them as preservers of order, and it makes the masses aware of God's stake in change.

The radicalizing of the Latin American churches under the impact of this theological shift is a familiar story. In many countries the church has moved to the forefront of those demanding change in the age-old patterns of political, economic, and military power that were once blessed by the church and declared to be the will of God. The fact that this vision of an alternative future was first introduced by the Marxists should not invalidate its truth, insist these theologians. In the Marxist analysis the church recognizes its own heritage in disguise. The church lays claim, therefore, to that which is rightfully its own on the basis of the critical power of the biblical message of the kingdom of God. Moreover, the church, insofar as it is true to its own vision, must champion humane means toward humane ends—something that often has been lacking in Marxist approaches.

---

[4]Moltmann, *Theology of Hope,* 25.

The implications for educational theory of this reorientation of the church's leadership role have been made clear by Brazilian educator Paulo Freire in *Pedagogy of the Oppressed*.[5] Whereas traditional education fits persons into a preexisting order by giving them information and skills that enable them to adjust and function productively within the needs of the present system, now education asks critical questions about the nature of the system itself. Previously, the education of the illiterate gave access only to means of communication programmed by the establishment. Thus education increased the efficiency of the system but did not question it. Now education includes practice in the art of critical thinking. Previously, culture, including its political and economic manifestations, was assumed to be a "given"—certainly not something to be enriched or changed by the lowly peasant. The process of "conscientization" now makes the peasant aware that culture is not divinely ordained but a human product. And as a human product, it is subject to change by human beings formulating more humane goals.

If the implications for education are already apparent, can we expect similarly far-reaching implications for the theory and practice of psychotherapy and pastoral counseling? What changes would result if human existence were seen not as a process of adaptation to a preordained world but as the interaction of a subject with his or her environment in the light of an alternative force? Admittedly, the motif of the kingdom has not been prominent in the approaches of most of those who have sought to do therapy or counseling from a Christian point of view and out of Christian presuppositions. There are several reasons for this, the most obvious being that the kingdom is a social rather than an individual category, and the preoccupation of much of psychotherapy has been with the individual. Within the helping professions themselves voices are being raised to ask whether the traditional approach to healing has been too centered on the self qua individual and has not taken sufficiently into account the social context within which illness occurs. Is it possible that the counseling profession has unwittingly been influenced by the pietistic heritage that has dominated both Catholicism and Protestantism over the past two centuries, which has focused on the salvation of the individual soul and has been scarcely aware of the social fabric and its conditioning power?[6] Certainly influences other than pietism have also been at work in shaping this individualism—Enlightenment rationalism, the influence of the frontier, the logic of capitalism,

---

[5]Paulo Freire, *Pedagogy of the Oppressed* (New York: Seabury Press, 1970).

[6]George V. Pixley argues that the kingdom of God, in contrast with its original meaning in Jesus' message and Palestinian Christianity, becomes inevitably individualized and privatized as it moves into the urban heterogeneity and rootlessness of the Roman Empire. *God's Kingdom* (Maryknoll NY: Orbis, 1981) 88-100.

and so forth—but pietism has been so pervasive and so successful precisely because of its hand-in-glove congruence with these other cultural factors.

One way to redress the balance would be to take a cue from the theologies of liberation and hope and begin with the kingdom, working our way back to creation. This is, in fact, the road we will take in the remainder of this chapter. Along the way we may discover that it is necessary to speak of the kingdom and of creation in one breath, as we find in the one the clues to the real nature of the other. And we may also discover that it is necessary to rethink the corporate as well as the individual aspects of the human condition.

THE KINGDOM AND THE SELF

When early Christians were called into discipleship, it was not so much to prepare for life in another world as to prepare for the coming of another world into this one. The kingdom was viewed quite concretely as divine intervention to bring about a new order that would defeat the forces of sin and corruption and usher in an era of God's rule over all flesh.

We cannot ignore the fact, therefore, that it is not the saved individual that stands at the heart of the gospel but a redeemed social order. In the kingdom the individual is saved as a participant in the reconciling power of positive social relationships. This presupposes, however, that the present order of things is negative, that social relations have broken down, and that kingdom power is missing, obscured, or ignored in our common life. If the kingdom is the answer to a problem and the kingdom is social, then the nature of the problem must also be social and not just individual. If this be the case, where then does the individual fit in?

In order to answer these questions, let us take a closer look at Jesus' call to repentance, a call that was intimately connected with his announcement of the kingdom. The call to repentance was addressed not just to the nation but to individuals. It thus can provide us an avenue for seeing how the sense of individuality and individual destiny emerged in Christianity without in any way abrogating the social nature of salvation.

"The kingdom of God is at hand; repent, and believe the good news" (Mark 1:15). This is the first account we have of Jesus' preaching. The message seems straightforward enough, but we have difficulty hearing it in its original sense. For us "repentance" does not seem to go together with rejoicing and good news; it has to do with sorrow, guilt, and remorse. It is important for us to see, therefore, that with this word Jesus offers in the first instance not condemnation but promise. *Repent,* in the Jewish sense in which Jesus is using it, means fundamentally "to turn."[7] And in the

---

[7]Neither the English nor the Greek words, *repent* and *metanoein,* in their literal meaning, reproduce accurately the sense of the Aramaic that Jesus used,

context of Jesus' message it means to turn toward the new source of power that is appearing on the horizon. This is why it is good news, "gospel." To be sure, it also means turning away from, and breaking with, the old powers of the present age. What is innovative in Jesus' preaching is not what he calls persons to turn from, however, but what he calls them to turn toward—toward the divine mercy and love that elicits and enables the turning. God himself turns toward human beings through Jesus' healing and saving activity, and his mercy makes possible our turning. It is good news because God, in this eschatological activity, is restoring the covenant with his people—not the covenant law as interpreted by the religious authorities in Jesus' time, but that which Jesus instead takes to be the original, gracious character of the covenant relation between God and human beings. Therefore, the dawning of the kingdom brings a recovery of God's original intention for creation.

To "turn" involves both thought and action. Thus salvation can never be reduced simply to a new self-understanding within the individual. It is insight into the destiny of the self as part of creation, that part which, because of its evolutionary development, is enabled to participate consciously with the Creator by playing a responsible role in the realization of the divine intention for the whole of creation. Repentance is effective as it becomes not just insight but action: vocation, calling, work. And action is most effective as it becomes communal, participatory. Insight is constantly deepened and reshaped as the self is at work in new situations, informed by the inexhaustible depth and resources of the divine intention and the vision of a common task. To speak of the divine intention, however, is to speak of creation and covenant, and this carries us back to a renewed consideration of these biblical motifs.

CREATION AND COVENANT

Covenant is the special Jewish understanding of the way in which God and human beings are related and, as such, provides clues to Jesus' own understanding of human nature, which he presupposed in his call to the kingdom. A covenant is an agreement entered into by two parties that binds them to each other and to the obligations that they assume under the agreement. Covenants come in many varieties in the ancient world, and the technical distinctions need not concern us here. The biblical covenants with Moses, Abraham, Noah, and Adam, despite their diversity, share the common note that God binds himself in faithfulness to human beings and thereby lends their lives stability and depend-

---

which could only have meant "to turn around." Johannes Behm, in Gerhard Kittel, ed., *Theological Dictionary of the New Testament* (Grand Rapids: Wm. B. Eerdmans, 1976) 4:999-1000. *Repent* is literally "being remorseful, having pain," while *metanoein* is to change one's mind. Thus the Latin *convertere* and the German *umkehren* reproduce more accurately the force of the Hebrew and Aramaic.

ability in the midst of threatening and unpredictable circumstances. They, for their part, bind themselves to God and covenant values and obligations that transcend their self-interest. The moral character of the Mosaic covenant meant that the self-interests of those who controlled political, economic, and religious power were no longer absolute; everyone, regardless of station, was answerable to a higher authority who relativized and restricted the power of rulers and institutions by a superior law of justice. God's justice became the plumbline by which to judge and expose political and even religious ideologies. According to George Mendenhall, this was "a development of utmost importance for the history of religion, for it places moral obligations above political and economic interests in the scale of religious values. The continued legitimate existence of any political and economic institutions was thus conditional upon obedience to the ethical norms stipulated in advance by the deity."[8]

This notion of covenant is seen in the creation itself by the authors of Genesis 1-3, and these chapters provide the most succinct statement of Hebrew anthropology. Human beings are singled out from the rest of creation to bear special responsibility for the order of the world under its Creator. This call to responsibility implies a creature "capable of being addressed" (Brunner) or, perhaps better, the call supposes "response-ability" on the part of the called. It is creative, therefore, in the sense that it calls into existence that which did not exist prior to it and could not exist apart from it. Humans are defined as those creatures who have their special quality of life not through a unique substance—they are "dust" like the rest of nature—but through the divine call to care for the world in which they have been placed. In the biblical sense, therefore, the "self" is not something self-contained but is activated in and through its relationships and responsibilities. The word that in the Old Testament is most commonly translated as "self" is *nephesh,* literally "breath," the life force that is received by the self from the Creator (Gen. 2:7). Hence the self is constantly dependent for its life principle on relations beyond itself. This dependency is not to be understood as slavish, however, as the term "image of God" in Genesis 1 makes abundantly clear.

The *imago dei* concept has become so central for the Christian understanding of humanity that it is perhaps appropriate to pause to examine it in its original biblical setting. Down through the ages the term has picked up some questionable nonbiblical meanings, so that today it is popularly understood as referring to godlike capacities with which human beings are endowed, such as reason or conscience. In its original biblical context, however, it may have meant something quite specific.

---

[8]George E. Mendenhall, in *Interpreter's Dictionary of the Bible* (Nashville: Abingdon, 1962) 1:719.

The term "image of God" occurs in a manuscript (Genesis 1) dating from the period of the Babylonian captivity (586-540 B.C.E.). Thus the term may have been borrowed from a Babylonian context in order to express in updated and more cosmic language an older Hebrew tradition (from circa 950 B.C.E.) found in Genesis 2. According to the Babylonian custom, when the emperor conquered a new territory, he set up an image of himself in the provincial capital that empowered the governor, as his representative, to bring order to the province and govern it ("subdue and have dominion"). Gerhard von Rad has suggested that this relationship of loyalty and authority was applied analogically to human beings, who were to be the sign of God's rule over the earth.[9] If that was in fact the intention of the authors of this passage, the term probably also served a polemical function, distancing the Hebrew story of creation from the Babylonian creation saga, *Enuma elish,* to which the first chapter of Genesis otherwise bears certain literary resemblances. In the *Enuma elish* human beings were created so the gods might have slaves to do their work. Nothing could have been more inimical to the sensibilities of the Jews—whose nationhood had been forged in the crucible of revolt from slavery—than to regard humans as in essence slaves. Their version of creation, by contrast, portrays humans as viceroys of the Creator, placed in a position of freedom and trust, and answerable to Yahweh and his laws alone. From their standpoint humans were never meant to be enslaved by kings or in bondage to the powers of nature personified in the pantheon of pagan gods. "As a creature man is ranged with all other creatures, but now, as the one whom God's Word meets, he comes to God's side and confronts the rest of creation."[10] This is not to say that humans have arbitrary control over nature. "The world of creation has its own laws . . . far beyond man's understanding" (cf. Psalms 19, 29, 104, 135, 147).[11] But the cosmos is not a capricious divine or demonic realm, as it was regarded in the ancient religions generally, to which humans are subject and which they must placate with magic and whatever other means they can contrive in order to survive in a predominantly hostile environment. The world is "creature" as they are, and not to be feared but declared "good" by the Creator and ultimately subject to the Creator's just laws. The effect of this was to desacralize the ancient world and reduce human allegiances to one—to Yahweh the God of justice, who faithfully keeps covenant with those who keep covenant with him. Thus the covenant concept ensured fundamental human dignity and defined the structures of human existence in a relational way. It relativized au-

---

[9]Gerhard von Rad, *Old Testament Theology* (New York: Harper, 1962) 1:146.

[10]Walther Eichrodt, *Man in the Old Testament* (London: SCM Press, 1951) 30.

[11]Ibid., 31.

thoritarian claims in this world at the same time as it recognized the legitimate claims of the Creator, the natural world, and fellow human beings upon that creature whose very existence is formed in the event of response.

The image of God, therefore, is not something indelible that we human beings "have"; it is not a possession any more than the covenant is a possession. It is a relation that for its actuality is dependent upon a continuing partnership that extends into the future, a relation with the one who is always ahead of us, calling us to new possibilities and responsibilities. An illustration from Sri Lankan theologian D. T. Niles clarifies this:

> The image of a king's head on a coin is part of the coin and cannot be separated from it. Even if the king dies, the image remains on the coin. But there is another kind of image. On a still and cloudless night we may see the image of the moon in the water of a lake. So long as the water is unruffled by wind, and the moon not covered by cloud, the image will shine out clear and beautiful. But if a cloud comes between the moon and earth, the image will disappear or if the water is ruffled by wind, the image will be scattered and distorted. Thus the image of the moon in the water does not belong to the water in the same way the image of the king on the coin belongs to the coin. The image depends upon a certain relation between the moon and the water. If this relation is broken, the image is distorted or lost.[12]

Hence the image of God in human beings could perhaps best be described as an eschatologically oriented process, understood in terms of the "ontology of the not yet." Jesus' call to the kingdom has the effect, structurally, of locating creation and covenant in the future in the sense that they enter human existence as new possibilities made available in the dawning power of the kingdom. And the kingdom brings "re-creation" and covenant renewal. To be sure, the term *covenant* does not appear as frequently in the New Testament as in the Old, with the exception of the Epistle to the Hebrews.[13] Nevertheless the basic character of the covenant relationship is written into the heart of the New Testament, and its substance is reiterated every time the community gathers to celebrate "the new covenant in my blood" (Matt. 26:28, 1 Cor. 11:25). It is not surprising, therefore, that the collection of writings about Jesus and his movement became known as the New Covenant (*testamentum*).

If such a positive understanding of human nature and covenant is found in the Old Testament, however, what is genuinely new in the New?

---

[12]In Lesslie Newbigin, *Sin and Salvation* (Philadelphia: Westminster Press, 1956) 16-17.

[13]Mendenhall suggests that this less-frequent use of the term *covenant* in the New Testament is because in the Jewish context *covenant* meant the Mosaic law that Christians understood to have been superseded through Christ, and in the Roman context *covenant* meant an illegal secret society (ibid., 722).

What distinctive accents emerge with Christianity? By Jesus' time the understanding of the covenant had in many respects become moribund, and the only way it could be recovered was not by looking to the past, which the religious authorities had sewed up in their interpretations, but to the eschatological future and the new covenant that was to be the sign of God's sovereignty over all the earth (cf. Jer. 31:31). It is this new future that Jesus announces, a future in which grace replaces the law as the basis of a relationship between God and humankind—without diminishing the call to justice and responsibility. This is the result of Jesus' reinterpretation of the kingdom as a gift, not conditional upon the perfect fulfillment of the law but received out of the Father's overflowing love and desire to reconcile. Hence those who stood most in need of mercy were the first to grasp the good news of the kingdom, and the oppressed and powerless were those who could rejoice most over God's identification of himself with their cause and their defense.

Moreover, the call is personalized and individualized. This is not to say that there is an absolute dichotomy between the old and new covenant communities in this regard. Obviously every individual had covenant responsibilities in Israel; and just as obviously the new covenant creates a people, the Body of Christ, and not just individual Christians. Yet undoubtedly individuality and a sense of selfhood intensified with the Christian understanding of faith as emerging out of the confrontation with the good news of the kingdom and the call to discipleship. In the closed civil and religious communities of the first century, this call to discipleship could be answered only by individuals or small groups such as families or friendship circles. The breakdown of the authority of the religious system under the impact of pluralism had opened up the possibilities for individuals to identify with alternative sources of meaning and to form conscious subcultures. Thus the emergence of the modern self as individual is at least in part traceable to the milieu that surrounds the birth of Christianity. The Jewish God, through the cross of his Son, overcame both Jewish traditional legalism and Hellenistic cosmic principalities and powers, making release possible from those forces of religion, culture, and the cosmos that previously had been considered determinative in the fate of the individual (Col. 2:13-15). Each person was invited into a covenantal relationship with the God whose Spirit is present through the love manifested toward every human being by the Son on the cross. Because this love was given without regard to traditional barriers of race and class, to participate in such love was to be enlisted in the cause of justice, which gives honor to each person not on the basis of merit but on the basis of the divine initiative that affirms the existence of each and calls into covenant even those who, by the world's standards, are of little account (James 2:1-5).

The primary community to which one belonged was no longer defined by the natural and cultural ties of clan and nation but, in a development that was quite new in human experience, became a matter of choice as one decided to cast one's lot with the Christian community. All of these factors combined to create a situation in which the self was viewed as an agent responsible for his or her own destiny in a way hitherto unimaginable as long as one's personal identity was submerged in a larger social unit.

One could easily overestimate the degree of individuality that came to birth in this process. Certainly most persons saw themselves not as heroic individuals in the way that Romantics of the nineteenth century did. They saw themselves instead as transferring their allegiance from one Lord to another and their social location from one sustaining community to another. To be sure, the tear in the social fabric occasioned by Hellenistic pluralism was later overcome as Christianity itself became dominant and coextensive with society. But the church always kept those earlier generations vivid in its memory through the documents that were produced and the stories of the martyrs. Hence the subcultural situation remained normative, at least in theory, even though for most of its history Christianity has fallen as predictably as any other religion into the role of guardian of the establishment. The notions of social counterculture and individual decision and responsibility were nonetheless so deeply etched in Christianity's sources that they proved again and again to be the inspiration for questioning the established order.

As the expectation for a radical transformation of this world waned, however, and as the church appropriated to itself more and more of the prerogatives of the divine kingdom, the notion of an alternative future for this world lessened and faith was diverted from hope for the future to hope for heaven. The *saint* then emerged as the answer to the routinization of Christian culture. The saint is one who by God's grace stands above the imprisonment of this world and its conventions because he/she already dwells in another world. The goal was heaven, which one reached only by the most strenuous individual commitment. The result was a shift from the kingdom model of the holy community to an elitist model of the holy individual. The results of this are still with us, seen for instance in the fact that the terms *call* and *vocation* are commonly reserved for those with clerical status, as if the whole people of God were not called. (Of course, the clergy in their obedience signify the obedience of the whole church. But the sign too easily becomes the substitute for a more universal covenantal responsibility exercised by the entire community.) The recovery of the eschatological orientation of the Bible provides an antidote to this tendency to divide Christians into the spiritual elite and the common "sheep." The Bible points toward a future for all human beings in a transformed world. Moreover, individual decisions and personal efforts are seen as contributing to social and not just individual spiritual goals. The call comes to "seek first the kingdom of God and his righteousness," and all other human concerns and priorities will fall into place. This is not to negate traditional spiritual blessings. They will find their proper location precisely in conjunction with, not in opposition to, material concerns for the well-being of humankind.

THE FALL AND ORIGINAL SIN:
THE BONDAGE OF THE SELF

In the discussion thus far, have we given sufficient attention to the other traditional biblical motif in the understanding of human nature, the Fall? Is it not a fact that most persons who seek help from priests and therapists are far from seeing themselves as robust images of God, happily exercising their covenantal responsibilities in anticipation of a better day? They feel themselves instead to be the victims of circumstances beyond their control. They are in bondage to forces and powers about which they feel helpless to do anything. Is there a way of viewing the traditions of the Fall and original sin that can give us insight into both the nature of the problem and the solution without abandoning eschatological hope as a genuine possibility for concrete human existence?

If human beings are created for covenantal relationships and cannot be finally fruitful apart from the kingdom of God, this must mean that they are created incomplete. This to-be-completed state is "good"; as such, it is not a deficient mode of being, for it is precisely what allows human existence to be a lifelong journey. Although conception is obviously the biological starting point, the "creation" of a human being is continuous, and the human being as the image of God is a lifetime in becoming. This incompleteness is the possibility for continuous creation by the Spirit, yet it is also the occasion for insecurity and anxiety. Blessing and curse, so it seems, come from the same structure. Incompleteness necessitates constant change, but change is threatening because it means that the future cannot be predicted or controlled from the present. This insecurity triggers the will to power that sets up situations of conflict that in turn intensify insecurity, raise defenses, escalate the need for control, and lead to the breakdown of the very relationships that support, sustain, and nurture the self in ways that enhance necessary growth. One of the negative manifestations of the human condition, as Augustine recognized, is the *cor curvum in se,* the heart turned in upon itself, which illustrates the "caughtness" character of sin. The heart in its anxiety is deaf to the voices outside itself that seek to affirm it. Or even more tragically in our world, the heart has no memory of positive, affirming voices outside itself—and has learned, therefore, to defend itself against further pain by rationalizing its dilemma or, in the more violent form of the same defense, by slaying all comers even before they have a chance to speak.

The traditional doctrine of original sin is the classic description of the fact that this condition exists. As an explanation of why it should be, the story of the Fall in Genesis 3 is not very satisfactory. The difficulty of tracing sin back to an actual first cause—if Satan, then who caused Satan to sin?—has led theologians to speak of the *mystery* of evil, for its origins seem lost in an abysmal realm that the mind cannot penetrate. More helpful, it seems to me, is to recognize that the possibility of human evil (and the breakdown of interpersonal and psychic life in general) is given in the very structures of insecurity and change that also make human fulfillment possible. It is the price paid for the potential for positive relations and growth. The alternative to freedom and change would be complete homeostasis, which would mean stagnation, boredom, and the death of existence as we know it. To be sure, constant instability has no meaning if it is not set within the context of an overall purpose and goal. The message of the kingdom provides the goal that gives both a directedness to all human activity and an assurance that the ultimate accomplishment of the goal is not dependent upon the preliminary success of human efforts. Both stability and goal-oriented change are necessary if our efforts are to be purposeful but not anxious and compulsive.

This kind of a universe involves risk. "God does not play dice," quipped Einstein. I believe it is not unfair to say, however, that God does take risks; God accepts the risks involved in creation that is not static but is moving toward the realization of its possibilities. The genuine independence that the creation has been granted is at once the precondition for partnership and for revolt. It is this fact that is graphically portrayed in the story of the Fall. When the Lord God revisits the Garden "in the cool of the day," after the man and woman have turned for their fulfillment toward the part of the world under their control—to guarantee their future without having to relate to one who is outside of themselves and beyond their control—it is apparent that a fundamental distortion of relationships has taken place. Tension and insecurity have entered a picture previously characterized by confidence and trust. The one who was not only their Creator but also their Lord and Friend has now become the most obvious threat to their existence. They hide themselves, and in their action lurks the wish that God were not there, the wish that God were not the future to be contended with—in short, the wish that God were dead. In this deceptively simple story we find portrayed all the essentials of the saga of human insecurity and conflict that every psychiatrist and counselor encounters daily in his or her ministry of healing. Adam and Eve appear to be better representatives of ordinary human existence than Prometheus. Most of what we encounter is not grand in scale, not a heroic battle against an irrational fate willed by distant gods. It is a breakdown of communication in the family—perhaps between husband and wife—or a "personality conflict" with the boss, just the kind of situation that is portrayed in the primeval Garden. "Adam, where art thou?" "I was afraid and I hid myself." The verbatim of Adam and Eve—naked and now self-consciously insecure—could be recorded by any therapist. "Who is at fault?" "Anyone but me." And Paradise is over, never again to be entered—until the kingdom.

Note that the usefulness of the doctrine of original sin is not just to provide a description of basic human misery. It serves an often overlooked therapeutic function as well. The story of the Fall recognizes that we bear the consequences of a sinful situation that we did not consciously choose or willfully create. It provides a way of dealing with guilt (therefore not denying the element of human responsibility) while also providing an opening for a nonjudgmental approach. The common way the church has dealt with sin is by assigning guilt. That may be satisfactory for single, isolatable deeds. What we usually are faced with, however, is a complex network of relationships gone awry. And any attempt to assign guilt results predictably in defensive reactions and denials of responsibility—just the opposite of the openness that we are attempting to build. In the doctrine of original sin, guilt is assigned to Adam. We bear the consequences of his sin; that is, we are allowed to see ourselves as victims of a situation without having to take personal responsibility for its cause. This defuses the situation because the anxiety about losing power and control is not attacked directly. The focus instead can be on what to do about the problem at hand. Our condemnation is not at stake, and so we can begin to assume responsibility for the existing conditions without losing face. Adam is the one to whom guilt can be assigned until we have developed the capacity and resources to face it ourselves. One therapist, in a conscious appropriation of Latin American liberation theology, calls this phase "bondage analysis," which is the clarification of the existing conditions without assigning guilt.

The next stage involves identifying the obstacles that stand in the way of healing. What would it take to remove them? And if they cannot be removed, is there any way to overcome them by another method? Here we must pass from the model of Adam to that of Christ. Adam provides the analysis of how things are; Christ is the one who removes the obstacles to the future by enabling us to trust the future and release our grip on the past. To let go of the past is only possible if the conviction concerning the trustworthiness of the future is powerful enough to sustain us in the midst of objective insecurity. Jesus announced that this power is present and that the first fruits of the kingdom are available wherever his word and promise of divine mercy and love are received as the foretaste of what is to come and in the end prevail.

For Christians, then, the first signs of the coming age are already present through Christ—that is, through his death and resurrection, the new covenant and Christian community he brought into being, and the healing forces he has generated in the world. But this is all proleptic and remains obscure to most of humanity. Where is the promised fulfillment for all humankind? Why the delay? As the bumper stickers say, why not "Parousia Now"?

I would like to think it is because God is creating a space in which psychiatrists and psychotherapists, counselors and priests, teachers and mothers, land reformers and political revolutionaries, can work. In other words, wherever the "dividing walls of hostility" are being penetrated and new possibilities opened up, the power of the kingdom is at work to enable the whole created order to realize the destiny for which it was called into being. God is still taking risks.

In this chapter we have described some of the changes taking place in theology today and the emergence of new ways of viewing the human condition. These changes, when added together, may indeed constitute the kind of paradigm shift to which Paul Pruyser refers in the first chapter of this volume. It is already evident that the recovery of the revolutionary implications of the biblical motif of the kingdom of God—for so many centuries lost from sight or interpreted in strictly otherworldly terms—is causing a fundamental reorientation in the method and content of theology. This reorientation may be the leaven that will gradually reshape the consciousness and practice of the churches and of those cultures where Christianity continues to exert a major influence.

CHAPTER THREE

The Human Condition in Biblical Perspective*

—•●•—

ROBERT S. BILHEIMER

Though the Bible has much to say about the human condition, it rarely speaks of humanity without speaking at the same time of God. Hebrew epistemology considers knowledge of God reciprocal with knowledge of humankind. God became clear to His chosen people and people gained clarity about themselves through God's graciousness, which led them out of bondage during the Exodus and into the promised land. Religiously understood as God's *purpose,* the idea of the promised land directs human concern away from a preoccupation with the past to a concentration on the present and the future in which that purpose is to be consummated.

Taking these relations between God and humanity as basic biblical premises, Bilheimer explores what further light Scripture throws on the human condition. He does so by taking a close look at the meanings of *people* and *peoplehood* in biblical literature. Human beings find their identity in community, and God's concern with community and "chosen people" is an embracing and expanding concern that extends to all peoples. Being "in a community" and "of a people" sets a limit to the scope and meaning of being human. Further limiting factors of the human condition are, in Bilheimer's view, the ever-corrupting impact of sin, the inescapable and history-shaping presence of "the powers," and the strong note of contingency that creatureliness injects into the human condition. No doubt, these limiting factors produce what one may well call the human plight of bondage to powers of various kinds. But the biblical message also takes human limits as situations in which, because of God's demonstrated emancipatory action, human freedom can be exercised in order to transform the world with all its peoples into the promised land.

———————————

*This essay is based on a portion of the author's *A Spirituality for the Long Haul* (Philadelphia: Fortress Press, 1984).

The attentive reader can scarcely escape the Bible's sensitivity and passion concerning the human condition. We characterize the third chapter of the book of Genesis as the account of the Fall, thereby giving it a dogmatic cast. Yet it is a powerful story that in caring, delicate language conveys feeling for the plight of human beings and uncovers its depth. The images of the Apocalypse and the Revelation to John impart the almost unbearable intensification to be wrought by the divine consummation of human life; yet these images speak poignantly, whether of the threat of death or the coming of life. The books in between—whether they recount history or tell truth by means of metaphor or myth, whether they discuss the collective or personal encounter with God, whether they be poetry or prose—exhibit unceasing interest in humanity and the conditions of life.

The reason for this biblical concern for human beings emerges indirectly yet clearly. The subject of the Bible is God, not humanity. The Hebrew knowledge of God, however, was not abstract nor drawn by the methods of abstract reasoning. Biblical knowledge of God arose from experience: encounter, struggle, worship, and the interpretation of these in a process that unfolded over a long period of time and within diverse historical circumstances. As it did, a fundamental consequence became clear. Knowledge of God produced knowledge of human beings. Biblical people, in a vital process of progressive disclosure, came to know God and also themselves.

Knowledge of God led biblical people to speak of God's graciousness.

> A wandering Aramean was my father; and he went down into Egypt and sojourned there, few in number; and there he became a nation, great, mighty and populous. And the Egyptians treated us harshly, and afflicted us, and laid upon us hard bondage. Then we cried to the Lord the God of our fathers, and the Lord heard our voice, and saw our affliction, our toil, and our oppression; and the Lord brought us out of Egypt with a mighty hand and an outstretched arm, with great terror, with signs and wonders; and he brought us into this place and gave us this land, a land flowing with milk and honey.
>
> Deut. 26:5-9; see also Josh. 24:2-13; Deut. 6:20-25

"We cried . . . the Lord heard . . . saw . . . and the Lord brought us out"—that is graciousness. This foundational passage, repeated as a creed in worship countless times over centuries, embodied the memory that shaped ancient Israel's identity and contained the central point of Israel's knowledge of God. God does not relate to humanity in the manner of a cosmic diffusion, spilling out from the source. God does not relate to the world as a clockmaker who produces the creation, sets it going, and then leaves it to run by itself. God is gracious and relates to the world and humanity in specific, although not merely momentary action.

In biblical knowledge the graciousness of God has its own structure. One part of this structure is clarity: the clarity of "the Lord brought us out," the clarity that impressed the disciples after the light, the cloud, and the voice of the transfiguration, when they then saw "Jesus only." Another part of the structure of divine graciousness is mystery.

> Moses said, "I pray thee, show me thy glory." And he said, "I will make all my goodness pass before you, and will proclaim before you my name 'The Lord,' and I will be gracious to whom I will be gracious, and will show mercy on whom I will show mercy. But," he said, "you cannot see my face; for man shall not see me and live." And the Lord said, "Behold, there is a place by me where you shall stand upon the rock; and while my glory passes by I will put you in a cleft of the rock, and I will cover you with my hand until I have passed by; then I will take away my hand, and you shall see my back; but my face shall not be seen."
>
> Exod. 33:18-23

Although there is a tradition in Scripture in which the glory of God is seen, the tradition of the word directly spoken is predominant. Even so, the word leads into things unseen and the glory that is seen is partial. Behind both, by the biblical account, stands the incomprehensible mystery, which is beyond human comprehension; and from the mystery both word and glory proceed.

Both clarity and mystery are to be found in the biblical encounter with God. Yet they are not simply two "points" made about the "nature of God." According to the biblical knowledge of God, mystery and clarity are united in the graciousness of God. In this extraordinary union, clarity leads into mystery and mystery issues forth in clarity.

Over the centuries knowledge of God led to knowledge of self, humanity, and the world, yet in a certain way. The biblical people and writers, for instance, were not scientists, either in the ancient or the modern sense of the word. Although, as I shall shortly suggest, what they discovered about themselves connects with much that modern science says about human beings, they were not concerned directly with scientific or philosophical inquiry into human nature. Moreover, the biblical people were not moralists. One need scarcely say that there is morality in Scripture, but it does not address the human being simply with moral maxims or from a moral viewpoint. And the same is true of politics and economics. The standpoint from which Scripture views human beings is its knowledge of God, and its interest lies in those aspects of human life that affect divine-human relationships.

Scripture proceeds with economy, for it concentrates upon realms of human life that matter in the relationship between the divine reality and the human reality. These are fundamental limits (in the sense of Tracy 1975, 92-95) or boundaries of human existence. These are limits that cannot be overcome except by the graciousness of God; and conversely they are the limits at which God meets human beings. That is their significance. The Bible thus primarily serves a pedagogical, teaching function rather than an analytical function concerning human self-understanding. The latter is there, but the Bible is not a sociological, anthropological, psychological, or geological textbook. It is concerned with the action of God at the limits to life and therefore is concerned that we know and appreciate what these limits are.

In this respect, the starting point from which the Hebrew knowledge of God developed and grew takes on importance. Taking account of the period of Abraham and the patriarchs, which was real but historically shadowy, Israel's clear historical experience with God began with the Exodus. This means that Israel's knowledge of God originated with the redeeming action of God's graciousness. This beginning experience, the basis of all that followed, was itself oriented to the future. God did not merely lead the Israelites out of captivity into either a general freedom or another bondage but into the promised land, an expression of divine purpose. Biblical knowledge of the future is not, therefore, speculative. Rather, the recognition that the future consists in the consummation of God's purpose derives from the historical, remembered, living experience of God's response to humans who cry out in affliction. Thus, contrary to much theology and church teaching, biblical understanding of human beings is not in the first instance grounded upon the past, in the account of the Fall, but upon a present knowledge of God's emancipating action oriented toward the future.

This sequence in the Bible indicates the tone and perspective that it conveys concerning the human condition. One is everywhere struck by a severe, unrelenting realism concerning humanity. However, with remarkable constancy the atmosphere of healing, or at least the beginning of healing in self-recognition, imbues this stark realism, for the latter has a purpose. This is to clarify those limits to human existence that are crucial for the relationship between God and humans, to make known the boundaries at which God meets human beings. Scripture's interest in the human condition is to demonstrate the methods to eclipse these limits, beginning now and culminating in the complete freedom of the new creation, the kingdom of God.

With this perspective in mind, I shall indicate the main elements that appear to compose the scriptural view of the human condition. These five elements are as follows:

PEOPLE AND PEOPLEHOOD

Biblical experience extended over a period of some 2,000 or more years in the Eastern Mediterranean world. From the beginning of recorded history, this world was the scene of the rise, mutation, and disappearance of many peoples. Israel's history began at the close of the third millennium B.C.E., during which the Mesopotamian empire and Egypt had arisen. The empires of Assyria, Babylon, Greece, and Rome appeared along with smaller peoples during the biblical period. Peoples lived, had intercourse and competed with one another, conquered, were subject to and jostled others in an ever-shifting scene. Moderns might say that it was an intensely *historical* environment. In the sense of a consciousness of diverse peoples and human history, this world was a global village in microcosm.

In this setting the ancient people Israel and the new people in Christ found their identity. One must pause to notice the meaning given to the term *people* in Scripture. It is a prominent term and appears in Bibles also as *nation* (or *nations*) and as *Gentiles*. The term indicates the peoples or nations surrounding Israel, and in a special way refers to Israel as God's people and to the church. In any usage in Scripture, the term refers to an obvious, experience-based human group among whom there is a union. Scripture uses the term to apply to such groups irrespective of their particular characteristics. A people is united by living together, sometimes as a tribe, or a national unit of common ancestry, and sometimes as a political unit defined by history or by constitution. In the latter case, a people is composed of varied peoples and the overall effect is of a layered peoplehood that is nevertheless bound together. People is a broad as well as a fundamental term.

In the historical setting of millennia of peoples, neither Israel nor the early church viewed "peoples" as a merely sociological phenomenon. Indeed, from first memory onward, the people Israel was understood to have originated with God. The voice to Moses in the burning bush (Exod. 3:1ff.) spoke of God hearing the cry of the afflicted and of God's purpose in leading the people into a new land. From this moment—through the history of wandering, settlement, development, division, exile, return, subjection; through the history of temple and law, wisdom and worship; through the extraordinary centuries of the prophets from Elijah to Ezekiel and onward to the apostolic age—people and God were associated. Moreover, this connection was based on more than the special situation of the chosen people and included peoples of both ancient existence or new.

In this unfolding experience, those who developed the traditions of Israel perceived something that belongs to the nature of humanity. The attention given in Scripture to peoples other than Israel or the church provides the clue to this universal law. The symbolic tenth chapter of Genesis, the Table of Nations, located in the "primeval history," suggests that humanity exists as peoples rather than as a conglomerate mass or as individualistic atoms, and that all are related to God. One is reminded of Margaret Mead's conclusion that "Homo sapiens is a species which can only survive in a man-made environment, using man's dependence on a culture as the species-characteristic statement" (Mead 1964, 68). In the prophetic tradition the symbolism of Genesis turns into living fire as the prophetic summons, the prophetic judgment, and the prophetic promise are addressed to the peoples, exempting none. Israel's originating experience is thus broadened: God's presence creates community and peoples, and God's purpose includes them all. This fundamental perception was assumed by the New Testament traditions.

Biblical experience, however, led further. The people, or community, was understood to be the matrix within which human identity is formed. Biblical experience entailed finding a distinctive identity. For ancient Israel, this was given by Torah, the revealed will of God, and for the new people identity was supplied by God-in-Christ. In both, though, the matrix of this identity was the people. The prophet Jeremiah particularly, followed by Ezekiel, spoke of "the law within them" (Jer. 31:33), thus showing the intimate and powerful connection between the principle that constitutes the people and the identity of the person. Henceforth, not only in the prophets but in the thought of Jesus and the apostolic age, the original perception deepened. "Peoples" was not only the form of human life, but the "people" provided the matrix of the human sense of identity.

Biblical experience also demonstrated that identity involves having both creativity and character. Creativity, the basis of culture, is both affirmed and taken seriously in Scripture. Scripture is not anticultural, but strongly insists that cultural effort and its products be put at the service of God. In the scriptural view, culture is a function of peoples. It is always a people, not merely a class or a race or a random group of individuals who use their achievements for or against the will of God; and within the people are, of course, individuals. Because the people is the matrix of identity, the people is the cradle of creativity. That is true also of character. From the time of Moses' leadership in the wilderness— through the development of the law, the growth of worship, the repetition and interpretation of Israel's history, and the thrust of prophetic leadership, leading up to the teaching of Jesus and apostolic writing— character is Scripture's bottom line. Character qualifies creativity and peoplehood, even as creativity and peoplehood produce character. "People," as used in Scripture, is thus a fundamental concept concerning the human condition. It is the form in which humanity is constituted to live and the matrix within which human identity is developed, creativity is achieved, character is shaped.

At the same time "people" denotes a limit to human existence. It is a necessity; without it human life cannot exist. One can observe that fact, but Scripture discerns this necessity on a more profound level. God's presence with humanity produces peoples. Humans have no option but to live together as a people and as peoples. Moreover, there is no other context for identity and the expressions of identity in creativity and character than this communal nature of the human being. One cannot find identity, achieve creativity, and form character apart from a people. In the modern phrasing of Erik Erikson, human identity is a product of a "psychosocial relativity" (Erikson 1968, 22-23) and thus limited.

SIN

Turning from the limit of "people" to the limit implied by sin, one moves into a different realm of human existence and discourse. "People" provides for life, enabling it to go on and to achieve creativity and character. "Sin" introduces one to the darker realism of life. The varied biblical language concerning sin speaks from within the human sense of dislocation, providing understanding and thus hope. One feels that, although the note of condemnation against both sin and the sinner is strong, the purpose of the manifold treatments of human wrongdoing is not to condemn but to warn and to provide human self-understanding.

Scripture is clear and direct when it mentions sin:

> Nathan said to David, "You are the man. . . . You have smitten Uriah the Hittite with the sword, and have taken his wife to be your wife, and have slain him with the sword of the Ammonites."
>
> (2 Sam. 12:7ff.)

> . . . there is swearing, lying, killing, stealing and
>   committing adultery;
> they break all bounds and murder follows murder.
>
> (Hos. 4:1-2)

> . . . they that trample the head of the poor into the
>   dust of the earth,
>   and turn aside the way of the afflicted:
>
> (Amos 2:7)

> . . . for they eat the bread of wickedness
>   and drink the wine of violence.
>
> (Prov. 4:17)

St. Paul is no less specific. By a "base mind and improper conduct" he means that

> they were filled with all manner of wickedness, evil, covetousness, malice. Full of envy, murder, strife, deceit, malignity, they are gossips, slanderers, haters of God, insolent, haughty, boastful, inventors of evil, disobedient to parents, foolish, faithless, heartless, ruthless.
>
> (Rom. 1:29-31)

Yet these and other references seem to point to something else. They imply some unity, some standard by which they are singled out. Everywhere, the authors of Scripture name wrongdoings and human evils against the background of their passionate faith in God and consequent knowledge of God's purpose and graciousness. That suggests one principle of coherence. One could say that these actions are simply distasteful to God, and that would be true, albeit insufficient. Put another way, if these be sins, what is sin? What common feature in these activities displeases God?

Various names and descriptions appear—missing the mark, making a mistake, rebellion, going astray, engaging in abnormal legal, moral, or religious behavior—but as experience lengthened these were understood to have common elements. *Sin* became a term that gathered specific actions together and provided greater meaning to them all. The immeasurable contrast between the light of God and the darkness of life was indicated not only by the single acts that humans perform, but by sin, a condition of human life itself. The term is understood in two related ways.

The modern word for the first aspect of sin is *compulsion*. In its psychological meaning, a compulsion is "a strong, usually irresistible impulse to perform an act that is contrary to the will of the subject" (*Random House Dictionary*). A classic scriptural text about sin says much the same thing:

> I do not understand my own actions. For I do not do what I want, but I do the very thing I hate. Now if I do what I do not want, I agree that the law is good. So then it is no longer I that do it, but sin which dwells within me. For I know that nothing good dwells within me, that is, in my flesh. I can will what is right, but I cannot do it. For I do not do the good I want, but the evil that I do not want is what I do. Now if I do what I do not want, it is no longer I that do it, but sin which dwells within me.
> (Rom. 7:15-20)

This penetrating confession is followed with the cry: "Wretched man that I am!" (Rom. 7:24). With a clarity not yet articulated, St. Paul understood the inner, compulsive power of sin.

A compulsion to do what? The answer to this question provides the second aspect of the biblical meaning of sin.

One must recall the story of Adam, Eve, and the Serpent (Gen. 3). The symbolism of the Serpent captures the compulsiveness of sin, depicting that aspect of sin that is not merely "I" but something with power to pull, to persuade against one's better judgment, to tempt. In the garden both the temptation and the result point to the center: the two ate "of the tree of the knowledge of good and evil." That was the act, and the meaning of it is understood because of the Serpent's comment, "You will be like God, knowing good and evil." The phrase "good and evil" was a way of saying "everything": "You will be like God, knowing everything." Moreover, "knowing" went beyond intellectual comprehension to a deeper knowledge as when a woman and a man "know" each other in sexual intercourse; and "knowing" also carried the meaning of being able to accomplish. Penetrating to these realms, the act disclosed its own momentous portent. Humans would know the corrupting power of hubris, the compulsive attractiveness of the urge to attain Godlike knowledge, experience, and ability.

The symbolism of Genesis 3 expresses the profound history of Israel's struggle with God and of the self-knowledge that resulted from it. That struggle imparted knowledge of a fundamental fact of human life: the human being is captive to a compulsive tendency to rebel, to usurp the role of God.

The ramifications are far reaching for the person and for society. A sentence of St. Paul states the principle succinctly. Speaking of people generally he wrote: "[T]hey exchanged the truth about God for a lie and worshipped and served the creature rather than the Creator, who is blessed for ever" (Rom. 1:24). Herein Paul points to the form of idolatry that goes far beyond formal obeisance to a false god in the sense of a golden calf or other. The idolatry that Paul indicates is endemic to human existence worships any entity (whether that be the self, the state, wealth, another person, an ideology) and is explosive, corrupting, and dangerous. Moreover, as Jeremiah's reference to the "inward parts" suggests and as Jesus' teaching shows, these idolatries become internalized, often in the form of supposed virtues.

The effect of such idolatry extends to every area of human attitude and activity, and not least to areas of concern in our age. Corporate achievement is understood to be susceptible to idolatry, as the story of the tower of Babel indicates (Gen. 11:1-9), and as the prophets from the eighth century onward insist. Jesus' extraordinary paradox, "For whoever would save his life will lose it; and whoever loses his life for my sake and the gospel's will save it" (Matt. 16:25; Mark 8:35; Luke 9:24), brings to mind our own painful inner tangles when we concentrate too heavily upon our own security, pleasure, and protection. At the same time it reminds us of the vulnerability we feel when we contemplate the risk of letting go of the self, losing it in a bigger and higher cause or even in the love of those close to us. This leads to the other portions of Scripture that indicate, sometimes in substantial catalogues (Cf. Gal. 5:19-21) the attitudes, postures, and passions of the troubled psyche. These are not listed as simply bad or naughty dispositions of the inner self. They appear rather as indications of what happens as a result of the profound idolatry that Paul defines and of which Scripture generally speaks. The connection between the troubled psyche and the idolatry of worshiping the creature is not spelled out in Scripture, but it is firmly made. In the connection thus established, one may discern a further aspect of the honor, dignity, and delicacy of the human constitution. From the high view of human life set forth by Scripture, one may conclude that the human creature is of such a wondrous texture that if worship is given to anything less than God, the human texture falls apart. The inner troubles are not inchoate. They possess the coherence of sin in its most profound sense.

In its scriptural meaning sin is not a moralistic term, denoting what is merely naughty. Sin is a descriptive category that illumines a fundamental human condition and its consequences for life. Locating the story of Adam, Eve, and the Serpent, which refers to the human being as such, and that of the Tower of Babel, which refers to collective achievement, in the primeval history indicates the conviction that sin is universal. In itself, sin is a condition of active orientation toward the self as the center, as contrasted with loving the neighbor as the self. The moral consequences of sin are serious, but the most far-reaching consequence is rebellion against the final reality—against God—in the interests of a partial reality—the self.

Sin therefore is a limit to life. In an important way, the limit imposed by sin differs from the limit imposed by "people" and by the "powers" and "creatureliness" to which I shall turn next. In scriptural experience these latter are all ambiguous, a part of the provisions of God for human life, yet subject to corruption. Of all of the boundaries to life encountered in the biblical experience with God, only sin is understood to be wholly and unequivocally bad. Moreover, there is no escape from the subtlety of sin or its power and pervasiveness except by the action of God's presence with humanity. Moderns have believed that human progress is achieved by the exercise of human energy and will, directed by reason. The acceptance of culture and the emphasis upon the character of a people found in Scripture suggest that in a highly relative sense and limited form progress would not be denied. The accompanying modern view, however, that human faculties can achieve a progress able to penetrate the boundary described by sin stands squarely athwart biblical experience. The latter would maintain that the elevation of human reason, whether in the form of science or another form, to the position of an ultimately saving force in human progress is in itself a manifestation of the idolatry that the word *sin* describes. That does not, of course, mean obscurantism or the rejection of science or rational knowledge. On the contrary, disciplines of human knowledge help mightily to illumine the human condition and improve human life, assuming that these faculties are held in their proper place as human and therefore subject to the limits of all human activity.

POWERS

In the Epistle to the Romans, following his treatment of sin, St. Paul turns to the power, hope, and life given by the Spirit of God, concluding with the following:

> For I am sure that neither death, nor life, nor angels nor principalities, nor things present, nor things to come, nor powers, nor height, nor depth, nor anything else in all creation, will be able to separate us from the love of God in Christ Jesus our Lord.
>
> (Rom. 8:38-39)

The flow and beauty of the language do not conceal the fact that surprisingly different entities are listed together, and this tendency appears in other references as well. One feels that definite realities are being considered, but in a way that seems imprecise. We read of "every rule and every authority and power," "all rule and authority and power and dominion," "thrones or dominions or principalities or authorities" (Cf. Rom. 13:1ff.; 1 Cor. 2:8, 15:24-26; Eph. 1:20, 2:1ff., 3:10; Col. 1:16, 2:15; Rev. 13). The language is strange, but before it is dismissed on that account, it is well to note Gordon Rupp's comment upon the tendency to throw out ancient language too readily:

> Modern man smiles at the old Cornish prayer:
>
> *From Ghoulies*
> *and Ghostlies, and long-leggity Beasties*
> *and all Things that go bump in the Night,*
> *Good Lord deliver us.*
>
> [A]nd as one who lived as a Methodist preacher in London between 1940 and 1945, I can assure you that "Things" still go bump in the night in an evermore frightening crescendo. (Rupp 1952, 15)

And those "Things," we might add, were experienced in the London night before the dark dawning of the nuclear age.

The varied biblical language refers to the same realities, and of the terms the basic one is *powers*. The concept is most highly developed by Paul, but the aspects of life and society to which it refers figure broadly in Scripture. As moderns do, biblical people lived in a power-conscious world. Along with us, they did not speak only of power in the abstract, but of power with tangible location and character. The "powers," for instance, are located in the institutions of history, as one sees in the numerous references to the state. Moreover, powers are to be seen in the events and forces of history. The "rulers of this age" (1 Cor. 2:8) or "world rulers" (Eph. 6:12) do not refer to Caesar or the heads of state, but rather to the forces of world history. Thus our world rulers, the rulers of this age, are not our successive presidents and their counterparts in other nations, but the forces of world hunger, nuclear deterrence, balance of powers, cooperating or conflicting national interests, oppression, and the like. The phrase, "the prince of the power of this air" (Eph. 2:2) issues from a then-current view of the heavens and the earth and the air. Nevertheless, "of this air" is an equivalent of the modern phrase about something being "in the air," used of course without the cosmological trappings. Moreover, many of the things "in the air" are powerful. For instance, the spirit of modernity, of enterprise, discovery, and confidence in human capacities was for a long time the prince of things that were "in the air," just as those who were in Nazi Germany can point to that dark ideology as the prince among the powers that were then in the air. Modern equivalents of "powers," in short, may be "power structures" or perhaps "structures of earthly existence" or "social forces."

"Powers" therefore belong to the sweep and movement of human history. Our language of structures, forces, and ideologies portrays the same elements of history known in the Bible and expressed in the New Testament language of principalities and powers. In addition, the powers do not seem to be accidental to life but a part of it.

The realities designated by "powers" and related language constitute a limit to human life. They are not an invention of humans, but are "ordained" (Rom. 13:1) or related to God's creative provisions for human life. It would, of course, be a mistake to draw the conclusion that the powers—even (or especially?) the state—have a moral or spiritual status independent of the purpose of God and that they therefore must be always obeyed. On the contrary, the ambiguity and the limit character of the powers suggest constant vigilance in order that the various forms of the powers serve the purpose of God. The powers operate both within and among "peoples," and the "people" give institutional, philosophical, and qualitative shape to the powers that inhere in their collective life. Further, as the powers are intertwined with the peoples, they are also related to sin. Whether they be institutions or ideas or social movements and forces, or constellations of these, the powers possess a magnetic force that draws human loyalties and energies to them; and in some powers—such as racism or sexism in the society and totalitarianism in its institutions—this magnetic force becomes absolute. Powers are not in themselves evil, but they are capable of being corrupted and of exhibiting corruption. An endemic element in human existence, the powers are a limit to it, their effect permeating every aspect of life. Indeed, they are a part of the totality that is subject to redemption.

CREATURELINESS

At the beginning of this chapter, we referred to the origin of biblical knowledge of God and humanity in the redeeming action by which God led Israel out of bondage in Egypt. We now return to this theme because of its importance for understanding the limit that creatureliness imposes upon human life. We noted that the biblical knowledge of the future grew from the redeeming action of God in the present. The same is true of biblical knowledge of the origins of humanity and world, of God as creator. The earliest creed, quoted from Deuteronomy 26:5-9, makes no mention of creation. From the knowledge of God's redeeming act in Egypt, however, Israel drew the further knowledge that God is the creator of the world and humanity. The significance of this sequence, by which the redeeming act provides knowledge of the origins as well as of the future, cannot be overemphasized. It means that the biblical understanding of God as creator is not speculative but rather grounded in the experience of delivery. Paul Ricoeur speaks of the great discovery of the myth's symbolic function. Of this myth one should never say that it is *only* a myth, but rather that it has the greatness of myth, "that is to say, has more meaning than a true history" (Ricoeur 1969, 234-36). By a "true history" Ricoeur means an account "coordinated with the time of history and the space of geography." The Genesis symbolism of God as the creator freed from the confines of a particular time and space arises from the history of Israel's encounter with the presence of God and expresses its meaning. How and by what process the connection was made between the divine redeemer and the divine creator is not spelled out in Scripture, but the overpowering conviction of the one led to knowledge of the other.

The sense of being created, of creatureliness, exerts a pervasive limit upon human life. Not only can the creature not be the Creator, the clay the potter, but the creature is contingent upon the Creator. Human feeling and activity cannot escape the contingency of life. Everywhere, the biblical traditions point to nature as the setting of life and to the mystery of birth and death as constant, unavoidable statements that human life is not self-sufficient but dependent. Jesus' attention to human anxiety, no less than the attention that he gives to true and false security, reveals the deep effect that creatureliness has upon the human spirit. Overall, the biblical theme of radical faith in one God is again and again stated as the final answer to human insecurity and anxiety.

Even so, human dependence desires to wear the cloak of autonomy. We are created, it is written, "in the image of God" (Gen. 1:27). This is not a reference to the moral or spiritual capabilities of human beings. The phrase refers to the person as a whole; hence stress is upon the capacity and task of humans to be the representatives of God in the creation and in relation to the rest of creation. The phrase refers to the human function in the nonhuman world: namely, we should have the same care for the natural world that God has because God saw that "it was good." It bespeaks a harmony in which human beings perform a divine, or at least a divinely appointed, function. Yet this harmony has given way to dissonance. An actual dependence upon God recedes in favor of a sense of human autonomy; the assertion of mastery over the nonhuman world takes precedence over the task of representing God in the nonhuman world. The capacities humans possess seem to warrant the autonomous use and management of the nonhuman world so far as that is possible. Thus sin infects the relationship between humans and their natural environment, for "autonomy" is little removed from the idolatry of self-worship.

The limit set by creatureliness, therefore, is far reaching. It is a clear source of anxiety and of fear. It is connected with sin. Strivings for autonomy clearly shape the character of the people, even as the latter affect the forms in which autonomy is sought. One limit thus involves the other in a web for which the most characteristic biblical words are "captivity" and "bondage."

THE FUNCTION OF HUMAN LIMIT

The limits under which human life proceeds have a double function. On the one hand, they describe the specific aspects of life in which limitation most fundamentally appears. The limits of "people" and "powers" provide the framework of the human historical struggle, in which identities arise, peoples form, decay, renew themselves, act upon one another, mutate, and give place to new peoples in a process exhibiting continuity as well as novelty. The limit imposed by sin creates the individual's spiritual, psychological struggle with God, self, and neighbor, even as the limitation of creatureliness defines the human struggle with the natural environment. Powers and creatureliness and the limits of sin derive specific shape and character from the "people" and at the same time powerfully affect the people and one another. It might be thought that this network is simply a part of the human condition, a mark of fate, but Scripture does not see it so. Constantly harkening back to the origins of its faith, Scripture uses the words "captivity" or "bondage" to describe the plight of humans. It could not do so without being aware that something lies beyond, in comparison with which human life is held captive.

The limitations to human existence show us, second, the realms of life in which human beings may achieve freedom. They say to us, "here and not somewhere else." Freedom from the limit is achieved at the limit. One may quickly aver that it is impossible on biblical grounds to be free *from* the people, or the powers, or sin, or the sense of contingency, and this is true. Freedom, however, has a deeper sense in scriptural experience than "freedom from" or even than freedom to choose. By *freedom*, Scripture means the capacity to transcend, to rise above the limits that confine life. The essence of the matter is that God touches human beings and shows them the divine and gracious purpose precisely where the specific limits of people, powers, sin, and contingency touch life. The touch of God, loving and powerful, creates an impassioned knowledge of a future beyond limitations, indeed of such a future beginning now. Because this is true, a further dimension of the overall human condition is also true.

If human life is captive to a network of powerful limits, human life is also capable of response to God. No matter how much the biblical traditions emphasize the captivity of human beings, the object of the biblical language is to show that precisely at these limiting realms, freedom from captivity is possible. The capacity of responding to God is the human basis of hope, and God's ceaseless search for the human heart is the guarantee of the hope. Yet there is more. The touch of God produces a new community, a People among and within the peoples of the world, a People both seen and not seen. Those drawn into the depth and power of the People know a new principle by which it is constituted. They know that sin is not the last word of life. Even though they continue to sin, the powers—however massive and attractive—are not final, nor are the frightening contingencies of life ultimate. From that knowledge comes the further recognition that life itself, and with it human history and the world, is even now being transformed. Although the Bible underscores our captivity, the human future with God provides transcendence, transformation, and freedom.

REFERENCES

Erikson, Erik. 1968. *Identity: Youth and Crisis*. New York: W. W. Norton and Company.

Mead, Margaret. 1964. *Continuities in Cultural Evolution*. New Haven: Yale University Press.

Ricoeur, Paul. 1969. *The Symbolism of Evil*. Boston: Beacon Press.

Rupp, E. Gordon. 1952. *Principalities and Powers*. London: Epworth Press.

Tracy, David. 1975. *Blessed Rage for Order*. New York: Seabury Press.

CHAPTER FOUR

Emerging in Love: Everyday Acts in Ultimate Contexts*

—————————— • ● • ——————————

MICHAEL A. COWAN

The appealing and simple title of Michael Cowan's chapter is entirely in line with the basic message it gives: human beings arise in and from acts of love, and thrive on loving and being loved. But to fully appreciate that message, a great deal of philosophical, psychological, theological, and cultural housecleaning is required. For Western persons are trained to think of themselves as more or less self-enclosed beings with a high degree of continuity, and these qualities may or may not be effective in relating to other beings. This culturally transmitted and constantly reinforced substantive model of personhood, Cowan thinks, cannot do justice to love understood as a dynamic matrix from which persons emerge.

Cowan does the housecleaning job with gusto and in an engaging way that turns it almost into a form of art. Adopting largely a first-person-singular style, he tells us what the housecleaner perceives, thinks, feels, and experiences at every step, what cobwebs he removes, and how different the house begins to look when he opens the curtains and lets the

———————————

*This essay was born in relationships. Its principal scientific, philosophical, and theological sources are cited in succeeding notes. Its more immediate roots are the transforming face-to-face relationships with which my own life has been blessed. The essay was prepared for an interdisciplinary consultation on religion and the social sciences convened at the Institute for Ecumenical and Cultural Research at Collegeville, Minnesota. The main title was suggested by my colleague Paul Pruyser; the subtitle is a paraphrase of Clifford Geertz from "Religion as a Cultural System," in *The Interpretation of Cultures* (New York: Basic Books, 1973) 122. I wish to acknowledge in a special way the appreciative and critical readings of previous versions of this essay by Richard Albares, Tim Reuland, Dick McQuellon, Anthony Ford, Colm O'Doherty, and Gerard Egan.

light shine in. But the chapter's footnotes and the numerical references in his text show us that he is actually doing a very thorough critical review of the ethos and tenor of traditional Western conceptions of personhood. In fact, he writes in support of a different ethos that he sees emerging in some leading thinkers and in his own experience. He articulates a process view of humanity and dwells on love as the most salient of all processes.

PROLOGUE
ACTING AND KNOWING

Our deepest sense of life's meaning emerges as we go about the day-to-day acts entailed in composing a life: being a child in a particular family, attending schools, forming friendships, working with our hands and minds, marrying, caring for our children, struggling with our enemies, praying or refusing to pray, participating in the larger civic and economic realities of our world, and facing death. This sense of how our lives proceed, which gave rise to this essay, was born in moments spent with persons whose lives leave them on or over the threshold of demoralization.

This essay moves in five interlinked steps, each one taking up a different perspective on our lives, much as one might move around a statue in an effort to appreciate it. (The great difference, of course, is that we never stand outside our living and move around it.) Each viewpoint that we take can only provide its measure of light and of shadow. We ought to expect no more and no less of it. The conviction gleaned from living that serves as the link among the perspectives of this essay is that the wellspring of all human life is meaning.

MODELS *OF* REALITY
AND MODELS *FOR* REALITY

As one whose life is emerging in the web of Western industrial societies and cultures, it is my deeply ingrained habit to take for granted a particular sense of who I am, of what being a person means. I will call this way of being human "maintaining self-identity." This guiding image of personhood supports and is supported by a similarly unconscious assumption about how persons relate to each other. I will call this habitual way of conducting myself in my relationships "external association."

Culture—"an historically transmitted pattern of meanings embodied in symbols . . . by means of which (persons) communicate, perpetuate, and develop their knowledge about and attitudes toward life"[1]—guides our lives in both so pervasive and so subtle a way that we ordinarily take its most basic assumptions and guidelines entirely for

---

[1]Ibid., 89.

granted. It is only when they fail to work or are subject to radical challenge that we step back and attempt to discern whether our particular ways of being women, or men, or loyal citizens, or productive workers, or faithful adherents of particular religious traditions are divinely inspired, or naturally required, or relative to our culture and history. Such symbolic upending is clearly exemplified in the current struggles men and women in our culture are undergoing regarding masculinity and femininity and regarding economic and familial roles in the light of such a definition. In our culture today the lives of many are torn or enriched—or both—by these issues, which only a generation ago seemed settled.

The symbols of a culture are always simultaneously models *of* reality and models *for* reality.[2] This means that a symbol both describes what something is and encourages us to see it in a particular way. For example, a trained architect could, upon carefully inspecting and measuring a house, produce a set of blueprints of its structure. The blueprints are a model *of* the house, a representation of its structure in another medium. Should they serve as the basis for constructing another house, they then function as a model *for* the new building.

The words *man* and *woman*, for example, name realities that we discover in our world. They represent those realities in the alternative medium of language: they are models *of* reality. But *man* and its culturally associated meanings throw me into an intricate and unacknowledged network of pathways for living as a "man" and for dealing with those others designated as "woman." Women, of course, are also models *for* reality, shapers of my self and relationships.[3]

The image that I share with other Western persons of human beings as self-identical individuals enmeshed in a network of external association is not merely a model *of* social and psychological reality, an attempt to portray the truth about being human; as with all true symbols, it is also a model *for* human lives. It contributes to the emergence of a particular variety of self relating in a particular way to others. "Maintaining self-identity" is both a way of describing personhood (model *of*) and a guiding image for being a person (model *for*). "External association" is both a way of describing our relationships with others (model *of*) and a blueprint for creating those relationships (model *for*). To be a Westerner is to take one's own identity and the external nature of one's relations to others for granted. It is to have "I continue to be the same person" echoing at the fringes of my awareness as I go about daily ac-

---

[2] Ibid., 93-94.

[3] The notion that being human is being-in-the-world is drawn from Martin Heidegger's analysis in *Being and Time,* trans. John Macquarrie and Edward Robinson (New York: Harper & Row, 1962). See esp. pt. 2, §§ 14-18.

tivities and also to have "these others are independent of me" resonating as I engage in everyday, face-to-face interaction.

These shared understandings of who we are and how we are related make it quite difficult to realize the extent to which we contribute to the ongoing creation of one another in everyday life. In what follows I want to bring that realization and its implications into a more focal awareness by examining our dominant cultural images of personhood and relationships and the concrete personal and social existences that tend to spring from and reinforce those images. I will contrast those interlocking images with an alternative vision of human development and relationships in everyday life. If all models *of* reality are at the same time models *for* reality, then this reconceiving of persons-in-relationship may offer a contribution to the more widespread emergence of ways of being human and relating to others that take account of the progress of our lives and the inevitably cocreative character of our relationships.[4]

MOMENTARY SELVES

My experience of self-identity—a sense of personal sameness through the course of my life—is not an illusion but rather an abstraction. Any abstraction leaves behind much of the full richness of the reality it names; self-identity is no exception.[5] As a participant in Western industrial society and culture, I tend to be highly aware of the threads of continuity that make my experience in the present moment specially related to my past.[6] I am also inclined to prize the psychological sense

---

[4]Bernard Loomer has urged the transformation of process/relational philosophy from a mode of thought into a mode of living in "The Future of Process Philosophy." See J. Sibley and P. Gunter, eds., *Process Philosophy: Basic Writings* (Washington D.C.: University Press of America, 1978) 538. This essay is intended precisely as a contribution to that effort. It hints at a "tale that might be told" in our lives together (see n. 31 below).

[5]The tendency to mistake our abstract conceptual frameworks for the fullness of reality is referred to by Alfred North Whitehead as "the fallacy of misplaced concreteness" in *Science and the Modern World* (New York: The Free Press, 1952) 51. It is likewise the basis of Korzybski's dictum that "the map is not the territory."

[6]Our sense of ourselves as having a continuous identity is understood within a process/relational or Whiteheadian framework as resulting from the particularly intimate relations between the drops of experience that center in our bodies. This intimacy of relating inclines each succeeding drop very strongly toward reenacting the dominant pattern of its predecessor. The following quote from William James, whose impact on Whitehead's thought was an important one, nicely illustrates this point:

Yesterday's and today's states of consciousnesses have no substantial identity, for when one is here the other is irrevocably dead and gone. But they have a *functional* identity, for both know the same objects and so far

of identity that results from this powerful sense of connection to a particular past.[7] Maintaining self-identity is the bulwark of my model of/ for being a person.

This strong consciousness and valuing of personal identity—this particular model of/for being a person tends to block my awareness that self-identity from moment to moment is a matter of degree, of "more or less." I can look back a few years and see "some changes in myself," but somehow from day to day and week to week I feel so much the same that not only immediate but also evolving differences in myself are hard to note.[8] Why am I so much more likely to be aware of how I am alike from

---

as the by-gone me is one of those objects, they react upon it in an identical way, greeting it and calling it mine, and opposing it to all the other things they know. This functional identity seems really the only sort of identity in the thinker which the facts require us to suppose. Successive thinkers, numerically distinct, but all aware of the same past in the same way, form an adequate vehicle for all the experience of personal unity and sameness which we actually have.

(From William James, *Psychology—Briefer Course* [New York: Henry Holt, 1892] 203).

[7]The classic psychosocial analysis of identity is found in Erik Erikson, *Identity: Youth and Crisis* (New York: Norton, 1963). For an important empirical study of the process of identity formation in the Eriksonian tradition, see James Marcia, "Development and Validation of Ego-Identity Status," *Journal of Personality and Social Psychology* 3:5 (1966): 551-59. A nontechnical "translation" of the psychosocial understanding of identity appears in Gerard Egan and Michael A. Cowan, *Moving into Adulthood* (Monterey CA: Brooks/Cole, 1980) ch. 6.

[8]In "The Development of Process Philosophy" Charles Hartshorne offers a counterpoint to our static vision of selfhood:

In the past that I recall, "I" was there, just in so far as what is important about "my" personal sequence of experiences was already in the earlier experiences. But why is it that we cannot remember our identical selves as small infants? Surely because in those early states what is now most important about us was not yet actual . . . we certainly cannot ever remember that in the past we were concretely and precisely what we are now, for that we were not! The "selfsame ego" is an abstraction from concrete realities, not in itself a fully concrete reality. To see this is the beginning of wisdom in the theory of the self.

(From Donald Browning, ed., *The Philosophers of Process* [New York: Random House, 1965] xiii.) The recent, strong interest in development as a lifelong phenomenon, which includes pioneering attempts to trace the anatomy of adult development in American culture, also moves counter to the image of static selfhood. See, e.g., Daniel Levinson et al., *The Seasons of a Man's Life* (New York: Knopf, 1978).

The term *development,* when used in a psychological sense, is a particular instance of the phenomenon of "process" understood in a metaphysical sense. Those interested in "human development" are challenged by the metaphysics of

day to day than of how I am different? Why am I so strongly inclined to prize stability rather than fluidity in myself?

The model *of/for* personhood that dominates my everyday experience as a Western person is powerfully shaped by a Greek heritage that assumed the universe is composed of independent substances.[9] To be a substance is to have a unique and fixed essence that remains the same however much surface aspects may change. When applied to persons and spread broadly in a culture like ours, it means that at the deepest level I share with you an image of human beings as entities with separate existences.[10] I exist independently and then relate to others. What is most important (essential) about me does not change over the course of my life. A variety of secondary (accidental) attributes may vary, but I am essentially self-identical: what really matters about me is not subject to transformation as I move from conception to death.

As an essentially unchanging self I am regarded as the subject of my feelings and actions. I am not constituted by my experiences but somehow underlie them. In Western, "substantialist" ways of thinking, the self has been variously regarded as: those aspects of existence that are particularly mine,[11] the organization of all the ways in which one sees himself or herself,[12] a rational agency that attempts to balance inner wishes and outer realities,[13] or even as a transcendental agent independent of the flow of experience.[14]

Whitehead to be mindful of the source of all becoming—relations (see § 3 below). An initial attempt to call attention to the importance of taking sociocultural structure seriously as the context of all human development is found in Gerard Egan and Michael A. Cowan, *People in Systems: A Model for Development in the Human-Service Professions and Education* (Monterey CA: Brooks/Cole, 1979). The present essay is a radical restatement of the "People in Systems" model in the light of process/relational metaphysics.

[9]This is the metaphysical stance of Aristotelian and later Thomistic metaphysics. It is embedded in the language and taken for granted in the dominant, everyday world view of Westerners.

[10]Heidegger has offered a powerful analysis of the problem of failing to distinguish the human from things in the world (*Being and Time*, 71-77).

[11]Gordon Allport, *Becoming* (New Haven: Yale University Press, 1955) 40. This classic statement bears a process orientation in certain aspects of its treatment of personality, but in the end does not slip its substantialist moorings.

[12]A. Combs, A. Richards, and F. Richards, *Perceptual Psychology* (New York: Harper & Row, 1976) 159. This is a revised version of an introduction to psychology from the perspective of the perceiving subject.

[13]This is the Freudian ego.

[14]This is the Kantian transcendental ego.

How did I come to take up this structure of existence, this particular way of being human?[15] An extended commentary on the genesis of the Western abstraction "self-identity" as a model of/for being human is beyond the scope of this essay. However, the growth in Judaism of a sense of personal responsibility for one's behavior before God and its continuation in the Christian tradition,[16] the interaction of this Judeo-Christian world view with Greek modes of thought,[17] and later with the development of the production modes that characterized the evolution of advanced industrial societies,[18] along with the individualizing of virtually all aspects of Western institutional life[19] contributed massively to the widespread emergence of individuals who both take for granted and nurture a strong sense of identity in themselves and others.

To be a thoroughly and contemporarily Western adult is to feel, perceive, value, think, and act—in short, to live—as if I first exist separately and then form voluntary external connections with other individuals like myself.[20] These connections with others may have an

---

[15]A "structure of existence" is a particular way of being human and of conceiving that existence. The conception of radically variable structures of human existence is the central construct of John Cobb's historical-comparative study entitled *The Structure of Christian Existence* (Philadelphia: Westminster Press, 1967). In that text Cobb analyzes what he takes to be the three major structures of human existence to date: primitive, civilized, and axial. Within the axial structure of existence he distinguishes and examines five subtypes: Buddhist, Homeric, Socratic, Prophetic, and Christian. Another powerful statement of the radical variability of human nature is to be found in Clifford Geertz, "The Impact of the Concept of Culture on the Concept of Man," ibid., ch. 2.

[16]Cobb, ibid., chs. 9-10.

[17]Regarding the differences and complementarity of Hebrew and Greek thought, see Thorlief Boman, *Hebrew Thought Compared with Greek,* trans. Jules Moreau (New York: Norton, 1970).

[18]The classic treatment of the role of religious doctrine in the evolution of industrial societies is found in Max Weber, *The Protestant Ethic and the Spirit of Capitalism,* trans. Talcott Parsons (New York: Scribner's, 1958). A critical assessment of the Weber thesis is found in R. W. Green, ed., *Protestantism and Capitalism* (Boston: D. C. Heath, 1959).

[19]This trend is described under the rubric of "fundamental democratization" by Karl Mannheim in *Man and Society in an Age of Reconstruction* (New York: Harcourt, Brace & World, 1940) 44-49. Mannheim's concept is applied by Morris Janowitz in the analysis of a variety of spheres of contemporary social life in Western industrial democracies. See *Social Control of the Welfare State* (Chicago: University of Chicago Press, 1977).

[20]The conception of "fictional constructs" as a model of/for reality is treated in Hans Vaihinger's *The Philosophy of "As If": A System of the Theoretical, Practical and Religious Fictions of Mankind,* trans. C. K. Ogden (London: Rout-

impact on me in a variety of secondary ways but do not affect who I am most fundamentally. In the process of prizing and nurturing this strong sense of personal sameness throughout my life, I learn to conceive of my strong sense of self-identity as *the* natural or essential way of being human. In this I am mistaken.[21]

Since I always already find my life thrown into a particular web of cultural pathways, a particular constellation of models *of/for* reality, it is inevitable that my initial sense of who I am will be shaped through being a person characteristic of my historical epoch.[22] Maintaining self-identity is the dominant model *of/for* being a person in the West at the moment, and our strong tendency is to live this way unreflectively.

A more adequate model *of/for* personhood must take account of the deeply processive character of human lives.[23] It has been suggested that the life of a person resembles a swimmer diving into a pool at one end and moving toward the other.[24] As I watch from above the pool, I can

---

ledge & Kegan Paul, 1924). According to Vaihinger, "It must be remembered that the object of the world of ideas as a whole is not the portrayal of reality—this would be an utterly impossible task—but rather to provide us with an *instrument for finding our way about more easily in this world*" (15).

[21]Cf. n. 15 above.

[22]Heidegger argues that authentic being-in-the-world is always a modification of our condition "primordially and for the most part," which is to be unthinkingly absorbed in the cultural pathways into which we are born (*Being and Time*, 237).

[23]The systematic statement of process/relational metaphysics is Whitehead's *Process and Reality*, rev. ed., ed. David Ray Griffin and Donald W. Sherburne (New York: The Free Press, 1978). The alternative images *of/for* personhood and relationships covered in this essay were nurtured by Whitehead's vision of reality. Cf. Bernard Lee, *The Becoming of the Church* (New York: Paulist Press, 1974). Chapter 2 of this text is a well-written introduction to many of the central categories of Whitehead's system. It is of particular use to those who approach process/relational philosophy with theological and/or pastoral concerns.

[24]This is an effort in translation: technical Whiteheadian language is confined to the notes. The danger in this approach is that a substantialist view of reality is so embedded in the structure of the English language that to use it is to adopt implicitly a substantialist view of reality. Whitehead developed his own vocabulary in order to force the reader to wrestle anew with what things really are, rather than merely continuing to see the world in the light and shadow of our Greek heritage. No true grasp of Whitehead's vision is possible apart from a serious encounter with Whiteheadian language. This encounter is guaranteed to be upsetting, in at least two senses; it is also the admission price to another world (see pt. 4 of this essay). Jay McDaniel, "Zen and the Self," *Process Studies* 10 (1980): 110-19. McDaniel draws suggestive parallels between Whiteheadian and Zen conceptions of life.

observe each individual stroke as well as the ways that strokes in the series are alike.

Creating an individual stroke is analogous to every moment in my life: I am deciding who I will be and what I will do now in a way that involves putting together events of my past, current influences, and goals for my life.[25] As the present stroke of the swimmer is marked by a past history of success and failure in swimming, the moment I am composing now bears the imprint of my successes and failures in composing a life. Just as the stroke of the swimmer is shaped by the conditions of the pool and other factors (e.g., whether this is a practice session or a championship contest), the moment I am currently composing is affected by conditions in my environment, including especially the quality of support and challenge available in my roles and in face-to-face interaction with others in everyday life.[26] As the stroke of the swimmer takes shape based on the swimmer's ultimate goal, the moment I am composing now must take account of my goals for life here and now.

The swimmer is most fully present not in strokes completed nor in the ones to come, but rather in the one now being created; I am most alive not in past versions of myself nor in those yet to be, but rather in the moment now emerging out of a past and heading into a future.[27]

The pattern of similarity among the strokes, the swimmer's unique style, is analogous to the patterns of sameness in the moments of my life. Each of the swimmer's new strokes bears the mark of the past; so too, each new moment in my life is importantly affected by past moments and is likely to bear resemblance to them. These are "family resemblances," that is, while this moment is like its predecessors in an often recognizable way, it is not exactly alike.[28] As daughters tend to resemble their mothers while remaining nonidentical, so adult moments of our lives can resemble earlier ones without exact correspondence. My self-identity, which is always partial, is this pattern of similarity in composing the moments of my life. In naming the partial similarity among

---

[25]In process/relational metaphysics there are no true contemporaries. All that I am taking in now is from the past. See A. N. Whitehead, *Adventures of Ideas* (New York: The Free Press, 1933) ch. 12.

[26]Recent studies of human development suggest that the presence of a blend of support and challenge are required for the ongoing development of persons. See, e.g., L. Knefelkamp, C. Parker, and C. Widick, eds., *Applying New Developmental Findings* (San Francisco: Jossey-Bass, 1978).

[27]"The creativity of the world is the throbbing emotion of the past hurling itself into a new transcendent fact"—Whitehead, *Adventures of Ideas,* 177.

[28]The notion of family resemblances has been employed by linguistic philosophers to capture the sameness and differences in various "language games." Regarding language games see, e.g., William R. Alston, *Philosophy of Language* (Englewood Cliffs NJ: Prentice-Hall, 1964) ch. 2.

those moments "identity," my culture stresses—and teaches me to stress—"similarity" in the term *partial similarity*. Because maintaining identity is such a powerful model *of/for* being a person in Western life, I am likely to be aware of and prize those things about me that remain the same and subtly but powerfully discount how this new moment is only partially similar to predecessors.

So what? If an observer above the pool failed to recognize that the swimmer was in the process of composing a stroke or that succeeding strokes have differences as well as similarities, we would consider such observation not simply partial but importantly flawed. If I fail to recognize that I am most fully alive in the moment I am assembling now and that my present mode is both like and unlike the ways I have assembled moments in the past, my sense of personhood is not only partial but seriously flawed. Maintaining self-identity as a model *of/for* being a person is constricting in precisely this way. The result, as any psychologically distressed person or practicing psychotherapist can attest, is that the hand of past moments of experience can press so heavily on the present that all too often the new possibilities for living that are present in a new moment cannot be felt or seen. This heavy-handedness of the past is only partly "in the nature of things." More crucially, my preoccupation with the identity between my past and present selves can severely limit the possibilities for who I might become. I am also prone to limit unduly what others might become and to perceive them as unnecessarily restricting the range and depth of my living.

At each new moment in my life, as in each new stroke by the swimmer, I make a choice about how I will put together the effects that have come to me from my world. This process of choosing, much of which is not present to my consciousness,[29] is where the element of freedom and spontaneity that I find in my experience resides. I am never able to finalize my existence into neat, finished structures. My life has a way of being more than the goals and roles into which I am forever trying to mold it.[30] I constantly entertain other "tales that might be told," other ways that my life might go.[31] My past, no matter how powerfully good

---

[29]The basic mode of perception according to Whiteheadian philosophy is "perception in the mode of causal efficacy." This basic feeling of events in our world is prior to the more abstract "perception in the mode of presentation immediacy," which is what we ordinarily mean by "perception." For Whitehead the latter mode is a derivative of the former. According to this analysis, our basic accounting of the world is done unconsciously. Cf. Cobb, *The Structure of Christian Existence*, ch. 2. See also n. 39 below.

[30]The notion of human existence as possibility, as always moving ahead of itself, is central in the ontologies of Heidegger and Sartre.

[31]The capacity for "propositional thinking," for envisioning novel ways that we might become, other "tales that might be told," is for Whitehead the source of the genuine creativity that we find in human experience. See *Process and Reality,* pt. 3, ch. 4, for a technical discussion of propositions as "lures to novelty."

or overwhelmingly bad, cannot dictate completely how I will respond to the offerings of the present. That response always contains an element of free choice, and for that reason always has the possibility of novelty present within it.[32]

As I choose in putting together this new moment, I do so with a feeling for the likely effects of that choice on my life and others. I cannot shake a sense that my present will have future consequences for myself and others.[33] In a processive model *of/for* personhood my life at the deepest level is an ever-flowing series of decisions: I compose my present experience out of a past and into a future, just as the swimmer moves toward a goal by creating one interdependent stroke after another.[34]

The moments of experience, the choices that make up my life flow into each other. A choice that I make at age forty is the descendant of a long line of previous ones whose effects now linger into the present. Subsequent choices may enhance or reduce the power of previous moments, but they do not completely eradicate them. My past choices live on into the present as an important part of its heritage. The relation of historical moments of experience to present ones is an *internal*[35] one: these past moments are not merely a bunch of causes and effects from somewhere in the past, but rather are part of the very stuff out of which I am composing a new moment. Their effects on my life are decided anew at each succeeding moment.[36]

---

[32]The immediacy and unity of a moment of experience is its "subjective form." This "moment of sheer individuality" is the "subjective" character of a drop of experience. See Whitehead, *Adventures of Ideas,* 177 and cf. n. 34 below. Robert Neville has stressed the importance of freedom in Whitehead's world view in *The Cosmology of Freedom* (New Haven: Yale University Press, 1974).

[33]This is the "superjective" character of a drop of experience. See Whitehead, *Process and Reality,* 87-93. Cf. n. 32 above.

[34]In Whiteheadian language, a human life is a society of momentary occasions of experience related internally.

[35]The notion of relations as internal, as contributing to the very depths of what is real, is the center of Whitehead's vision of the meaning of being related. See *Adventures of Ideas,* ch. 13. The image of relationality that has had the most powerful effect on my thinking about and feeling for the world is Bernard Loomer's "web of life." See, for example, Loomer, "The Future of Process Philosophy." Cf. n. 75 below on the interpretation of Marx from the perspective of a philosophy of internal relations.

[36]In classical Whiteheadian metaphysics the goal to which a drop of experience orients itself is its "subjective aim" and has its beginning in the offering of an ideal possibility in the form of an "initial aim" to the drop by the primordial nature of God. See esp. pt. 4, ch. 2, § 2 of *Process and Reality.* My own feeling is that a deeper internalization of Heidegger's conception of worldhood (see n. 3 above) would obviate the need for enormous reliance on the conception of eter-

From the beginning of my life I am a succession of moments of becoming. The web of relationships out of which I am continuously emerging provides the "raw material" from which each new moment emerges. This process of becoming, of composing a new moment out of the welter of environmental influences, is the core of reality in a processive vision of what is.[37]

As a Western person I am constantly invited by my language, customs, roles, and institutions to absolutize the maintenance of self-identity as a model of/for personhood. And, as noted, sometimes the weight of who I have been presses so heavily on the new self seeking to emerge that possibilities for transformed selfhood offered by the present are defeated by the prominence of my past selves.

In contrast, a sufficiently fluid perspective results in a person of integrated experience who has a particularly intimate awareness of the pattern of his own past moments.[38] In our culture a tendency to reenact this pattern has become a way of life, and "self-identical" individuals whose "nows" are too often held captive by the events and decisions of the past are the result.[39] The new selves struggling to be born at each moment must swim not only against the current of their personal histories but also against the tide of our collective preoccupation with the maintenance of self-identity.

FACE-TO-FACE INTERACTION
AND THE COCREATION OF SELVES

Our experience of relationships as external—of ourselves as existing independently and then relating as we choose to others—is not an abstraction but rather an illusion. Any illusion deceives us into accept-

---

nal objects as the basis of genuine novelty that seems to characterize much of process thought. Especially in the human realm, forms of definiteness seem to me to be: 1) the legacy of history and culture in a most concrete sense, and 2) themselves in process, not fixed or "envisaged" once and for all.

[37]The coming together of many influences in a momentary occasion of experience is termed a "concrescence." See *Process and Reality,* pt. 3, chs. 1 and 2. In every concrescing moment "the many become one and are increased by one" (ibid., 21). This line has been referred to by Bernard Lee as "the story line of reality" in Whiteheadian metaphysics (Lee, *The Becoming of the Church,* 63).

[38]See n. 6 above.

[39]The concrete ways in which the past maintains its hold in the present have been insightfully captured under the rubric of "life-script theory" within transactional analysis. Cf. Claude Steiner, *Scripts People Live* (New York: Grove Press, 1974) and Eric Berne, *What Do You Say After You Say Hello?* (New York: Grove Press, 1972). The text that has most powerfully affected my sense of the fluidity of human selfhood with regard both to the power of our pasts over our presents and radical openness to the experience of others is John Cobb's *Christ in a Pluralistic Age* (Philadelphia: Westminster Press, 1975). See esp. ch. 13.

ing something false or imagined as a matter of fact: "external association" is no exception. In this conception of relationships we may influence and be influenced in a variety of secondary or accidental ways, but never to the extent of contributing to the "essential" or "inner" constitution of each other. Independent individuals, relating to each other out of necessity or free choice while always maintaining our fundamental self-encapsulation: this is the symbolic image, the model *of/for* relationships to others, that we enact in our deeply ingrained collective sense of relations as external.

It is now our habit, as persons whose cultural heritage includes the substantialist vision of personhood described above and the highly individualistic ethos that is its companion,[40] to assume that the critical determinants of one's identity and basic assumptions and feelings about self, others, and world are to be found in the first segments of life.[41] We also tend to presume that these critical determinants are principally located in families of origin and their immediate surroundings. We are inclined to think that identity is relatively fixed in a "normal" life after late adolescence or early adulthood, and that this is but one of an ordered series of developmental crises that are waiting to unfold barring serious failures in our environments.[42] In this we are mistaken.

Few today would argue with the assertion that interaction in the family of origin during one's early years will result in a trajectory that is massive in its effects on subsequent experience. As a practicing psychotherapist I stand in awe of the power of the decisive familial encounters in infancy and early childhood to shape a stabilizing world of assumptions. That world prevails until later encounters reshape it.[43] Even in our radically individualized culture subsequent moments in friendship, marriage, religious community, work, education, and psychotherapy do contribute to the deep and ongoing restructuring of iden-

---

[40]On the mutual reinforcement of ethos and world view in culture, see Geertz, "Religion as a Cultural System," 89-90.

[41]This is a fundamental position of psychoanalytic thought. For an excellent tracing of the process of individuation in our culture from this perspective, see Margaret Mahler et al., *The Psychological Birth of the Human Infant* (New York: Basic Books, 1967). A translation of Mahler's research that frees the reader from the burden of psychoanalytic jargon can be found in Louise J. Kaplan, *Oneness and Separateness* (New York: Simon and Schuster, 1978).

[42]The classical treatment of this unfolding-pattern image of human development through life is Erik Erikson's "epigenetic principle" in *Childhood and Society,* 2d ed. (New York: Norton, 1963) ch. 7.

[43]The image of "decisive encounters" comes from the child psychiatrist J. Cotter Hirschberg of the Menninger Foundation. The conception of the "assumptive world" is drawn from Jerome Frank, *Persuasion and Healing* (Baltimore: Johns Hopkins University Press, 1973) ch. 2.

tities and assumptions. Yet we tend to see even someone in an extensive process of positive change as the same person now divested of emotional baggage or fouled-up thought processes or old bad habits.[44] While it is no doubt the case that sameness and continuity remain in such a person's life, often enough the differences so rival the continuities that we are forced to choose between seeing people as basically the same regardless of change or allowing for greater fluidity in our vision of who we are.

The choice that we tend to make is clearly for the first alternative: underneath people remain who they became in early life. This choice both comes from and reinforces our underlying cultural image of persons as independent entities with fixed essences, which is the model *of/for* personhood discussed above. But it also operates to shape our hopes, expectations, and actions in friendships, marriage and family life, and relations in work, education, religion, and psychotherapy. Our models *of/for* these relationships and the depth of effects they can (and cannot) be expected to have are profoundly tied to our image as independent and largely unchanging.

In fact, our individual and collective identities do not exist prior to our relations; they arise out of them. Our identities are not fixed after young adulthood; they remain open to the last moment of our existence.[45] The web of relations out of which we emerge initially and from which we continue to emerge for the balance of our lives is our perpetual core.

We understand the constitutive presence of places, symbols, persons, and things in our lives when we recognize that our lives are the ongoing experience of them and that integration of them into new moments will in turn affect our future as well as that of others and the world.[46] To think of and act in our relations as if they are internal or constitutive is to perceive the source of the "continuous becoming" of the self, the nexus of physical, social, and cultural interconnections out of which an individual's life is always emerging.

In a particularly powerful way our personal and collective identities arise initially and emerge continuously from the web of concrete human relationships in which we are constantly immersed. This perpetual relational web is at root a commingling of spirits or styles. The

---

[44]Perhaps the most pernicious form of this assumption is to be found when problems in living are understood as illness, i.e., in the medical model of psychopathology.

[45]The openness of human existence to possibility until death is most powerfully treated in Heidegger. See, for example, *Being and Time* on "the temporality of understanding" (385-89).

[46]"The many become one and are increased by one." Cf. n. 37 above.

"whats" (or content) of our lives—our particular tasks, roles, vocabularies, and uniforms—are less powerful in shaping identities than the "hows" (or manner)—our tones of voice, facial expressions, postures, and gestures toward others.[47]

My identity, which is continuously emerging, is in large measure the joint result of my interaction with others at the level of spirit or manner and the way I "provisionally"—for no aspect of the self is fixed—regard the input of these others.[48] This is why we sometimes experience other persons as, for example, so pervasively angry or demoralized that this becomes the dominant way in which we understand them. It also accounts for the fact that angry or demoralized persons sometimes change and begin to have other kinds of presence in people's lives. They have allowed a new manner or spirit into their experience, usually a loving one.

Identity-generating relations rooted in spirit or manner constitute the cocreative web of our lives at the deepest level. "To be in relationship" means "to be creative of" and "to be created by." Our personal and communal response to this pervasive and cocreative relating, as primordially evidenced in the manner of our everyday lives, is our identity at the deepest level. Our stories are not a part of a history possessed by us totally: they are all part of a history possessed by us partially.[49]

LIGHT AND SHADOW

A process of emerging out of relatedness characterizes everything that is real.[50] What makes humankind unique is the symbolic activity by which we put together our moments of becoming, the crucial role

---

[47]Research on the relative effects of verbal vs. nonverbal components of a message makes this clear. See, e.g., Mark Knapp, *Nonverbal Communication in Human Interaction* (New York: Holt, Rinehart and Winston, 1972) chs. 1 and 4-6. An excellent technical summary of scientific theory and research on nonverbal communication can be found in Robert Harper et al., *Nonverbal Communication* (New York: Wiley, 1978).

[48]Cf. Bernard E. Meland, *Faith and Culture* (Carbondale IL: SIU Press, 1953) 37. "In our bodies as evidenced by the turn of the head, the look, the stance, the way we receive other people, and more hiddenly still, the probabilities of response, the apprehensions, the concerns, yea the sensibilities—in all that gives character to the person—we carry the fund of valuations that give the total, existential meaning of ourselves as person." Meland's conception of "structures of experience" (cf. Cobb's "structures of existence," n. 15 above) offers an insightful analysis of culture's impact on how we experience our worlds (see ch. 6).

[49]This sentence is a paraphrase of Teilhard de Chardin, who wrote: "*My* matter is not a *part* of the universe that I possess *totaliter:* it is the *totality* of the universe possessed by me *partialiter.*" From *Science and Christ.* Quoted in Lee, *The Becoming of the Church*, 133.

[50]The notion that inanimate matter, e.g., a rock, is in a process of becoming

played by the meaning of things, events, and people in our experience.[51] Worlds of symbolic meaning—the constellation of cultural models of/for reality discussed above—are the medium within which we live, move, and have our becoming.[52] It is not simply "how things are" that shapes our experience, but what we interpret them to mean.[53]

An example may help to illustrate this interpretive way of perceiving the world and how this affects our experience. I am looking at what I would describe as a striking photograph of bleached white buildings clustered against the blue background of the sea. Had I spent time in this place, memories of those moments might be triggered. If I had shared that time with a person who was quite special to me, then he or she might well be a factor in my experience now as I regard the picture. That presence might even be dominant in shaping who I will become in this moment. Who has not been lifted out of (or into) a moment of despair or meaninglessness by an object, picture, or text recalling a person or event with the power to touch us so deeply as to transform our mood?

As a matter of simple, physical fact (and even this statement bears a huge load of interpretation) the object on the wall in front of me is a piece of glossy paper roughly two feet wide and three feet high with blotches of various color on its surface. To be human is to operate almost constantly out of an ingrained sense not of what things *are*, but of what they *mean*. In fact, quite a lot of discipline is involved in learning to go "back to the things themselves": to concern ourselves with bare forms, textures, colors, and so forth.[54] I am born into worlds of symbolic mean-

---

jars our everyday Newtonian consciousness, but is quite consistent with the image of reality now emerging in the theory of the quantum. See, for example, Gary Zukav, *The Dancing Wu Li Masters: An Overview of the New Physics* (New York: Morrow, 1979).

[51]Perception in the mode of symbolic reference is a synthesis of the two pure modes discussed briefly in n. 29 above. For a readable treatment of the Whiteheadian conception of the two pure modes and their synthesis in symbolic perception, see A. N. Whitehead, *Symbolism, Its Meaning and Effect* (New York: Macmillan, 1927). A technical and scholarly analysis of the evolution of Whitehead's theory of perception can be found in Paul F. Schmidt, *Perception and Cosmology in Whitehead's Philosophy* (New Brunswick NJ: Rutgers University Press, 1967).

[52]In *Toys and Reasons* (New York: Norton, 1977) Erik Erikson discusses stages in the development of "symbolic competence."

[53]In *Truth and Method* (New York: Crossroad, 1982) Hans-Georg Gadamer offers a powerful statement of the foundations for an adequate understanding of the act of interpretation. Cf. also Charles Taylor, "Interpretation and the Sciences of Man" (*The Review of Metaphysics* 25 [1971]: 3-51) for an analysis of the implications of hermeneutics for the understanding of human behavior.

[54]This is Edmund Husserl's dictum for phenomenological method in philosophy. See, e.g., *The Idea of Phenomenology* (The Hague: Martinus Nijhoff, 1973) 1.

ing; I live continually in them; I participate in their ongoing transformation; I will die amidst them. Those who survive me will understand my death in symbolic terms, and that understanding will shape both their initial reactions and subsequent responses.

The person perceiving a chair and sitting on it, the infant learning to recognize and name "Mama," the revolutionary organizing a network for the violent overthrow of an oppressive political regime in the name of social justice, and a community of persons gathered around a table to break bread and share a cup in order to identify with the life of Jesus: these are all human beings composing present moments of experience in the light and shadow of worlds of meaning, of symbols, of models of/for reality.[55]

To be human is always to live in cultural worlds of meaning. To exist in particular webs of meaning is also to internalize thoroughly and unconsciously a disposition toward living, a unique set of moods and motivations that give a particular tone and style to one's experience.[56] When we speak of the detachment of the Buddhist or the reserve of the British or the romanticism of the Celt or the discipline of the German we are trying, however clumsily and partially, to point to the "deep stories" that persons are born into and live out as members of a culture.[57]

My argument in these pages has been that our dominant and interrelated models of/for personhood and relationships in the West skew our version of human living in a particular direction. While in reality the maintenance of self-identity is always a matter of degree, we are culturally disposed to make it absolute; while emerging continuously out of a particular group of relations is our existence, we are culturally disposed to prize independence as a way of life. The passion for individual achievement, for example, stems from seeing our identity as *the* issue and our independence in pursuing it as a given. One troubling instance of our overly individualistic disposition is the incredible amount of damage to family life that is routinely inflicted by persons intent on the pursuit of success in their occupations. At the level of international re-

---

[55]The use of "symbol" throughout this essay is oriented to the analysis of Suzanne Langer's *Philosophy in a New Key* (Cambridge MA: Harvard, 1957) esp. ch. 3. Clifford Geertz's conception of symbol and meaning is indebted to Langer; Langer's conception was heavily influenced by Whitehead.

[56]See C. Geertz, "Religion as a Cultural System," 94-98.

[57]For culture understood as story cf. C. Lévi-Strauss, *Myth and Meaning* (New York: Schocken, 1979) and Stephen Crites, "The Narrative Quality of Experience," *Journal of the American Academy of Religion* 39 (1971): 295-311. With powerful results John Shea has taken up this perspective in theological reflection on the Christian tradition in *Stories of God* (Chicago: Thomas More, 1978) and *Stories of Faith* (Chicago: Thomas More, 1980). Cf. also John Dominic Crossan, *The Dark Interval* (Niles IL: Argus Communications, 1975).

lations we are faced continually with the possible, some would say inevitable, destruction of human life through our inclination to employ unilateral power in pursuing *"the* national interest" within the community of nations.[58]

How we respond to other persons depends upon what we can and cannot allow them to mean to us. Recall, again, that to be human is to be concerned not primarily with what things are but what they mean. In my dealings with you it is not my intentions and behaviors in themselves that will elicit your reaction, but your enculturated reading of their meaning. That reading in turn emerges from the meanings of the countless other similarly enculturated moments in your life that preceded it. In order to understand the effects of my presence in your life, I must hear you describe that presence *as experienced by you.* This principle of the centrality of meaning in human action is summarized in the classic dictum of sociologist W. I. Thomas: "If (people) define situations as real, they are real in their consequences."[59]

If my effects in your life and yours in mine depend on our reading of the meaning of events between us, then what sorts of relations are possible for us? I would like to describe briefly four orientations in relationships from the standpoint of the type of meaning that we allow others to have for us. I will call the orientations *transferential, contemporaneous, instrumental,* and *appreciative.*

Transferential describes relationships in which my perception of who you are is so dominated by the effects of persons from my past, especially parents or other figures of authority from childhood, that what you mean to me has little relationship to what you are actually intending and feeling.[60] Such a relationship involves unconsciously misidentifying you with an influential past figure. It has been perceptively described as a mode of relationship in which "we must grope around for each other through a dense thicket of absent others. We cannot see each other plainly. A horrible kind of predestination hovers over each new attachment we form."[61] In trans-

---

[58]A profound analysis of the character of unilateral power and its paradoxical relationship to "unilateral love" is found in Bernard Loomer, "Two Conceptions of Power," *Process Studies* 6 (1976): 5-32.

[59]From *The Child in America* (New York: Knopf, 1928) 572. This statement of Thomas has been described as "perhaps the only proposition in social science that approaches the status of an immutable law." U. Bronfenbrenner, "Toward an Experimental Ecology of Human Development," *American Psychologist* (1977): 513-31.

[60]On the psychoanalytic conception of transference, see R. Greenson, *The Technique and Practice of Psychoanalysis* (New York: International Universities Press, 1967) 1:152-55.

[61]Janet Malcolm, *Psychoanalysis: The Impossible Profession* (New York: Knopf, 1981).

ferential moments my past, rather than who you are, determines what your presence in my life can and cannot mean.

Contemporaneous names a type of relationship in which the meaning that you have for me is not determined by my history but draws primarily on what is transpiring between us in the present. In this orientation novel possibilities of meaning are not automatically crushed under the weight of the past. I will allow you your uniqueness. In contemporaneous moments who you are in our present, rather than who someone else was in my past, determines what your presence in my life can mean.

Instrumental is a mode of relationship in which what you mean to me is determined by the ways that you fit (or fail to fit) into my agenda for future hopes and goals. Put most simply, this is an orientation to relationship in which you are primarily a means to my ends. American culture has been described as one of "instrumental activism."[62] In this view our most basic characteristic as a people is that we are always looking for ways to shape the world to our purpose by using things as tools.[63] In a culture with strong tendencies in this direction, it is not surprising that face-to-face interaction between people should take on a tincture of instrumentalism, that we should routinely become tools for one another. In instrumental moments my agenda, rather than yours or ours, determines what your presence in my life can and cannot mean.

Appreciative signals a pattern of relationship in which what you mean to me emerges from bridging your world of meaning and mine in a way that is not dominated by what I wish to accomplish at the moment. I seek to understand and deal respectfully with your experience as we meet.[64] In appreciative moments the meaning, qualities, and possibilities of your life, rather than mine alone, determine what your presence in my life can mean.

The four patterns of relationship, of letting someone else have meaning in the becoming of our experience, were described thus for the sake of clarity. In fact, at any moment in our lives when another approaches, we receive her or him with a mixture of the four attitudes just discussed. Our reaction will be affected by the important relationships

---

[62]Cf. Talcott Parsons, *Personality and Social Structure* (New York: The Free Press, 1964) 196.

[63]In *Being and Time* Heidegger argues that our everyday attitude toward entities encountered in the environment is to see them as there in order to be useful, manipulable, at the service of our projects, etc. In *The Question Concerning Technology,* trans. W. Levitt (New York: Harper & Row, 1977), Heidegger explores the roots of Western culture's instrumental tendency in Greek antiquity.

[64]"Appreciative consciousness" has been successfully explored in Bernard E. Meland, *Higher Education and the Human Spirit* (Chicago: University of Chicago Press, 1953) ch. 5.

in our histories and is therefore partially transferential; it will take some account of the actual presence of the person here and now and is therefore partially contemporaneous. The person's meaning to us will be shaped by the ways that he or she affects our plans and hopes and is therefore partially instrumental; it will involve some measure of receptivity and understanding, however minimal, and is therefore partially appreciative. The question, I think, is this: in what proportions are these orientations to be found in our typical disposition toward others?

In Western culture our inclination to take the maintenance of self-identity as the model *of/for* personhood and to see external association as the model *of/for* life with others predisposes us to nonmutual relationships of the transferential and instrumental varieties. That is, we tend to interpret who someone is largely on the basis of critical events from *our* past and how well the person fits *our* agenda for the present moment. When self-identity looms too large in our sense of what personhood is, it is difficult to avoid using our need for maintaining identity as the key to interpretation. It is likewise quite difficult to allow others to be who they are rather than being something that fits our personal history and goals.

In contrast to our overly individualistic and separatistic models *of/for* human life, I have offered images of ourselves and our relationships from the framework of process/relational metaphysics. As a model *of* reality this world view stresses that becoming is the deepest characteristic of being real and that every instance of becoming emerges from relationships. But what does process/relational thought offer as models *for* being a person and being-in-relationship in such a world? What manner of living does this world view advocate?

To follow these models *of/for* reality is to proceed as if oneself, others, and the universe are eternally pilgrimaging—always emerging out of past moments of relating and into new ones. It is to treat the web of relationships that is our universe with the reverence due to the womb of all becoming. It is to believe that the capacity to be affected within relationships is as powerful as the capacity to have effects.[65] It is to be disposed toward appreciative moments that contain the novelty offered by every new present.

The dominance of transferential/instrumental or nonmutual modes of making meaning is not an essential characteristic of human nature. It is rather one way of being human that emerges within particular cultural and historical circumstances. There have been, are, and can be other ways of making meaning—of being human.[66]

---

[65]Cf. Loomer, "Two Conceptions of Power."

[66]This point is made dramatically in John Cobb's *The Structure of Christian Existence*. See n. 15 above.

DYING AND RISING
IN EVERYDAY LIFE

By *size* I mean the stature of a person's soul, the range and depth of (your) love, (your) capacity for relationships. I mean the volume of life you can take in and still maintain your integrity and individuality, the intensity and variety of outlook that you can entertain in the unity of your being without feeling defensive or insecure. I mean the strength of your spirit to encourage others to become freer in the development of their diversity and uniqueness. I mean the power to sustain more complex and enriching tensions. I mean the magnanimity of concern to provide conditions that enable others to increase in stature.[67]

The process/relational model of/for reality cries out for a nonindividualistic version of personhood and against the nonmutual stance that fosters and is fostered by our individualist ethos. The Christian understanding of love is for me a style of life that counters our deep collective predisposition to distort the meaning of others and the universe itself and then to behave toward them on that distorted basis.

By love I mean the capacity and commitment to let the emerging stories of others matter to us even as our own stories naturally matter. Worlds of meaning are transformed, made larger and enriched qualitatively, in the effort to let what is "outside" us enter our experience on its own terms.[68] This struggle to let the universe and other people affect us and to affect them in a nondistorted way is always an encounter with the limits[69] of what we can be: it is not something that can be managed and accomplished decisively, but is rather a continuing movement toward a horizon that moves with us, a way of becoming rather than a goal to be achieved. A loving stance is possible only when we are deeply and internally disposed to let something or someone else's tale matter to us in a degree that approaches how it matters to them.

At times what we hear and feel in loving moments will affirm our deepest convictions about ourselves and about what is and what ought to be. At other times faithfully taking in the events and feelings of another story will bring our understandings and plans to the brink of destruction and over it. Our speaking will have both kinds of effects in the experience of others. To love is to commit oneself to the belief that even

---

[67]From Bernard M. Loomer, "S-I-Z-E Is the Measure," in *Religious Experience and Process Theology,* ed. H. J. Cargas and B. J. Lee (New York: Paulist Press, 1976) 70.

[68]The power of symbols to transform and integrate experience is treated expertly in Henry Nelson Wieman, *The Source of Human Good* (Carbondale IL: SIU Press, 1946) 17-23.

[69]Cf. David Tracy, *Blessed Rage for Order* (New York: Seabury, 1975) 105-109 for a treatment of the limit quality in human experiences.

the upending of our worlds of meaning, no matter how painful, signals the emergence of something that can be trusted—which is that we will be enriched because we have been willing to stop clutching our own stories long enough to hear and speak to one another.[70]

Tad Guzie has made this point powerfully from the standpoint of Christian theology by saying: "A materialistic understanding of the light or bread or life that Jesus gives obviously does not work. Nor does a materialist understanding of his death and resurrection. Christian faith does not affirm that life is *resumed* after death. It affirms something much more profound, namely that life comes *out of* death."[71]

The deaths from which new life emerges are the losses of cherished beliefs about ourselves, others, the universe, and God. Once again, the question for us is not primarily what life is—that is, biological realities—but what life means. Deaths of meaning, in which we can so often fail to discern the birth pangs of new and fuller meaning, are the sort that affect us most nearly.[72]

Our earth cradles an incredibly pluralistic web of meaning along with the technological capacity, both military and otherwise, to hasten dramatically the end of all worlds of meaning. The primal expression of love in this context is embodied in the commitment to understand and speak authentically, to bridge worlds of meaning even at the cost of ongoing deaths to the self.[73] Those who would nurture the disposition to love in a pluralistic age must begin supporting the development in ourselves and our institutions of the capacity to listen deeply and appreciatively to others' meanings and to communicate our meanings powerfully and respectfully to them.

The past twenty years have seen an explosion of practical and effective methods for training persons in the skills of listening accurately and deeply and speaking clearly and constructively to others.[74] These methods have been resourcefully applied to enhancing the communications skills of psychotherapists, doctors, teachers, ministers, business managers, spouses, parents, elementary school children, and many other groups. In so doing we have again demonstrated our incredible gift for

---

[70]On parables and the upending of worlds, cf. John Dominic Crossan, *In Parables* (New York: Harper & Row, 1973).

[71]See Tad Guzie, *Jesus and the Eucharist* (New York: Paulist Press, 1974) 91 and passim for a development of this theme.

[72]Cf. Ernest Becker, *The Birth and Death of Meaning* (New York: The Free Press, 1962). See esp. chs. 7-13 on the centrality of meaning in human life.

[73]Cf. Cobb, *Christ in a Pluralistic Age,* ch. 13.

[74]See, e.g., Gerard Egan, *The Skilled Helper,* rev. ed. (Monterey CA: Brooks/ Cole, 1981) for an excellent example of a "skills-based" approach to preparing persons for the helping professions.

giving people tools—instruments—for accomplishing their goals. Unfortunately we have also discovered anew that methods drawn from the sciences, in this case the behavioral sciences, are very strong in answering "how-to" questions, but too often superficial or even dangerous in their (typically implicit) treatment of "whys." We may be nurturing a generation of persons who see active listening as a tool to be employed in order to insure effectiveness in the pursuit of their goals, entirely missing the spirit and cost and reward of making oneself present to another in a demonstration of mutuality. When this occurs, the deep instrumentalism of our way of life has once again asserted itself.

In societies whose economy is based on production for profit, a tendency to view the environment and other people as a means to ends will not abate.[75] In societies whose political systems and international relations are grounded in the unilateral employment of power, a tendency to maintain stereotyped and therefore distorted pictures of "the enemy" will not go away.[76] My belief is that leadership and moral authority in addressing the intertwined issues of our day—peace, economic well-being, and social justice on a worldwide basis—lie not with those whose motives are to make a profit or build scientific knowledge or exercise national political power, however necessary the responsible exercise of all three functions are in complex modern societies. Such leadership rests with those whose commitments are to the ultimate value of sustaining life of the body and the spirit for all persons. Such leadership will show itself in the quality of relational life within communities themselves, in the manner of their presence and openness to groups and persons outside their boundaries, and in their influence on the world's economic, scientific, and political systems.[77]

From a Christian perspective, "Anyone who proclaims Jesus' death by eating the bread and sharing the cup commits himself (or herself) to the work of unity, to the work of making a body."[78] That work is the cre-

---

[75]Cf. the Marxist analysis of alienation in capitalist societies in Bertell Ollman, *Alienation,* 2d ed. (Cambridge: Cambridge University Press, 1976). Ollman's text is particularly germane to the present essay in that he draws explicitly on a philosophy of internal relations (cf. n. 35 above) as an interpretive key to understanding Marx.

[76]Cf. Loomer, "Two Conceptions of Power." For an alternative to a unilateral stance in the process of negotiation, see R. Fisher and W. Ury, *Getting to Yes* (Boston: Houghton Mifflin, 1981).

[77]The "liberation theology" movement is one instance of an attempt to exercise such influence emerging from Christian communities. The larger social role of the important associational groups of our everyday lives ("mediating structures") is thoughtfully discussed in Peter Berger and Richard Neuhaus, *To Empower People* (Washington D.C.: The American Enterprise Institute, 1977).

[78]See Guzie, *Jesus and the Eucharist,* 101, for a treatment of the Christian sense of "one body."

ative transformation and integration of worlds of meaning, of models *of/ for* reality. In the work of shepherding meaning, which is uniquely ours as human beings,

Every act of authentic speaking
makes one life a gift to the becoming of another.

Every act of hearing deeply
increases the size of the listener's spirit.

Every act of responsible challenge in a spirit of understanding
is an invitation to an increase in stature.

Every act of nondefensive exploration in response to challenge
reflects a commitment to a life of larger dimensions.

Anyone struggling to nurture the discipline and tenderness and resilience of spirit that such giving and receiving demand, knows well the moments of dying that they entail and the intensity of living that arises out of them. To speak to one another and hear one another in this spirit of deep mutuality is to place the everyday acts of face-to-face interaction in the ultimate context of love.

CHAPTER FIVE

The Early Developmental Matrix of Self, Other, and the Divine
—————————————— • ● • ——————————————

J. ALFRED LEBLANC

As adults reading this book, the self that each of us is now experiencing is the outcome of a fairly long and perhaps arduous growth process that had its beginning in our conception, went quickly through fetal existence to the upheaval of birth, and then took years of hard care and hard work to become articulated. In the chapter that follows, LeBlanc, a psychiatrist and psychoanalyst, gives a summary of professionally respected developmental studies that address the question of how the self originates, what factors affect its deep structure, what impingements may thwart the course of its growth, and from what relationships it slowly emerges. LeBlanc's portrayal will make it clear that the human individual does not start with a clear-cut self that subsequently has to learn to engage in relations with others; rather, in the beginning there is only a peculiar kind of relationship out of which self and others slowly become articulated.

This chapter also takes us into the religious self, namely whether and how any self might become involved in a "dialogue with God." Using some modern poetry and giving us a brief clinical case, LeBlanc emphasizes the human need to trust, to hope, and to believe; he also sketches the disastrous effects on the self when these dispositions are absent or undermined.

One can hardly come to faith in God without successful passage through a first step of self-formation and a second one of dialogue (or the development of a capacity for object-relationships). These first two steps are themselves complex processes that I will describe briefly from a psychoanalytic perspective. The transition to a consideration of faith from the same analytic perspective can then be made coherently. In the final part of this chapter I will address the allegation that religious practice and adherence are themselves regressive experiences.

STEP ONE:
FORMATION OF SELF

Self-awareness is a function of the body and intellect working together. Both assist us in grasping reality, and each person is both a subjective and an objective reality. A loss or diminution of either component of that reality leads to psychological impairment or disorganization. Absence of a sense of wholeness or integration is experienced as threatening to survival and entails anxiety, a signal of danger.

How do we come by our subjective and objective self-awareness? How do we know ourselves and others (and later perhaps God)? Though some presume that these are innate givens, psychopathology teaches differently: What of autistic children who do not relate to or know others? What of others who first display a sense of personal identity and self-awareness only to lose it later, inexplicably, in psychotic states?

Spitz (1951) has shown that a failure of emotional bonding in the first six months or year of life can result in death or severe debilitation, even when otherwise healthy care, food, medication, and physical warmth are received. If the deprivation of emotional bonding occurs in later months, autistic states or childhood psychosis occur. And still later deprivations appear to result in adult personality disorders. This necessary physical and emotional environment, without which the child cannot thrive, constitutes what Hartmann (1958) has called "the average expectable environment." It entails first a loving, caring relationship between the mother and child. It also entails consciously or subliminally a recognition by the caretakers of the infant's needs at each phase or developmental step and some approximate, timely response to those needs. Harlow's experiments (1966, 1971) with mother-deprivation in monkeys confirmed Spitz's finding with human infants. His subsequent experiments offering cloth-and-wire mother substitutes worked initially, but little attachment and bonding occurred. As these monkeys reared with cloth mothers grew older, however, they became just as deviant in their play, defense, and sexual behavior as animals reared in bare cages without surrogates. Without an average expectable environment psychological life and thriving will not occur in animals and humans.

Allport, speaking of social interaction, noted: "It is the actions of the other to which he differentially adjusts that force upon a child the realization that he is not the other but a being in his own right" (Allport 1954, 44). His emphasis suggests that external reality (or mother) impinges on the child and sets the limits whereby the self becomes defined. While his statement is correct, it points only to a single phase in a much longer process that Mahler (1968) has vigorously explored. Before and with the social *No!* to which Allport alludes, there must occur much nurturing and many a *Yes!* Mahler has titled this sequential process that leads to the emergence of the self "The Psychological Birth of the Human Infant" (1975).

Though psychological birth is not synonymous nor coincident with physical birth, the two are analogous. Both births are critical events, the happy product of a genetic program and a set of environmental conditions that produce a cohesively functioning human infant. Physical birth is not only a beginning but also a culmination. Months before, there is evidence of cells, organs, and limbs in formation, of body rhythms and heart beat, of movement—in a word, of life. It is the final externalization of this process, the coming forth in a state of readiness that marks physical birth. Psychological birth has its antecedents also. These extend through the first two years of physical life and culminate within the third year, when a sense of self or identity normally crystallizes. What was previously a kind of closed mother-and-infant system (as was the intrauterine state preceding physical birth) becomes transformed into the open system of the child gaining a truly separate selfhood. And as with physical birth, the quality of "prenatal" care and attention given to the child by the mother and others decisively affects the psychological birth process.

The physically newborn child is buffered from excessive external stimulation by a "stimulus barrier" much as the infant in utero is buffered by the amniotic sac and maternal womb. Sleep predominates. Within this barrier or "autistic shell," the newborn rests, initially oblivious to much of his external surroundings and very sensitive to internal body stimuli. Since the brain has no barrier to internal stimuli comparable to the one it has for external stimuli, the internal stimuli will exert disproportionate force on the new infant. The instinctual urges and body sensations from within are the first contributors to the sense of self (Freud, 1920).

Phase I:
The Body Self (Early Infancy)

First sensory perceptions arise in the alimentary tract and by kinesthetic sensation in joints and muscles (Spitz, 1965). These sensations and the rhythm of their changes give rise in turn to a primitive sense of self whose core is one's body (Benjamin, 1961). With the ripening of neuronal tracts, the sensations of taste, touch, smell, temperature and pressure, and later vision and hearing contribute their input to the child's expanding consciousness.

Gradually, a shift in consciousness from internal to external perception sets the stage for a number of developments. The oral, tactile, kinesthetic, visual, and vestibular impressions begin to discriminate between inside and outside. The capacity for "double touch" (Hoffer, 1950)—that is, touching and sensing one's own fingers and other body parts—provides a schema of the spatial configuration of our body. A central aspect of "double touching" is the recognition of one's own vitality and animation. Stirnimann (1947) speaks of the innate discrimination present from birth between animate and inanimate objects. Harlow (1971) obtained similar findings with monkeys reared on surrogate wire-and-cloth mothers. The data derived from the external senses become integrated with the primitive internal body impressions to form an image of the self. The skin becomes visualized as the "envelope" or border dividing inside and outside. In comparison to the earlier, "gut" sense of a diffuse reality, the second-level perceptions form more convincingly our awareness of an articulate external, objective reality that surrounds the body-self and fosters adaptation.

Activity—measured by muscle tension, position, and pressure receptors—augments the awareness of specific body parts, which become integrated into functional units (e.g., eye-hand coordination). These functional units contribute to a total body image experienced as an action center. The sensorimotor functions involving parts under voluntary control are more readily incorporated into the total body image than those regulated by the autonomic nervous system (Lofgren, 1968). The sexual organs (e.g., the male penis, the female clitoris) have no voluntary intentional movement and obtain their objective quality by association with the whole body-self. The penis thus remains insecurely anchored, for there is a sense of powerlessness vis-à-vis involuntary movements. (I will comment in a later section of this essay on the restorative and integrative aspects of sexual and physical activity in the consolidation of the sense of self.)

Phase II:
The Establishment of a Symbiotic Bond

Though perceptions emanating from the body itself contribute to the formation of a self-concept, the development of a reliable sense of self is not at all possible without the affective coloring and impetus of a nurturing person. By virtue of the mother's repeated care and responsiveness, visceral relief and satiation are linked with an external nurturer. The infant repeatedly takes pleasure at the nipple and gazes at the mother's face. A perceptual and affective link becomes established and reinforced. With memory traces established, the satisfaction can be anticipated and the mother's return expected. When such a link is established and experienced with confidence, then we may say a symbiotic bond has been established.

The warm, cradling tenderness of mother (Hoffer, 1950), the mutual cuing in voice, expression, and gesture (Spitz, 1965), the playful engagement in mirroring activities with toes, fingers, body, and face imbue the child's body with a sense of value and love (Winnicott, 1962). The growth of a satisfied self reflects the soundness of the caring mother; this reciprocal interchange is the basis for the development of bodily integration and the feeling of being alive. The symbiotic bond replaces the infant's autistic hallucinatory and magical grandiosity by a more modest sense of sharing in the perceived omnipotence of the mother. In the next period this sense of omnipotence gives way to realistic perceptions and discrete attachments.

Phase III:
Differentiation (6-10 Months)
and Practicing (10-16 Months)

With the ascendancy of the distance receptors of vision and audition and the momentous shift from internal body sensations to external perceptions, the stage is set biologically and psychologically for differentiation, namely a clearer distinction of self from other. *On condition that the affective interchange of the symbiotic phase has been emotionally positive and sufficient in intensity and duration,* the innate thrust to differentiation will occur without damage. The successful handling of internal needs and crises and the enhancement of pleasure and well-being in the use of the external senses and of the motor system encourage the child's movement to the outside world. While venturing out the child retains a "safe anchorage" (Mahler, 1968) and will oscillate between seeking intimacy with the symbiotic mother and exploring the wider outside world. The child checks back with the mother during and after periods of exploration. Boldness alternates with caution; "customs inspections," comparisons of self and other, of mother and nonmother, and primary identifications through imitation or mirroring occur. Rizzuto (1979) has described the role of imitation and mirroring in the child's first images of God. The affective climate set by the mother's moods facilitates some of the child's evolving functions and retards others unevenly, thereby shaping the child's individual personality.

The inevitable occurrence of frustration or displeasure is a further prod to differentiation and development: the occasional absence of a pleasure or need satisfaction conveys the reality of what has been lost and stimulates the child's attempts at recapturing it. Freud (1933) held that sensations of a pleasurable nature do not have anything impelling about them whereas unpleasurable ones do in the highest degree. The latter stimulate change. This is the basis for secondary identifications in which the child assimilates the mother's care-giving capacities, after experiencing the complementary pleasures and deprivations. The previously cited commentary by Allport on socialization in the child—"It is the actions of the other to which he *differentially* adjusts that force upon the child the realization that he is not the other"—invokes differentiation. After pleasurable experiences of mothering and tolerable frustration, the child can differentiate himself by identification. In Anna Freud's terminology (1946) we would speak of a joint identification with a positive nurturer and with an aggressor. But it is the child's change from passive recipient to active doer that specifically enhances adjustment.

Locomotion also greatly enhances the differentiation process, for it widens the child's orbit. The child can scamper away from mother, stand upright, and so test and explore the world on his own. The toddler's energies now shift still more to his or her own body skills. The child becomes less enamored of mother and gains a growing sense of his or her own importance and initiative. Again, there is a transition from passivity to activity. The sense of escape from symbiotic fusion and engulfment accounts for the elation of this period. During the period of perceptual differentiation children retain some sense of omnipotence by sharing in their mothers' powers; now, moving away from or towards mother at will, they claim a sense of power for themselves.

While physically their standing is firm, psychologically the elation of standing alone, freely, can give way to crying and panic at losing mother. Toddlers typically will need opportunities to check back with their "other symbiotic half" for "refueling," or they may simply maintain contact from a distance by hearing and vision. This other half, the mother, must ultimately renounce her child's body and mind, letting go physically and psychologically in synchrony with the child's readiness for separation. Such letting go is an act of love. If primitive affective needs or insecurity of the mother result in prolonging the symbiotic tie, clinging and fearfulness will result. Similarly, if she hastily abandons the child in a panicky anticipation of loss, a precocious "self-sufficiency" may ensue. The natural reaction of the child to experiencing mother's occasional absence during this phase is a bearable level of longing, or "low-keyedness" (Mahler, 1975). Again, it is the quality and quantity of a mother's loving and understanding presence that regulates the outcome and makes initiative, self- and world discovery possible.

Phase IV:
Rapprochement (16-25 Months)

Propelled from mother by the thrust of their own motor skills, endowed with sharpened perceptual and representational capacities, these youngsters now recognize distinctly their separateness and identity as persons. They are more and more able to untangle their own emotional experience from their mothers'. Their "I" crystallizes. But this is a time of crisis, for their greater awareness also makes them conscious of their vulnerability. Their sense of sharing in the parental omnipotence and their need for symbiosis have diminished. They become painfully aware of the delusional character of their own assumed grandeur and relinquish it, but not without dramatic fights with mother (Mahler, 1975).

The role of the word "No" at this time, when verbal communication is ascendant and when some restraint on physical activity is often imperative, greatly enhances the awareness of separateness and of limitations (Spitz, 1965). It gives birth to new internal regulating structures, in identification with and in imitation of the governing parent. A "No" that takes into account the *child's* need for self-regulation and guidance will help; one vested in *parental* need for continued symbiotic attachment or control will crush the child's vulnerable separate identity. This is the time of "shadowing" and "darting away" behaviors. The children follow and woo their mothers; aware of their limitations, they fear losing her love. Alternating with explorations of the outer world they draw close to her, seeking approval and guidance; hence Mahler's term *rapprochement* (1975). But too much closeness may threaten the still-tenuous sense of separateness and dampen the impetus for "darting away" to prevent reengulfment. The mother's capacity to tolerate such ambivalent behavior and to be flexibly available (with love predominating over expressions of frustration, anger, or disapproval) assures optimal adaptation and grants the child an increasing measure of autonomy. When the mother shares the child's interests and explorations, the child in turn is encouraged to imitate her, identify with her, and internalize the qualities and behaviors of their mutual relationship.

With increased diversification of emotions and the capacity to experience and express feelings, the *sadness* of separation also emerges. Defenses against this sadness may occur, but a capacity for empathy may also be stimulated; for the child who has experienced longing in a situation of separation can identify with others in similar distress. In prior stages of symbiosis and omnipotence this empathy would not have been possible.

DIALOGUE

It is this capacity for empathic understanding of the other that makes dialogue possible. Empathy occurs where there is individuation and some measure of object constancy.

One stage of the self's emergence (Mahler, 1982) occurs at about age three when a sense of autonomy is first established. Successive developmental and psychosexual tasks provide new opportunities for mastery. Stimuli from the erotogenic body zones (oral, anal, and genital) create new conflicts; struggles in holding on and letting go appropriately, in initiating action and in mastering skills (Erikson, 1950) provide for further growth and stabilization of the self. Mahler (1975) has noted that the capacity for free upright locomotion, for "standing tall," parallels the boy's pleasurable discovery of the penis, its involuntary tumescence and detumescence. Sexual differentiation and assertiveness have a major share in one's evolving self-concept. For the girl, a developing capacity to capture or entrap, a sense of an inner space, an "inside genital" (Kestenberg, 1956) delineate her femaleness. The progress of these multiple differentiations through successive developmental phases, in the course of regressions and advances, with varied and unending conflicts, solidifies the sense of self. A self with wholeness and distinct boundaries can achieve intimacy without blurring and it can tolerate sameness without loss of self.

The second precondition for the exercise of empathy is some measure of object constancy. We have emphasized that a loving emotional bond is imperative for the child's growth. After the provision of an "average expectable environment," the combination of repetitive nurturing experiences with appropriate or naturally occurring frustrations safeguards the positive bond while catalyzing differentiation and growth. The mother here continues the task of stimulus barrier, fending off catastrophic or otherwise painful doses of external reality. As noted, occasional deprivations motivate the child to regain what has been lost by taking an active approach to what had previously been passively experienced. Active mastery also provides a sense of euphoria and well-being. The experience of loss through deprivation and its identification with the pleasure-giving or "good mother" facilitate the child's active return of love, feeling, and empathy. As the mother values the child's body, feelings, thought, wishes, and sensitivity, so will the child be apt to acknowledge in kind her wishes, her joys, her sorrows, and her sensitivities.

I visualize dialogue as a line of communication between first two, later possibly more, figures. The figures are *ideally* equidistant from a shared point of objective reality (if so, the parties experience good consensual validation), but *in practice* they may be different distances from this point of reality. What Bion (1977) has called a "work group" depicts the ideal. Dialogue can meaningfully occur (not give way to babble, incoherence, attack, or silence) when the distance between respective figures is not too great to break the bonding between them, or when one party can accommodate the other's "subjective" reality for some purpose. In the latter case the accommodating figure will feel some strain.

Pruyser (1974, and this volume), Rizzuto (1979), and Meissner (1984), all elaborating on Winnicott's (1951) concept of the transitional sphere, have broadened our understanding of the domain of reality to include objects that are at once real and unreal, inner and outer, illusory yet not hallucinatory. There is between our inner experience of a subjective reality and the so-called "cold cruel world of external reality," which clashes often with our subjective sense, an intermediate breathing space—part real, part creatively inspired—in which we may seek solace. This is the domain of symbols, stylized in art, religion, poetry, and other forms of culture.

Speaking of transitional objects, Winnicott describes their function as providing room for the process of accepting difference and similarity (i.e., differentiation and later intimacy). This process begins some time after four months of age and persists throughout life. Of the child's illusory object, for instance the blanket or fuzzy, he states:

> I am therefore studying the substance of illusion which is allowed to the infant and which in adult life is inherent in art and religion, and yet becomes the hallmark of madness when an adult puts too powerful a claim on the credulity of others, forcing them to share a respect for illusory experience that is not their own. We can share a respect for illusory experience and if we wish, we may collect together and form a group on the basis of the similarity of our illusory experiences. This is a natural root of grouping among human being. (Winnicott 1958, 230-31)

In the transitional sphere the mother willingly and temporarily subjugates her objectivity to the child's subjective, wishful fantasy. This symbiotic gratification permits engagement of the dialogue. In increments a shift occurs towards sublimation, from absorption in one's own unfulfillable wishes to sharing cultural pleasures. When the mother's grasp of reality is so precarious or tense that she cannot regress easily with her child to the transitional sphere, any attempted dialogue may be aborted or become inadequate.

It is the mother's loving constancy that enables her to follow her child into the realms of subjective experience and shared exploration of transitional worlds. Piaget (1937) has observed that at eighteen to twenty months of age, a persistent image or memory of the mother can be sustained, preceded much earlier by object constancy for inanimate objects. In contrast, what Mahler (1975) means by object constancy refers to a highly emotional bonding with the mother that values her as a stable identity even during different moods. It produces a state of relative emotional continuity in which basic love for the other can be sustained in the face of stormy emotions. With such object constancy the dialogue with the other who is recognized as distinct and separate can be continued.

GOD

If a metaphysician, starting with doubt, questions "the validity and reliability of whatever we sense, of all that tradition and authority hold for certain" (see Nachbahr's chapter in this volume), a clinician must of necessity start not from doubt but from love and hope. How might these disparate perspectives, both addressing questions of faith, God, or dialogue with God, be reconciled? Küng offers a bridge between these perspectives. Concerning belief in God, he writes: "This unproved assertion rests ultimately on a *decision* which is connected with the basic decision for reality as a whole" (Küng 1976, 73). Küng speaks of the *radical uncertainty* of any reality, noting it may be chaos, absurdity, or illusion. This uncertainty affords the possibility of despair and of refuge in nihilism. But rather than as an excuse for inaction, it could serve also as an opportunity for decision making and action. People are not only thinkers but also hopers and believers, and they may believe in no god at all and be racked with doubt and despair. Whatever their beliefs, they will tend to cling to them.

From a psychoanalytic perspective the passage through a series of developmental phases and subphases may bring the child or adult to a point of decision regarding faith and God. Winnicott (1963) has described this point of decision very well:

> To a child who develops "belief in" can be handed the god of the household or of the society that happens to be his. But to a child with no "belief in," god is at best a pedagogue's gimmick, and at worst a piece of evidence for the child that the parent figures are lacking in confidence in the pro-

cesses of human nature and are frightened of the unknown. (Winnicott 1965, 93)

A scrutiny of several Whitman verses where there is a lack of "belief in" may be helpful.

A Child's Amaze

Silent and amazed even when a little boy,
I remember I even heard the preacher every Sunday
put God in his statements,
As contending against some being or influence.

(Whitman 1912, 232)

Thought

Of obedience, faith, adhesiveness;
As I stand aloof and look there is to me something
profoundly affecting in large masses of men
following the lead of those who
do not believe in men.

(Whitman 1912, 232)

In "A Child's Amaze," the preacher does not differentiate himself from God but maintains a symbiotic fusion and protects his sense of goodness by projecting badness to others. We can appreciate the paradox for the little boy: which side should he be on? "Thought" depicts the absence of true constancy, illustrating only a pedagogue's gimmick.

The poet Anne Sexton, lacking conviction of her own human worth, describes her tortured efforts to arrive at belief.

Then there was life
with its cruel houses
and people who seldom touched—
though touch is all—
but I grew,
like a pig in a trench coat I grew,

....

and God was there like an island I had not rowed to
and still ignorant of Him, my arms and legs worked

....

but there will be a door
and I will open it
and I will get rid of the rat inside of me,
the gnawing pestilential rat.
God will take it with His two hands
and embrace it.

....

The story ends with me still rowing.

(Sexton 1975, 417-18)

Anne Sexton had proofread the galley sheets for this poem the afternoon prior to her suicide. "There will be a door / and I will open it / and I will get rid of the rat inside of me / the gnawing pestilential rat" clearly describes the yearning for relief through suicide. The metaphor "cruel houses" conveys a memory of hurtful and bad relationships. If people "seldom touch," there is little communication of love and tenderness and no sense of value of person and body. Anne Sexton knows this: "touch is all." Without good introjections she grows distorted "like a pig in a trench coat." She has a good sense of herself on a motor level—"my arms and legs worked"—but her self cannot be consolidated. She has too many repulsive and indigestible self-images: for instance, herself as evil, worse than Hitler, a pestilential rat, a crab. With her lack of clear differentiation or boundaries, she hates and accuses God for the destruction in the world; she confuses his destruction with her own and sees him fragmented as she is. Through many of her poems there is a poignant plea for contact, for touching, but her God is distant and not responding. She must undergo "the awful rowing towards God." Her inference is that she cannot be valued; she is a rat. God will heal her badness by "embracing" it, but this has not yet happened.

CONSTRUCTIVE REGRESSION AND REALITY

If, as noted above, the function of the transitional object and experience is to make room for accepting differences and similarities, and if Anne Sexton's repetitive efforts at family harmony failed, we must infer that the preliminary phases—consolidation of self, differentiation and constancy— were inadequate in her case. By her own testimony they were. Memories of early harsh and disillusioning relationships thwarted her self-development. There was no permanent sense of trust in and differentiation from others. She returned again and again to the symbolism of the transitional world; her symbols were full of destruction and loathing.

Her repeated return to the transitional sphere seems to have offered her some hope. "God will take it with two hands and embrace it" means that He will love even the worst of her. Such repetition of painful experiences has been described by Freud (1920) as a quest for resolution. Sexton's quest for God was also a regression in the service of the ego (Kris, 1971). This is a sort of regrouping process in which we temporarily permit ourselves the suspension of high intellectual functions, trusting that the more primitive strata of our mind will provide clues for problem solving. Bettelheim (1976) has described how children may solve everyday problems and fears through the controlled regression induced by listening to fairy tales. Freud (1900) had discovered the same mechanism in dream formation and described its role in adult sexual intercourse (1905). The mark of mature sexual functioning is the capacity to integrate in the sexual act the physical and psychological aims of earlier developmental phases (such as oral, anal, and phallic acts and sensations) under the dominance of genitality. There is a danger of arrest at one or another stage of foreplay that can give rise to sexual perversions and disturbances in character. But there is also a danger of failing to integrate both physical and psychological foreplay into the sexual act, thereby curtailing its richness and regenerative power. The self is continually (re)developed and (re)integrated throughout life, not only by virtue of a forward and upward maturational pull but also from behind and below by the readaptational use of earlier developmental formations.

CONCLUSION

There is a constructive form of regression that helps us in our task of accepting reality, and it is distinct from pathologic regression. It occurs in joking, for example, when we leave aside reasonableness and indulge in absurdity. It occurs in play where we may be carefree and free of responsibility. It occurs in sleep when we dream. For those who have already passed through the transitional level of experience, a refueling in faith is such a constructive regression.

Anne Sexton had achieved some measure of maturity and accomplishment prior to her illness. In crisis, she sought solace and strength within her transitional sphere to ward off the internal persecutors that afflicted her. She experienced a pathologic regression, with loss of body- and self-boundaries, depression and severely impaired self-esteem, disturbed interpersonal relationships and chaotic introjective-projective confusion, but she experienced a constructive regression as well. Her poem, I think, reflects the struggle and balance between these two forces.

REFERENCES
• ● •

Allport, E. W. 1954. *Becoming*. New Haven: Yale University Press.

Benjamin, J. 1961. "Some Developmental Observations Relating to the Theory of Anxiety." *Journal of the American Psychoanalytic Association* 9: 652-68.

Bettelheim, B. 1976. *The Uses of Enchantment*. New York: A. A. Knopf.

Bion, W. R. 1977. *Introduction to the Work of Bion*. New York: Aronson.

Deri, S. 1978. *Transitional Phenomena: Vicissitudes of Symbolization and Creativity in between Reality and Fantasy*. New York: Aronson.

Erikson, Erik. 1950. *Childhood and Society*. New York: W. W. Norton & Co.

Freud, A. 1946. *The Ego and the Mechanisms of Defense*. New York: International Universities Press.

_____. 1965. *Normality and Pathology in Childhood*. New York: International Universities Press.

Freud, S. 1900. *The Interpretation of Dreams*. Standard ed., vol. 4. London: Hogarth Press, 1953.

_____. 1905. *Three Essays on Sexuality*. Standard ed., vol. 7. London: Hogarth Press, 1953.

_____. 1927. *The Future of an Illusion*. Standard ed., vol. 21. London: Hogarth Press, 1953.

_____. 1933. *New Introductory Lectures*. Standard ed., vol. 22. London: Hogarth Press, 1953.

Harlow, M. F. and M. K. Harlow. 1966. "Learning to Love." *American Scientist* 54: 244.

_____. 1971. "Psychopathology in Monkeys." In *Experimental Pathology: Recent Research and Theory*. New York: Academic Press.

Hartmann, Heinz. 1958. *Ego Psychology and the Problem of Adaptation*. New York: International Universities Press.

Hoffer, W. 1950. "Mouth, Hand and Ego-Integration." *Psychoanalytic Study of the Child* 3:4. New York: International Universities Press.

Juni, S. 1985. "Religiosity and Preoedipal Fixation." *Journal of Genetic Psychology* 146:1:27-35.

Kestenberg, J. S. 1968. "Outside and Inside, Male and Female." *Journal of the American Psychoanalytic Association* 16: 457-520.

Kris, E. 1975. *The Selected Papers of Ernst Kris*. New Haven: Yale University Press.

Küng, Hans. 1978. *On Being a Christian*. New York: Pocket Books.

Lofgren, B. L. 1968. "Castration, Anxiety and the Body Ego." *International Journal of Psychoanalysis* 49: 408-10.

Mahler, M., F. Pine and A. Bergman. 1975. *The Psychological Birth of the Human Infant.* New York: Basic Books.

Mahler, M. S. 1968. *On Human Symbiosis and the Vicissitudes of Individuation.* New York: International Universities Press.

_____. 1979. *The Selected Papers of Margaret S. Mahler.* New York: Aronson.

_____and J. B. McDevitt. 1982. "Thoughts on the Emergence of the Sense of Self, with Particular Emphasis on the Body Self." *Journal of the American Psychoanalytic Association* 30: 827-48.

Meissner, W. W. 1984. *Psychoanalysis and Religious Experience.* New Haven: Yale University Press.

Piaget, J. 1954. *The Construction of Reality in the Child.* New York: Basic Books.

Pruyser, P. W. 1974. *Between Belief and Unbelief.* New York: Harper & Row.

Rizzuto, A. M. 1979. *The Birth of the Living God: A Psychoanalytic Study.* Chicago: University of Chicago Press.

Sexton, Anne. 1981. *The Complete Poems.* Boston: Houghton Mifflin Co.

Spitz, R. A. 1951. *Hospitalism: An Inquiry into the Genesis of Psychiatric Conditions in Early Childhood.* New York: International Universities Press.

_____. 1965. *The First Year of Life.* New York: International Universities Press.

Stirnimann, F. 1947. "Das Kind und seine früheste Umwelt." *Psychologische Praxis* 6: 1-72.

Whitman, W. 1912. *Leaves of Grass.* New York: E. P. Dutton & Co.

Winnicott, D. W. 1958. *Collected Papers: Through Pediatrics to Psychoanalysis.* New York: Basic Books.

_____. 1965. *The Maturational Processes and the Facilitating Environment.* New York: International Universities Press.

CHAPTER SIX

Sexual Aspects
of the Human Condition
—————————— • ● • ——————————

A. W. RICHARD SIPE

In the following chapter Richard Sipe frankly addresses a fact of human life that has caused some Christians to seek salvation by mortifying the flesh. That fact is that human beings are either male or female and experience sexual stirrings that have much to do with the whole complex business of attaining personal identity and engaging in relationships with other people. Because of sexuality's vastness, complexity, and profound impact on emotions and relationships, it is rightly considered a mysterious aspect of the human condition.

Being a personal counselor as well as an instructor in sex education classes, and having firsthand experience of both mandatory celibacy and the marital state, Sipe has become fascinated by how people talk about sexuality. He finds that the linguistics of sex often break down into a Babel of tongues that adds perplexity to what is already an inherently mysterious quality of experience.

Starting from the confusion of juvenile sex talk (which many people carry over into adulthood), Sipe discovers that there are three organized ways of talking about sex. He calls these "voices" and describes an objective, a lyrical, and a normative voice. These voices are often at odds with each other and sometimes appear intermixed in a shrill cacophony. Hence Sipe finds himself longing for an integrated voice and challenges theologians to help create one that will keep the experiential complexity of sexuality fully in the picture.

Is any subject more discussed than sexuality? I am not referring to excesses, aberrations, and the emotionally charged and politically tinged controversies that often surround the topic. Discount them for a moment. What I have in mind are the more everyday verbal expressions, explorations, and researches of ordinary human beings and various institutions.

Observant parents hear questions about sexuality coming from a three-year-old. The child's sexual interest, explorations, and observations are apparent even before his vocabulary is well developed. One does not have to depend on Freud to establish a historical record of infantile preoccupation with sexuality. Philippe Ariès quoted at length from the diary of Héroard, Henry IV's physician, which recorded the details of Louis XIII's young life. Héroard described the toddler-prince's frank references, in the presence of courtiers and attendants of both sexes, to his mother's genitalia; he recounted that when the little boy was betrothed to the Infanta of Spain, he gestured toward his penis and called it the Infanta's best friend.[1] But Ariès missed the point when he interpreted the child as only responding to his elders. It is clear from the texts that children were quite aware of their own and other's sexuality, while elders were also relating to the infant's awareness and questions.

This awareness has not diminished with the centuries. The origins of babies are discussed by six-year-olds on playgrounds and young adults in college dormitories. The painful sexual anxieties of adolescence are too familiar to review. The core concern for all persons is: "Am I normal?" The need to be "oneself" and yet "like everybody else" in one's sexual identity often reaches some resolution before marriage. Even so, courtship and marriage do not diminish talk about sexual matters. The focus, audience, and level of intimate exchange may shift; but the talk goes on throughout human development into midlife and old age. Thus it has been across the ages. And the discussions about sexuality take place not just among ordinary people and not just on an individual basis. Increasingly in the last thirty years, researchers in universities and medical schools claim to speak authoritatively on sexual matters. Certainly ecclesiastical pronouncements on sexuality have never been difficult to come by.

Why so much talk about sexuality? As one university student recently put it to me, "Talk about sex fills the air the way the clang of bells resounded in medieval Paris—reverberating everywhere and demarcating every segment of daily life." Even though talk about sex is so pervasive, its discourse is little understood. A noted researcher in human sexuality observed, "We know so little about sex at the present time that we do not know what research questions to ask." He also stated that he has never found anyone responding to sexual talk entirely "naturally."

In this chapter I hope to suggest a context that will help other students of sexuality to frame some productive research questions. I intend to do this by analyzing not *what* we talk about when we discuss sex, but *how* we talk about it—and how we *should* talk about it. I believe that the multivalent mystery of sex can only be appreciated through a variety of perceptual modes and discussed in a variety of voices. This con-

[1]Philippe Ariès, *Centuries of Childhood* (New York: Random House Inc., 1962) 100.

viction grew out of my experiences as a teacher and a psychotherapist; a sketch of this growth is the focus of part one. Some norms for successful "sex talk"—suggestions on how we might best articulate our thoughts and understanding of sex—are proposed in part two. In part three I describe what I believe are the main "voices" or approaches to sex talk. In part four I discuss myth as a synthesis of these many forms of talk. Finally, I propose a goal for sexuality discussions that I hope will challenge Christian thinkers.

SEX: A MYSTERY OF MANY VOICES

Two experiences have influenced my thinking about sex talk: teaching a college seminar on human sexual development and the practice of psychotherapy. Class preparation made me aware that sexuality can be approached from many disciplinary perspectives, each capable of offering only a partial view. I chose to approach sex education, as did many others in the early 1970s, from a multidisciplinary vantage point.[2] And student reactions to discussions about sex made me ponder. Students repeatedly remarked that they valued very much the chance to "talk" about sex. "This is the first time I ever really talked about sex or heard others talk about it." What could bright, articulate college students mean by such statements? At first I thought they were merely expressing relief at the open acceptance of subject matter that previously had been "forbidden." I surmised that they considered their talk about this subject, even with the same people, to have previously been somehow "dirty," but now magically sanitized by the college curriculum. In addition, however, I realized that by acknowledging the validity of their various perspectives, I was approximating in the classroom the students' experience of their own sexual development. This led me to a growing awareness of the diverse "voices"—which may be thought of as utterances, perspectives, or modes of perception—that must be used if sex is to be adequately characterized.

The students' reactions also led me to reflect on the experience of psychotherapy, during which many people talk about sex. How does frank talk about human sexuality in the classroom resemble similar talk in the consulting office? The subject matter and questions are much the same. Sexually related learning and growth can take place in both settings. What had previously eluded my attention, however, was the significance in both settings of the "voices" used to explore human sexuality. One could take various stances in approaching the same phenomenon, with the result that each stance offers some new (or different) understanding of the phenom-

---

[2]James Leslie McCary, *Human Sexuality* (New York: D. Van Nostrand Co., Inc., 1967); Herant A. Katchadourian and Donald T. Lunde, *Fundamentals of Human Sexuality* (New York: Holt, Rinehart & Winston, 1972); American Medical Association, *Human Sexuality* (Chicago, 1972).

enon. I slowly became aware that a range not only of subject areas but also of voices had to be used to form an integrated or organized sense of sex. In short, I found that in both the classroom and therapy settings no one single voice could encapsulate the reality of sex. This is not just because sex is a multifaceted reality, bridging each developmental stage. Nor is it solely because sex is a universal condition of our human embodiment. It has also to do with the mystery of sexuality—its potential, its limitation, and its essential incompleteness.

Therapy, however, differs from classroom study in that it attempts to help the individual put together his or her own biography. In therapy, personal history is reviewed in an immediate way and evaluated against perceived shared norms. This process does not come all in one piece or all at one time; instead, it is the product of an individual's groping for a personal way to integrate and organize his total experience. I may be speaking of a relatively simple albeit frequently ignored process, namely the felt and expressed journey in which the past, present, and future of a self are experienced in transition and transformation. To grapple in psychotherapy with the reality of one's sexuality is to put together a paradoxically incomplete whole from many parts.

In the effort to talk about sex, patient and therapist—indeed, all of us—face three levels of the sexual mystery. First, there is no simple or unified way to speak about embodiment. How can we give voice to the reality that consciousness and sensation are intrinsically and inextricably bound together? No single mode can give it utterance. Second, an incompleteness that simultaneously may be a wholeness confronts us when we talk about human sexuality. To be fully a man or fully a woman—that is, to realize one's human potential—is to realize that potential only as a man or only as a woman. Third, talk about sex faces us with the fact that man and woman are equally incomplete. Each sex is incomplete in relation to the other, even though each is wholly male or wholly female. Differences between the sexes are futilely translated into arguments over superiority or inferiority. Nor can superiority be gained in the incorporation of both genders. Denial of the need for or the value of one sex or the other is merely a refusal to acknowledge a part of reality. Most sexual controversies and aberrations involve a refusal to acknowledge one or more of these mysteries of our human embodiment.

SEX TALK: PITFALLS AND OPPORTUNITIES

If we are to talk fruitfully about human sexuality, we must respect the validity of diverse perspectives. We must expect the future expansion of knowledge. And we must become conscious of the voices used to express knowledge. To speak as if there were no perspective other than our own, or as if one perspective had absolute supremacy, impoverishes the fund of human knowledge as well as risks the loss of credibility. The same result ensues if one presumes that any perspective has exhausted the limits of sexual understanding. And to speak about sex as if its reality could be expressed in a single voice is to deceive ourselves as well as our listeners.

No one voice can encapsulate the mystery of sex, for no one voice can adequately speak about both behavior (what a person does) and being (what a person is). Relationships as well as identity contribute to human sexual reality.[3] The multifaceted nature of sexual experiences that span a lifetime and the complicated sexual aspect of human identity humble any speaker trying to describe these realities. In addition, we now know that the roots of sexual identity and behavior are preverbal: we experience sexual stirrings even before we can name or describe them. Identity and relationships—sex being an inevitable part of both—are dependent upon an individual's early personal history, when one forms essential human relationships (as between child and parent) and when one begins to shape a fundamental sense of self as different from other persons.

Sexuality is a necessary given of the human condition. It is impossible to identify oneself as human except as a sexually embodied being. At the same time, physical sexual behavior exists only in the context of a psychic reality. An eminent researcher insisted that there is no such thing as a purely physiological human sexual response and a purely psychical one.[4] The old dualism that reduced the person to body versus soul, carnal self versus spiritual self, is no longer effective in helping us understand the reality of our existence. Though justly maligned today, dualism handily described, via the opposition of eros and agape, a developmental process that extended from birth to death. Dualism usefully reflected a dynamic tension both within the psyche, between opposing tendencies in need of reconciliation, and within society, between individuals waging the battle of the sexes.

Today its shortcomings render the dualist mode quite useless, and as a result we literally have no Christian language for human sexuality. In the absence of such a language, we easily slip into arrogance, glibness, or hypocrisy. Arrogance ensues when one speaks from a dogmatic position, as if one's own perspective, perhaps valid within limits, represented the whole. We see such dogmatism when science is held to determine morality or when a moral perspective is imposed as scientific. The various ways of speaking must not be confused. To do so produces a discourse as scrambled as a mixture of English words and Chinese ideograms. Each perspective has its proper speakers and auditors. To quote Scripture, say, on a purely biological point is as inappropriate as to pound a nail into a plank with a pipe wrench: the wrench makes an indifferent hammer, and if damaged during such misuse, it

[3]Robert J. Stoller, *Sexual Excitement* (New York: Simon & Schuster Inc., 1979).

[4]William H. Masters and Virginia E. Johnson, *The Pleasure Bond: A New Look at Sexuality and Commitment* (Boston: Little, Brown & Co., Inc., 1974).

loses its efficiency as a wrench. Likewise, the use of religious categories to discuss cellular biology results in a distorted view of science.

Glibness in talk about human sexuality occurs when one speaks, even though validly, from one's own position but fails to take into account other perspectives in formulating that pronouncement. For example, recent papal dicta and certain statements of Hugh Hefner both have struck a similar tone of moral glibness; yet each proceeds from a potentially valid position. For example, when discussing morals Hefner appeals to empirical reality: "This has been observed." The pope appeals to norms presumably shared within the Christian community; we "should value" such and such an action. Neither speaker, however, acknowledges the perspective represented in the alternative voice.

Hypocrisy in attempting to find a Christian language for human sexuality results from the inevitable discontinuity between reality as it is lived and reality as it is talked about. This hypocrisy is evident in all those well-worn "do as I say, not as I do" pronouncements. Double standards, which abound in matters sexual, are vestiges of this outmoded way of thinking and speaking. Many sexual problems, such as birth control and mandatory clerical celibacy in the Catholic Church, have become institutionalized because of this way of speaking.

There is, therefore, much value in struggling to differentiate the voices of sex talk, that is, the ways in which we can talk about sexuality. This clarification of perspectives will not provide a Christian language for sex talk; but it will ease the pursuit of that language so that we can talk about the mystery of sex, and it will facilitate the attainment of sexual integration for individuals who now struggle with conflicting choices.

THE VOICES OF SEXUAL EXPERIENCE

I have proposed that three voices can be used to speak about human sexuality: the objective, the lyrical, and the normative. No one of these in itself gives a complete understanding of sexuality. Yet each is necessary if we are to understand an essential aspect of our sexuality.

The Objective Voice. In calling this voice "objective," I have in mind a descriptive rather than a philosophical definition. Some may think of this voice as scientific description or value-free language. Sex is often spoken about today in this mode. The scientific process produces knowledge by objectification, and its object of study is, so far as possible, quantified; the scientist expresses knowledge in terms as near to neutrality as he or she can manage. Scientific description generally uses the language of the third person; it attempts to produce conclusions that any qualified person can replicate, given the same conditions of the observation. Michel Foucault held that the modern "scientia sexualis" (his term) grew from the Church's practice of regular confession, instituted as a sacrament in the thirteenth century, which probed every aspect of a Christian's life and became increasingly focused on sexual thoughts and practices.[5]

---

[5]Michel Foucault, *The History of Sexuality* (New York: Pantheon Books, 1978) 1:60-61.

Sexuality, as the dimorphism of human beings (everyone is either male or female) and the interactions of the two sexes, may be studied objectively on many levels. The cellular manifestation of sexuality, the dimorphism observed in eighty-six percent of somatic cells, can be examined by cytobiologists. Differences in morphology and physiology can be categorized by physiologists and biochemists. The dimorphism of the human nervous system can be pursued by neurologists, and the differences in the ways boys and girls learn to think and the ways men and women act are explained by developmental and clinical psychologists. Differences in sex roles within and among societies are described by sociologists and anthropologists.

There is, of course, considerable overlap in these areas. For instance, take current investigation of the influence of hormones on sexual preferences. Recent research suggests that a surge of certain hormones in the mother's blood during the development of a fetus's cerebrum predisposes the child to homosexuality.[6] The evidence is far from conclusive, but if it could be proven that a sexual preference is influenced by certain levels of specific hormones during fetal life, such a demonstration would profoundly affect the inferences made by developmental psychologists and sociologists. Obviously, this information would be significant for moral theologians too.[7] Because cells, organs, and hormones determine the limits of behavior, social scientists must be concerned with the findings of research in cytology, anatomy, and biochemistry; because psychic states such as erotic interest determine endocrine and organic functions, anatomists and physiologists must be aware of advances in psychology.

Scientific description, then, offers a picture of how "third persons" act in the present, how they have acted in the past, and how they are likely to act in the future. By itself, scientific description cannot consider free human choices. Nor is the objective voice immune from the tenor of the times. A cursory examination of eighteenth- and nineteenth-century textbooks on sexual matters, such as *Onania, or a Treatise upon the Disorders Produced by Masturbation*,[8] indicates how a hysterical tone can pervade a "scientific" description; a look into the recent Hite Reports reveals how a titillating tone can invest an "objective" survey.[9]

---

[6]Jon K. Meyer, ed., *The Psychiatric Clinics' of North America Symposium on Sexuality* (N.p., n.p.: 1980) 6-10.

[7]Marc Oraison, *The Homosexual Question* (New York: Harper & Row, 1977). Andre Guindon, *The Sexual Language* (Ottawa: University of Ottawa Press, 1977). Anthony Kosnik, ed., *Human Sexuality: New Directions in American Catholic Thought* (New York: Paulist Press, 1977).

[8]Katchadourian and Lunde, *Fundamentals of Human Sexuality*, 231.

[9]Shere Hite, *The Hite Report* (New York: Dell Publishing Co., 1981). Shere Hite, *The Hite Report on Male Sexuality* (New York: Alfred A. Knopf Publishing Co., 1981). Gay Talese, *Thy Neighbor's Wife* (New York: Dell Publishing Co., 1980). Nancy Friday, *Men in Love* (New York: Dell Publishing Co., 1980).

The advantage of the objective voice is that it can explore such highly charged areas as homosexuality, sexual identity, and masturbation with a modicum of dispassion.[10] By imposing distance—the use of the third person—one can transcend grosser biases to some degree. An example of the disadvantages of insufficient use of the scientific voice can be seen in some Islamic cultures, which condemn and forbid attempts at objective study of the Koran, insisting instead on a devotional and literalist approach. The unfortunate consequences of this repression of the scientific voice have become only too apparent in recent years.

Psychotherapy usefully employs this scientific, objective stance, though with a difference, because it uses words as instruments. Psychotherapy is not an exercise in linguistics, but an attempt to explore and explain the unifying (and therapeutic) effect of words as they communicate an emotional reality. This psychotherapeutic exploration does not represent so much the grammatical use of the third person as its representational use. For instance, in therapy the development of the "observing ego" is a necessary part of the therapeutic process. The individual must look at himself, the past, and significant people and events in his development with a certain amount of dispassion and distance; one must objectify that intimate past. Whether the patient speaks in first or third person, he must play *with* and *in* the objective voice to achieve a therapeutic or integrative effect. This objective vocabulary is especially useful in coming to terms with sexual development and identity.

Still, the limitations of any scientific study are practical, theoretical, and ethical. Among the practical limitations is the notorious human proclivity toward bias. Even if causes could be linked to effects with certainty, the scientists would still have to reckon with the fact that, while experiments may be objectively carried out, they are never objectively set up. Michel Foucault, in *The Archaeology of Knowledge,* argued that any description should include what behavior is observed, where such behavior emerges (meaning, in the case of human behavior, the workplace, the family, the church, etc.), who made the observation (for instance, doctor, employer, or priest), the vantage point of the observer, and which "grids of specification" pinpoint these observations.[11] By considering these questions, Foucault asserted, scientific description can be corrected for bias.

The need for such a correction points up an obvious limitation of science: that external observation does not take into account interior, felt impressions. To consider the primary ways by which men and women

---

[10]Alan P. Bell, Martin S. Weinberg, Sue Kiefer Hammersmith, *Sexual Preferences* (Bloomington IN: Indiana University Press, 1981). Sandra S. Kahn and Jean Davis, *The Kahn Report on Sexual Preferences* (New York: St. Martin's Press, 1981).

[11]Michel Foucault, *The Archaeology of Knowledge and the Discourse on Language* (New York: Harper & Row, 1972) 50-53.

experience sex (instead of the actions that can be observed), we must turn to another "voice." We are so accustomed to scientific speech that we tend to regard a scientific report as the norm for good discourse. But there are other voices just as informed and informative as the scientific though they are different from it.

The Lyrical Voice. In his latest work, *The History of Sexuality,* Foucault noted one kind of "archaeological analysis" that reveals "the regularity of a body of knowledge": a study of "ars amatora." An erotic art, Foucault said, is the usual way for a civilization to make sense of its knowledge about sex. He pointed to the existence of such artistic expression in Etruscan, Roman, Arabic, Persian, Indian, Chinese, Japanese, and many other civilizations but not, alas, in the Christian.[12] Although examples of Christian erotica are not abundant, there has been some progress toward defining more exactly sexual elements in Christian art.

In a recent study Leo Steinberg explores the visual presentations of Christ in the Renaissance.[13] He makes a strong case for the explicit and deliberate acknowledgment of Christ's sexuality. There is, of course, no literary deposit in Renaissance literature to parallel this visual heritage. Caroline Walker Bynum has researched medieval spirituality and in her reading finds an awareness of Christ as a sexual being—especially Jesus as "mother"—in monastic circles.[14] A fresco from the apse of the basilica of Torcello that dates from A.D. 1230 reads: "SUM DEUS ATQUE CARO PATRIS ET SUM MATRIS IMAGO NON PIGER AD LAPSUM SET FLENTIS PROXIMUS ADSUM." ("I am God and man the image of father and mother. I am not far from the offender, but I am near the penitent.")[15] These erotic expressions suggest a lyrical voice in expressing human sexuality, however faintly it is sounded in Christian tradition.

By the lyrical voice (some might call it the poetic voice), I mean our personal explorations of sexual knowledge—our first-person communications that involve our emotions.[16] Wordsworth's classic statement in the preface to *Lyrical Ballads* addressed this point:

> I have said that poetry is the spontaneous overflow of powerful feelings: it takes its origin from emotion recollected in tranquility: the emotion is contemplated till, by a species of reaction, the tranquility gradually disappears, and an emo-

---

[12]Foucault, *The History of Sexuality,* 1: 57.

[13]Leo Steinberg, *The Sexuality of Christ in Renaissance Art and in Modern Oblivion* (New York: A Pantheon/October Book, 1983).

[14]Caroline Walker Bynum, *Jesus as Mother. Studies in the Spirituality of the High Middle Ages* (Berkeley: University of California Press, 1982).

[15]Antonio Niero, *The Basilica of Torcello and Santa Fosca's* (Venezia: Ardo/ Edizioni d'Arte, 1968).

[16]B. C. Lamb of the University of Maryland was especially helpful in formulating elements of the lyrical voice.

tion, kindred to that which was before the subject of contemplation, is gradually produced, and does itself actually exist in the mind.[17]

Whether or not we call this expression the lyrical or poetic voice, it reveals our inner, naked selves, something private that is uniquely ours—what many call a "feeling" because it originates deep within us.

Indeed, feeling is our connection with the physical world. Our bodies, the French philosopher Merleau-Ponty said, "synthesize" the world before consciousness does and present the world to us in the form of sensations or "affects."[18] The finer aspects of muscle coordination are integrated by the cerebellum in operations that never reach conscious awareness; yet the operations are there. We learn to judge distances through repeated acts of reaching; we learn about physical space through the data supplied us by our muscles and our eyes. The senses interrelate and synthesize the physical world for us before we are ever conscious of it. Sexuality forms one unity of our senses, for it draws together a multitude of observed facts and personal experiences.

A case of brain damage illustrates the body's essential link to our lyrical experience by showing us what happens when that connection is disrupted. Merleau-Ponty, in *The Phenomenology of Perception*,[19] described at some length the case of a German veteran of World War I whose vision was damaged and whose kinaesthetic sense was destroyed by an "occipital wound of limited extent" caused by a shell fragment. Schneider, the patient, could tell that he was standing up, if his eyes were closed, only by the sensation of pressure on the soles of his feet. Yet he could not describe a circle with his eyes closed. He could not trace a circle when asked, although once his hands chanced to make a curving motion, he recognized the motion and continued it. If required to move his arm, he began by moving his whole body and gradually narrowed down his motions until he located his arm.

Such kinaesthetic damage had serious consequences for the patient's intellectual and emotional life. According to Merleau-Ponty, Schneider wanted to hold religious and political beliefs, but the disturbance of his senses prevented him from thinking abstractly. He was also sexually dysfunctional. He was capable of erection and orgasm if his penis or inner thighs were stroked; however, he never initiated sexual intercourse. He experienced no sexual excitement from a kiss nor did he fantasize about sex. If his partner stopped caressing him, he would not pursue the exercise. In fact, he was always ready to discontinue inter-

---

[17]William Wordsworth, *Poetical Works,* ed. Thomas Hutchinson, rev. Ernest De Selincourt (London: Oxford University Press, 1966) 740.

[18]Maurice Merleau-Ponty, *Phenomenology of Perception,* trans. Colin Smith (London: Routledge and Kegan Paul, Ltd., 1962) 155.

[19]Ibid., 136.

course. We might say that because Schneider had constantly to fix and refix his physical position, he was unable to establish his psychic position relative to the objective, physical world that he knew to be "out there." Unlike Schneider, most of us are in better contact with the world, which appears to us as immediate and contiguous, though not always coherent. Indeed, some of the people who make up our social world appear contradictory, enigmatic, and irrational.

Literature can serve as an investigative enterprise by translating our lyrical experience of the outside world into words. Unlike a scientific description, which may note supposedly contradictory impressions but which itself must be consistent, a work of literature attempts to replicate the complex feelings of the subject. The goal of literature is to use such strategies as metaphor and metonymy to plunge the reader directly into the psychic state that the author intends—to move the reader from a third-person experience (detached, Schneider-like) to an involved, felt, first-person experience.

By moving the reader into a first-person position, an author can quickly sketch out a complex problem without the lengthy logical proof required of a scientist and without worrying about contradiction. Andrew Greeley, a sociologist turned novelist, is an unusual example of a writer who has moved between the two voices. He has spoken with some clarity from the objective stance of sociology; yet he has had to turn to the genre of the novel to express a "truth" that the objective voice could not handle.

Similarly, the lyrical voice can associate our personal lives with those of men and women we have never met. *Intimate Relationships: Marriage, Family, and Lifestyles through Literature,* edited by Rose Somerville, is a collection of short stories and poems that focus on sociosexual problems.[20] In it, "The Best of Everything," by Richard Yates, depicts the difficulty of changing from an adolescent "gang" society to marriage. "Tell Martha Not to Moan," by Shirley Williams, focuses on the problems of a pregnant, unmarried woman in the unstable culture of poverty.

Yet it is easy to attribute to the lyrical voice a force greater than it actually possesses. To be sure, its immediacy and intensity give it an allure and a sense of instant intimacy that, although elemental and valuable, is illusionary if isolated or if depended upon too heavily. Most novels and stories, however much they aspire to mythic integrity, are actually lyrical statements about real people in a real world. Greeley's novels are again good examples. Still, these literary excursions by Greeley, Yates, Williams, and others can help us to understand some problems of modern American society, if we pay attention to this interaction between the objective and lyrical voices.

---

[20]Rose Somerville, ed., *Intimate Relationships: Marriage, Family, and Lifestyles through Literature* (Englewood Cliffs NJ: Prentice-Hall, Inc., 1975).

The step inward from the third-person, scientific voice to the first-person, lyrical voice is a useful vehicle for conveying what we know about sexuality. Yet, just as the scientific voice has its limitations, the lyrical approach has its dangers. As Katchadourian wrote, Donatien de Sade and especially Mirabeau have given us powerful experiences of sadomasochistic feeling, but pure lyrical description cannot advise an individual on how to manage the sadomasochistic drives that appear to be a normal component of the human psyche.[21] "Under my cloak, I kill the king" goes an old Spanish proverb; but in order to choose a course of action "outside the cloak," an adult must consider not only his impulses but also the likely consequences of his actions. He must draw together the "he thought" with the "I thought."

Philosophers often consider impossible the synthesis of first person and third person, of subject and object. Sartre, for instance, differentiated sharply between the *pour soi* subject and the *en soi* object. There is currently heated debate over whether language is primarily an instrument of communication among persons (the so-called "instrumentalist" position) or primarily a means of giving form to and organizing one's thoughts (the "formalist" position). Not surprisingly, debate over sexuality splits along similar lines: sex as primarily an interaction, a way of contacting another person; and sex as primarily an internal, organismic, subjective system of feelings. Many feminist philosophers take the latter position, which is analogous to the formalist position on language. Alan Soble, in *The Philosophy of Sex,*[22] presents essays that take both these positions. The commonsense resolution of this dichotomy would be to say that sex is both internal and external: it is both a system of feelings for the individual and a means of contacting the world. Indeed, one sphere of experience depends on the other: without a stable relationship with the world, one cannot be in touch with oneself, and vice versa. Hence, sex talk demands both a subjective and an objective voice.

The Normative Voice. With the terms *objective* and *lyrical* I am striving to be descriptive rather than philosophical or scientific. Similarly, I do not intend to identify the word *normative* exclusively with its moral-theological meaning as symbolized by, let us say, the Mosaic Law. Rather, I wish to suggest that the normative voice in its mature form includes a prophetic dimension—that it integrates the Law and the Prophets and internalizes rules, transforming them into values.

Western culture today has made a good beginning for a scientific understanding of sex, and this culture's secular tradition of lyrical language about sex—though flawed by sexism and sensationalism—is rich

---

[21]Katchadourian, *Fundamentals of Human Sexuality,* 381-82.

[22]Alan Soble, ed., *The Philosophy of Sex* (Totowa NJ: Roman and Littlefield, 1980).

and deep for those with the education and the opportunity to explore it. But the normative voice seems in trouble. At one extreme we have those who insist that there are or should be no sexual norms—or that the only norm should be whether a given behavior "feels good" and seems at the moment to hurt no one. At the other extreme are those who advocate a return, if not to a literal adherence to Old Testament sexual norms (death for adultresses), at least to the dualisms of the Middle Ages (flesh evil, spirit good), or to the sexist and prudish standards of a vague yesteryear. How can people today, who have access to a better scientific understanding of themselves and to a more subtly nuanced, lyrical understanding of themselves than was available to their forebears, speak to each other and to their own hearts in a credible normative voice? How can the young be guided toward fulfilling sexual behavior but also helped to avoid scrupulosity and self-hatred?

I will suggest some criteria for a credible normative voice. We might deduce from the structure of the Old Testament that a mere code of thou-shalts and thou-shalt-nots, of "shoulds" and "oughts," is insufficient. Supplementing the Law were the Prophets, who exhorted the people to repent and return to a "Law-full" life and tried to provide a motivation for doing so by expanding people's awareness of God's love and closeness to them. Often this consciousness-raising language took the form of sexual lyricism: the communal experience of God was in some sense a sexual experience, affirming the importance and dignity of individual sexuality. Before he could speak out, the prophet had in some radical way to experience in his own flesh the message he was to deliver to others.

For Christians, the New Testament supplements both the Law and the Prophets. The Pentecost event can be interpreted as foreshadowing the essence of Christian maturity, the development of the normative voice beyond texts and codes: for one who "worships in spirit and in truth," the law of the Lord is written in the heart. Far from becoming a mimic of institutional regulations, a mature Christian weaves a fabric of values based on a faithful, honest experience of life, an evaluation of that experience, and an integration of his own discoveries with those handed down from the past. The past too, with its norms, is seen as subject to reevaluation based on more current understanding. One does not go about telling others what to do, but rather speaks to one's own heart in the normative voice.

Among Christian writers George Fox, the founder of Quakerism, is the clearest exponent of the underlying principles of the normative voice.[23] He espoused the authority of the "Inner Light," especially when

---

[23]George Fox, *A Journal or Historical Account of the Life, Travels, Sufferings, Christian Experiences, and Labour of Love, in the Work of the Ministry, of that Ancient, Eminent, and Faithful Servant of Jesus Christ, George Fox* (Philadelphia: Friends' Bookstore, c. 1849).

"individual judgment as to truth, right and duty is (thus) checked against the common judgment."[24] Attentiveness to the inner light resulted in the development of the "Inward Monitor" as a positive guide for life and action.[25] The normative voice was not merely conscience and certainly not legalism. It was the base of authority deeply rooted in awareness of the reality of self and other as part of active creation. The normative voice has its own authority and goal. The basic authority of the objective voice (third person) is in observation and its goal is primarily intellectual integration; the authority of the lyrical voice (first person) is the imagination and its goal is primarily emotional integration. The authority of the normative voice (second person) is an inner light that is a guide (you singular and plural shall and shall not) for action.

For a mature person who happens to have authority or command over others (parenthood, teaching, administrative supervision), the use of the normative voice is ideally less a process of saying "thou shalt" and "you must not" than it is a process of nurturing subordinates' discovery of the "I shoulds" and the "I should nots." There is something regressive about the military life-style precisely because it allows so little room for this development—so little room to err and learn from one's error. Such a nurturing process is carried out in the awareness that the human condition imposes on superiors and subordinates alike a common moral context, while at the same time the uniqueness of each person's life story imposes on individuals the privilege and responsibility of working out their own best response to that context. Developing a good normative voice is thus both grammatically and psychologically more complicated than is working with the objective and lyrical voices. The *psychological* process of internalizing values involves a shift of *grammatical* person. It is a movement from responding reflexively to "you must" and "you must not" exhortations to thoughtful, sometimes painful, decision making about what "I" must or ought to do.

Just as psychotherapy can help one to develop a more objective understanding of oneself and one's context and a greater awareness of the interplay of lyrical feelings with objective reality, so also can it assist its clients in this process of developing a normative voice of their own. The sad fact is that the sexual norms proposed by traditional Christianity can do little, beyond invoking the Golden Rule against exploitation, to help individuals in or out of psychotherapy to organize the multivalent reality that is their sexual lives. So many unconscious strivings find expression in sex: the need for play, the drive to create and procreate, the thirst for consolation and companionship, and the hunger for ec-

---

[24]Elbert Russell, *The History of Quakerism* (New York: Macmillan Publishing Company, 1942) 55.

[25]Ibid., 207.

stasy. These are such painful desires that they often only find their way into waking reality as preoccupations with other things or as obsessions. There is both a sameness and a uniqueness to each person's sexual strivings. It would be helpful if Christian moralists addressed themselves to the multivalent sameness, to the complex generalities of sexual life. With a cue from them, psychotherapists might then be able to help their patients recognize the ways in which their own experience is coordinated with the general norms and can be helped to fulfillment by them.

But instead of flexible norms reflecting the multivalence of sex, we have dos and don'ts proclaimed as absolutes, and we tend to zero in on a few behaviors labelled, almost capriciously, as aberrant: masturbation, youthful sexual exploration, birth control, "impure thought" (having sexual fantasies, especially if one is unmarried or a child), rape, homosexuality, abortion—but not sexism! These are all lumped together as seriously sinful, with little regard to the facts of human development or the circumstances of the individual. Norms for *good,* meaning approved sexual behavior, on the other hand, are inspiring only to those who really do have fun raising large families.

Some moralists defend this approach to sexuality by distinguishing between public and private forums. This is an inadequate defense for two reasons. First, the idea of the two forums, in effect, means that the Church speaks with a forked tongue, reinforcing a dangerous split between its public image and its internal reality, which everyone knows to be quite divergent. Second, the two-forums approach automatically places individuals needing to diverge from the public norms in the category of the un-ideal, the damaged, in need of compassion.

As a consequence of this disarray in Christian sexual norms, some clients present themselves for psychotherapy with problems springing from the disjunction between these norms and the realities of their own sexual experience. Psychotherapists must often labor to help these people free themselves from what are to them invalid or impossible norms. Sensitive persons who come into psychotherapy troubled by discrepancies between the proclaimed Christian norms and their own lived experience face the herculean task of developing their own normative "sixth sense" almost *de novo.*

While the normative voice in its maturity is internalized—the Socratic *daemon,* the Christian conscience, the spirit or Spirit of counsel within the heart—its call appears to originate not *from* ourselves but from somewhere *beyond* ourselves, urging us to regard truths more universal than our own. In some ways the Spirit reminds us of the metaphysical explorations of philosophers: "This is how I must act now," it says, "because this is what I hope is to come." Thus it orients our minds and hearts to eschatological expectations.

Yet the normative voice cannot be sounded and heard alone; indeed, a credible normative voice cannot even exist apart from the objective and the lyrical response to sexuality. A would-be normative voice that feeds on itself alone is only an echo or a compulsion that remains external to ourselves. Instead of being a source of enlightenment and clarity, it becomes darkly oppressive in its moralism and crushing to the self, which cannot integrate such an alienating voice.

PUTTING IT TOGETHER:
SEARCHING FOR AN INTEGRATED VOICE

Thus, there is value in distinguishing more precisely the voices by which we speak about our sexuality, so that we may reach a more complete understanding of its complexity. Although there is now no voice that integrates the objective, lyrical, and normative stances by which we may speak of sexuality, there have been attempts to find one in the past. Myth, which allows us to build a bridge between the real world and its larger truths, is such an attempt. Mythic language can speak about our sexual nature in a positive or negative way. Certainly, and unfortunately, we have no positive Christian sexual mythology that accepts us as we are. Mary is described as conceived without sin; Jesus as conceived without human intervention; the "holy family" as without sexual exchange; the Savior as fully human but without any trace of sexual interest. We are asked to anticipate with pleasure a future reward where there is no giving or taking of another person in marriage. In the face of such teachings, a young patient of mine put the problem eloquently: "It sure is hard to get sex and love together."

The problem of sexuality has been the subject of much mythopoetic treatment. Aristophanes, in Plato's *Symposium,* jokingly proposed a myth of sexuality that, despite its comic origins, revealed much about the problem. Human beings, laughed Aristophanes, were originally round with four arms, four legs, two faces, and so on. But they were powerful and proud, and when they tried to scale Mount Olympus, Zeus split them into two separate, incomplete kinds of beings, male and female. Since that time, said Aristophanes, we have been trying to rejoin at the genitals.[26] Despite its jesting tone, Aristophanes' myth sought to integrate the ways in which we talk about sexuality. He blended objective observations about reality (the interlocking function of the genitals, the similarity-dissimilarity of men and women), immediate lyrical feeling (the compulsion of the sex drive), and a normative dimension (amused approval) to produce a coherent view of reality.

Indeed, Freud's observations about sex may carry the weight they do today precisely because of their mythic quality. Freud combined thousands of specific observed details about his patients' lives to produce psychoanalysis, which is not merely a scientific theory but also a method, based on talking, for integrating such details. That is, he drew

---

[26]Plato, *Symposium,* 189a-192a.

a normative blueprint for a course of action grounded in objective observations of external and internal reality and mediated by lyrical (interior and subjective) involvement. Many of Freud's examples have the pithiness and artistic coherence of myth; for example, we could speak of the myth of the battered child who develops a sadistic perversion. Freud seemed aware of the mythic force of his discourse by the very fact that he looked to Greek mythology for the names of some of the dynamisms he identified, such as narcissism and the Oedipus complex.

This ambiguity of discourse has led Paul Ricoeur and others to struggle with the question of "proof" for psychoanalysis.[27] Scientific explanation, however, is neither the only nor perhaps the highest criterion for the evaluation of psychological truth. The communication fostered in psychoanalysis and other therapies offers a person the chance to create his or her own myth of the sexual self—the opportunity to join sex and love.

A rather more elaborate example of an approach to a mode of discourse that joins objective description, lyric, and normative speech is Chaucer's protonovel *Troilus and Criseide*. Chaucer's goal, according to Elizabeth Hatcher, was to create a context within which the possibility of psychological growth through sexual experience could be recognized—as it had not been in the sexual practice Chaucer observed in the world around him, in the literature and history he had read, and in Christian doctrine. He lived in an ecclesiastical culture whose "Lords spiritual" condemned all sexual acts except marital intercourse undertaken for the purpose of procreation. According to Hatcher, Chaucer did this by inventing a "myth of love," by which the young man Troilus progressed from childish solipsism to a heroic apotheosis through his sexual passion for the young widow Criseide.[28]

Chaucer was a poetic genius who has had few equals in any age, and the special bent of his genius was an insight into human nature that might stagger even Freud. He acquired this not by learning everything his civilization had to teach (actually, his education was rather eccentric), but by a keen interest in human detail and a powerful mythopoetic mind. Hatcher's point is that in *Troilus* Chaucer was breaking away in quite unheard-of fashion from what his civilization had to teach about love and human sexuality. The poet did not quite succeed, for at the end of his poem, he turned in dismay from his love story and urged his readers to abandon earthly love and seek Christ. So in the last analysis, he too left intact the dichotomy between eros and agape. He tried to integrate his objective, lyrical, and normative voices, but finally this "prophet" of new norms retreated to the shelter of Church doctrine.

---

[27]Paul Ricoeur, "The Question of Proof in Freud's Psychoanalytic Writings," *Journal of the American Psychoanalytic Association* 25:4 (1977): 835-71.

[28]Elizabeth Roberta Hatcher,*"Troilus and Criseyde:* Chaucer's Myth of Love" (Ph.D. dissertation, The Johns Hopkins University, 1970).

How is it that modern man, who knows so much more about the objective facts of sexuality than did Chaucer, produces only fragmentary and inadequate descriptions of it and multiplies these descriptions infinitely? Part of the reason is the vast increase in knowledge; in classical and medieval times, the field of knowledge was so small that one person could (and sometimes did) know all his civilization had to teach. Today, of course, a scholar must specialize to say anything important. Part of the reason, too, is that our society, intoxicated by its success at tracking down proximate causes and effects, has not exercised fully the voice that seeks to unify—the voice of theological reflection. Theology attempts to penetrate the mystery without trivializing it.

CHALLENGE TO CHRISTIAN THEOLOGY

The critic Vernon Ruland, in his book *Horizons of Criticism*, drew the following diagram:[29]

(The Experience)   (The Symbol)   (Reflection on the Symbol)

religious exp. ———> religion ————> theology

aesthetic exp. ———> literature ———> literary criticism

Theology, like literary criticism, represents a privileged third-person voice—third-person because it "objectifies" myths and privileged because it respects (or should respect) the feelings that feed into the myths.

Folk religions are said to have no theology precisely because they are the product of nonliterate cultures; therefore, there is no way for their priests to compare texts and resolve inconsistencies.[30] Every great organized religion is said to have a general theology. Some systems stress a person's integrity; they emphasize a person's bodily health and peace of mind. These "inner-directed" religions include Buddhism, Taoism, Hinduism, and Stoicism. Other religions place greater emphasis on the community of believers, since an individual's social conditions strongly influence his actions and happiness. These "other-directed" religions include Confucianism, Islam, rabbinic Judaism, and perhaps contemporary Marxism. Christian theology has tried to proceed along both fronts at once, emphasizing a person's integrity in his dealings with others.

One of the primary tasks of theology is to extricate the normative voice—the voice not only of law but also, in a fuller sense, of prophecy and of the spirit—from its cultural constraints and to give it concrete expression. When theology tries to explain things, it sometimes degenerates into

---

[29]Vernon Ruland, S.J., *Horizons of Criticism* (Chicago: American Library Association, 1975) 4.

[30]Richard M. Dorson, *Folklore and Fakelore: Essays toward a Discipline of Folk Studies* (Cambridge MA: Harvard University Press, 1976) 127-44. Cf. also "Folk Religion," in *Folklore and Folklife: An Introduction,* ed. Richard M. Dorson (Chicago: University of Chicago Press, 1972).

legalism, which functions well only in an invariable world. Indeed, the legalism of Hinduism indicates how far theology can stray from prophecy. As Gandhi pointed out, the Hindu scriptures nowhere sanction the caste system, and yet the legalism of that system is now ingrained in its culture.[31] Similarly, centuries of theological misinterpretation of the Bible have conferred upon Christian tradition a superannuated legalism in matters of sexuality. From this legalism Christians seem able to free themselves at best only individually and with difficulty. Maybe sexuality is always going to be a particular problem for Christian theologians, for it represents the primary level of contact with another person, based on structures inherent in our human reality but keyed to our external, physical world.[32] And sex is the one biological function that does not exist solely for the benefit of the individual: it remains incomplete until it can touch the other, for the sake of the species.

The Middle Ages hammered out a coherent theological world view that was moderately consistent in its scientific, lyrical, and legalistic aspects. Its Aristotelian science exemplified the unity of medieval thought. Medieval theologico-scientific teaching on the subject of sexuality was also conditioned by Platonic dualism and a culture in which women had a subordinate role and infant children were an economic asset. The subordination of women was reinforced, not balanced, by the cult of Mary, who was revered for her submission to a patriarchal Father-God. Her son was praised because He did not "abhor the Virgin's womb."[33] Thomas Aquinas, for instance, thought along these lines:

In Thomas's scheme, a woman was an incomplete man who dragged "real" man—that is, humankind—down the ladder of sensuality and away from his spiritual self.

Medieval science and society, however, are not modern science and society. Would we as twentieth-century people say that plants are more sensual than animals? To be sure, a modern thinker might argue that people

---

[31]M. K. Gandhi, *All Men Are Brothers,* ed. Krishna Kripalani (Ahmedabad: Navajivan Publishing House, 1960) 11-12.

[32]James B. Nelson, *Embodiment: An Approach to Sexuality and Christian Theology* (Minneapolis MN: Augsburg Publishing House, 1978).

[33]Erik Routley, "The Gender of God," *Worship* 56:3 (May 1982): 231-39.

feel more acutely and hence more subtly than do animals, thus making people more "spiritual." But others might argue that we are ignorant of other species and have no idea how subtly animals "feel." After all, the Pacific salmon returns to lay and fertilize its eggs in the very same river where it was itself spawned, apparently finding its way by its memory, now several years old, of how the water smelled. If so, that is pretty subtle and pretty acute behavior. Add to this the sight of a male blackbird, fluttering by the roadside and crying out in panic over his mate who has just been killed by a car. American Indian culture, which our ancestors brutally destroyed, sought spiritual health and knowledge from animals and the earth; perhaps we modern Americans would be less arrogant toward the rest of nature if our European forebears had respected the Indians and had encouraged an interpenetration of cultures.

While biological and physiological research documents some objective differences in the ways men and women feel and think, who today would seriously argue that women are lower on the scale of being than men? Yet modern theology would do well to pursue the quest for an integrated voice to speak about our human complexity that medieval thinkers attempted. The least we can do is support dialogues among scientists, artists, and prophets in order to broker discoveries that will change our culture, whether we like the change or not.

At the same time we must be critical of the outcome of the medieval efforts. Medieval thought failed because it was unable to develop beyond a hierarchical view of reality, and therefore it was trapped even by the stance of the privileged third person. If the therapies that emphasize speech have something to add to the understanding of the human condition, it may well be that their contribution lies in their development of the first-person plural—the "we"—as the voice of integration. When we can observe ourselves, our own behavior, and our history with some distance and yet experientially, and with empathy for others; when we can struggle with feelings and not get lost in them; when we can accept norms neither as shackles nor as tools of domination— then we can legitimately speak of "we." The first-person plural envelops both personal integrity and community.[34] It expresses the preconditions of the "covenant," which engages us in a personal and relational way. The reality of relationship lies in the "I and thou" and at the same time in the "we," which supersedes both.

---

[34]Jerome P. Theisen, *Community and Disunity* (Collegeville MN: St. John's University Press, 1985). This insightful study of original sin explores community and disunity as symbols of grace and sin. It forms the substructure for the application of these symbols to Christian sexuality.

CHAPTER SEVEN

The Tutored Imagination in Religion

————————— • ● • —————————

PAUL W. PRUYSER

In the following essay the human condition is approached from a special angle called psychology of religion. Throughout history and in all cultures, people have been religious in one way or another. Life has taught them that there are limits to human power and comprehension, and in response to this realization they have developed elaborate patterns of symbolic thought and action that address such ideas as transcendence, mystery, God, eternity, or ground of being. In a word, people are or become religious, or seek to extricate themselves from that "taint"—in either case acknowledging that religion is "around." But how is religion around, how does it get transmitted, and how is it being appropriated or protested?

It is suggested that religion is around as an imaginative undertaking. Like the arts, the sciences, literature, and music, religion is a major domain of human culture. And like these other cultural achievements, religion is an illusionistic enterprise that cannot be reduced to either the world of private, untutored, solipsistic fantasy such as prevails in dreams, or to the sensory presence of things and nature in the outer world. The great "goods" of culture, including religion, have a special ontological and epistemological status that constitutes a third world of symbolic or illusionistic entities. Access to that world depends on acquired skill in illusion processing that has much to do with a capacity for imaginative playing.

But the integrity of the delicate illusionism of religion is constantly threatened by intrusions from the world of personal autism and the world of sensory reality. It requires a special, tutored, and skillful use of the imagination to keep religion intact.

Religion, like art, deals with peculiar entities that are neither utilitarian things in the external world nor inexpressible private ideas in someone's head. Even when natural entities such as mountains, trees, or animals are objects of religious worship and devotion, their alleged divinity lifts them above the condition of being mere specimens of geology, botany, or zoology. Two technical terms have been used to allude to the special ontological and epistemological status of these peculiar entities of religion: *transcendent* or *mysterious.*

Despite the highfalutin' intellectual aura of these terms, which makes them unsuited for discussions with young children (and quite a few adults), experience with religious education shows that children themselves have no serious problem in recognizing, appropriating, and dealing with the peculiar entities to which religion refers (and defers). Cognitively and emotionally, children can live with gods and accept various manifestations of deity, no matter how transcendent or mysterious these entities or events are. Similarly, so-called primitive peoples appear to have been able to live with their god(s) and accept various manifestations of the divine, around which they have typically engaged in ritual action. The notion of "object" appears to be quite fuzzy in children and primitive man: it includes intangibles, chimeras, dream fragments, and other "fancies."

In later phases reflexive thought may be distanced enough from these peculiar objects themselves, and people's habitual dealings with them, to raise questions about their peculiarity: What kind of objects are these religious entities? Do gods exist? What am I doing when I pray? The focus shifts from the *objects* themselves to the *ideas* of transcendence and mystery: What do *transcendence* and *mystery* mean? What kind of cognition and recognition pertains to these terms and what kind of observations or experiences do they address? (Elsewhere in this book Nachbahr will expound further on mystery.)

LIMIT SITUATIONS

The concepts of transcendence and mystery are tools for coming to terms with limit or "borderline" situations (Jaspers 1949, Tracy 1975). These limit situations, when deeply experienced and reflected upon, can lead to the acknowledgment that there is a gap in being between the human subject and the divine object. The limit encountered in certain existential situations (such as birth, death, awesome events, conversion, guilt, confrontation with exquisite goodness or evil) becomes variously defined as: coming up against one's own limited power, limited authority, limited knowledge, restricted action radius, narrow scope of perception, failure of reasoning, inadequate means of expression, failure of nerve, captivity, etc. When people experience their dependency on powers beyond human control, they may find that a gap separates their frail existence from a mightier cosmic Being that is felt to be its own cause.

From this recognition the insight may arise that limit situations produce a momentary shift in the customary cognitive subject-object relations: the experiencing subject no longer cognitively dominates *his* or *her* object but finds himself or herself *known by it, grasped by it,* and *confronted by it* as a feeble, frail, groping, and bungling entity that cannot lay claim to self-sufficiency. Otto (1917) has sought to reconstruct the phenomenology of limit experiences in religion, specifying the forms in which contingency is experienced when one encounters the Holy. Otto's phenomenology includes the momentary subject-object reversal in which the religious person acknowledges the prior existence and overwhelming dynamic self-affirmation whereby the Holy poses itself and reduces a person to its object, which now undergoes an ambiguous state of awe and bliss. The crucial feature is the Holy's dynamism, which cannot be matched by anything human.

When we are satisfied with such descriptions of limit experiences (which need not be dramatic incidents), can we venture a psychological interpretation of them? Can psychology contribute to an understanding of people's relation to religion's peculiar entities? I think it can, especially by using a developmental approach.

CHILDHOOD DISCOVERIES

I have said that young children do not appear to have serious trouble in entertaining, and acting upon, the notion of God. Like most other children, I was introduced to religious ideas and attitudes through stories told by adults and by watching adult religious behavior such as saying grace before meals. Whether the home avails itself of the Bhagavad Gita, the Koran, or the Bible, the essential transmission of religion to children takes place through storytelling and engagement in ritual: without stories, no religion (Pruyser 1968, Wiggins 1975). In the story, some aspect of the structure and dynamism of the universe is conveyed in the form of a happening, a narrative, an evolving plot. Along with religion, I was at the same age introduced to the arts (Pruyser, 1976): the books had pictures, the prayers had rhythm, special diction, and voicing; the body postures assumed in ritual had aesthetic qualities approaching those of dance; some passages in the stories were poetic; and worship involved singing or listening to great music.

As a toddler I played with blocks, putting them on top of or alongside each other not only to make certain lineups but to pretend that the resulting patterns were towers or trains or houses. I discovered that I could play at being an animal and that even serious-minded adults entertained the thought that animals could feel, speak, and act in human ways, with pictures in books to prove it. I found out gradually and with delight that certain shapes, such as a short upright line or a curved line, denote something that is neither just a whimsical subjective thought nor an ordinary thing, but the letter "I" or "C"; and that one of these letters, the "I," undergoes a metamorphosis of status and meaning when it is taken for the number "1." After I had learned to read, I discovered that some words, read backwards, produce another word: "God" becomes "dog." Grown-up people would affirm these discoveries, but with a proviso: "I" was only "one" when one talked about numbers and never when one dealt with letters; "God" could never be spelled backwards in a prayer! And so I got my first inklings of language games.

As these novel worlds emerged and as I began to practice the skills and thoughts and words appropriate to each, I found them to be mutually reinforcing. Between the inner world of my private, fanciful images, as in dreams and reverie, and the patently outer world of perceptible things that fill space, a whole set of new worlds took shape that contained mostly intangible entities; yet they proved to be shareable, and they could be talked about in a certain language that was different from "this is a table" and "here is a tree." When I said: "Our Father who art in heaven," no one called me stupid or crazy or unrealistic, and even I myself did not confuse the referent of this phrase with the referent of another, nearly identical phrase, which said that my natural father, who had died, was alleged to be in heaven. In fact, only by leaping into a third language game, pertinent to joking and mockery, could I gigglingly utter the prayer phrase while casting a glance at my father's photograph, supported by the laughter of my siblings and instantly checked by the dismay of my mother.

It will surprise no one when I summarize these reminiscences from childhood by saying that I exercised my *imagination;* engaged in thought, speech, and acts with *imaginary* beings; and received much approval and help from adults in keeping traffic with the *imaginable.* Of course, approval was dependent upon my thoughts, words, and acts proving to be shareable with other people, or better, touching a responsive chord in them.

TRANSITIONAL OBJECTS
AND THE TRANSITIONAL SPHERE

The title of this section apposes two concepts introduced by the British pediatrician and psychoanalyst Winnicott (1951). This observer of children noted that older infants temporarily exhibit a strong attachment to some "thing" from their environment: a piece of blanket, a soft toy, a rag doll. They keep it close to them in moments of duress, cuddle it when they are excited, finger it when they doze off, or stick it into their mouths when they are frustrated. The "thing," called a "transitional object," functions as a tangible contour that marks off the child's inner world from the outer world, but also brings the two together. Winnicott astutely called attention also to the special cognitive and emotional attitude that family members assume toward the child who claims this transitional object: the adults do not dispute the child's special claim to that piece of blanket or rag doll, but indulgently allow for the intimacy with it. Wise mothers know that the transitional object cannot be rudely taken away from the child (e.g., to be laundered, or put into the toy chest for neatness' sake); they also know that in moments of distress their emotional access to the child can be aided by approach through the transitional object. In a word, the whole family knows, undoubtedly from their own childhood memories, that the child regards the transitional object not just as a thing among other things in the world, but rather as a quasi-sacred, ritual object that is to be handled with reverence and solemnity. It is a transcendent, mysterious, symbolic object. Through the transitional object, family members will seek contact with the child and engage the child in play. The family deals with the transitional object just as ritualistically as does the child. A special pattern of stylized human interactions ensues that is different from ordinary reality testing. The whole network of actions and interactions having to do with the child's chosen symbol, which approaches the nature of a liturgy, is what Winnicott calls the transitional sphere.

TWO WORLDS OR THREE?

A large body of developmental psychological and psychiatric writings describes the neonate's inner world as autistic. Drives, affects, longing, and kinesthetic sensations predominate, constituting what Freud (1911b) called the *primary process.* It is the world of dreaming, suffused with fantasies that are extremely subjective, essentially solipsistic, and ineffable. In deranged adults, unchecked indulgence in the primary process accounts for psychiatric delusions and hallucinations. In the autistic world everything is possible as long as it is imaginable— it is designed by the omnipotence of thought. Traces of this infantile omnipotence persist in adults: if one does not like one's current situation, one can daydream (fantasize) a better one.

As the mother's initial hyperadaptive attitude gives way to a more normally adaptive or "realistic" set of ministrations, frustrations increase for the infant, who becomes forcefully aware of the outer world as a mixed pattern of positive and negative stimuli with which one has to compromise. A distinction between "me" and "not-me" will slowly emerge, with increasing awareness of discernible external entities such as food, bathwater, people, and qualities such as light, colors, sounds, and temperature. Coming to terms with this outside, objective world elicits the *secondary process,* which is cognition based on objectivity, reasoning, reality testing, and logic. This process is evident in the child's use of words with firm denotation value in a stable, consensually validated language pattern. For years to come, the child will receive much guidance in practicing and perfecting this secondary process according to culturally recognized timetables.

Thus, the psychological literature on development grants status to two worlds: the inner and the outer, the subjective and the objective, the autistic and the realistic. Developmental literature states the goal of growth and of pedagogy as giving up the autistic world and embracing the realistic world, or as reality curbing the promptings of fantasy. The leitmotiv of development is that the secondary process shall overtake the primary process. Reason shall triumph over affect, order shall replace disorder, instincts shall be tamed, and man shall become civilized.

Spurred on by my own childhood reminiscences and enlightened by Winnicott's concepts, I find that this two-world vision of traditional psychology amounts to a truncated statement of the options for growth and development. Beyond or between the autistic and the realistic world lies a third world (Pruyser 1974) that has entities and events of its own, foreshadowed by Winnicott's transitional sphere and its transitional objects. It is the world of *play*, the world of the imagination, the world of *illusion*. I shall call it the *illusionistic* world (Pruyser 1976). And to give a provisional definition of terms, I quote from Freud (1927):

> These (religious ideas which profess to be dogmas) . . . are illusions, fulfillments of the oldest, strongest and most urgent wishes of mankind. The secret of their strength lies in the strength of those wishes. . . . An illusion is not the same thing as an error; nor is it necessarily an error. In the case of delusions, we emphasize as essential their being in contradiction with reality. Illusions need not be necessarily false, that is to say, unrealizable or in contradiction to reality.

There it is: illusion is neither hallucination nor delusion, though it can deteriorate into those states. Illusion formation is a unique process that derives from the imagination. However, it need not be captive to the autistic process and cannot be locked into the reality-testing procedures prescribed by common sense, let alone what Woodger (1956) calls the "finger and thumb philosophy" of positivism.

While Freud spoke of illusion in religion, Gombrich (1962) devoted a large book to *Art and Illusion*. Art is not the representation of reality, but a thoroughgoing transformation of stimuli from the inner and outer world. As creations of the imagination, both religion and the arts will have to be distinguished from reality in the ordinary sense and from solipsistic subjectivity. If too natural, too "thing-ish," too realistic, art vanishes into mere representation and religion into mere rationality (or fundamentalistic double-talk about an unseen world that must be taken as literally as the sensory world). If too subjective, too autistic, art and religion will fail to get a hearing since they come too close to delusion and hallucination. Everything depends on using the imagination in such a way as to keep its products linked with, but different from, the realities of the outer world and the common human stratum of the inner world. The culturally successful use of the imagination must be coupled with adequate reality testing so as not to deteriorate into madness.

THE ILLUSIONISTIC WORLD

In the following chart, taken from my essay on creativity (Pruyser 1979), I have sought to compare the three worlds outlined in the previous section. I have put the illusionistic world between the autistic and the realistic worlds not only to suggest an ideational space for it, but also to correct the genre of thought that imposes a forced—and I think false—choice between autism and realism.

AUTISTIC WORLD	ILLUSIONISTIC WORLD	REALISTIC WORLD
Untutored Fantasy	Tutored Fantasy	Sense Perception
Omnipotent Thinking	Adventurous Thinking	Reality Testing
Utter Whimsicality	Orderly Imagination	Hard, Undeniable Facts
Free Associations	Inspired Connections	Logical Connections
Ineffable Images	Verbalizable Images	Look-and-See Referents
Hallucinatory Entities or Events	Imaginative Entities or Events	Actual Entities or Events
Private Needs	Cultural Needs	Factual Needs
Symptoms	Symbols	Signs, Indexes
Dreaming	Playing	Working
Sterility	Creativeness	Resourcefulness
Internal Object (Imago)	Transcendent Objects Prefigured by the Child's Transitional Object	External Objects

Illusionistic objects transcend the other two, albeit certain traces of internal and external objects may codetermine their form and content. They are not products of whimsical private fantasy, nor replicas or representations of sensory data. They evolve from a tutored fantasy rooted in the collective imagination of the human mind and its history.

Much of the "relatedness" that Cowan emphasizes elsewhere in this book occurs through this collective imagination. Illusionistic objects and illusionistic thinking are *sui generis,* irreducible to the strictly private, ineffable, autistic, and essentially solipsistic mind, or to the public, demonstrable, look-and-see entities of the realistic world. Between autistic dreaming and realistic working lies the opportunity to play and to engage in symbolic[1] transactions, shared with and supported by other people who are civilized. Illusionistic thinking pertains to symbol systems such as religion and the arts and, as Polanyi (1958) and Kuhn (1970) have demonstrated, to the spirit of science. What else is a "paradigm" in science but a playfully entertained contract inviting certain believers to engage in a game, abide by its rules, and be excited by the prospect of some intellectual "payoff"?

---

[1]I use the words *symbol* and *symbolic* in the sense given to them by Tillich (1952), namely, that they participate in the power to which they point.

ILLUSION PROCESSING IN RELIGION

If Winnicott was correct in his programmatic statement that religion and the arts are developmentally rooted in the child's practicing with transitional objects in the transitional sphere, and if my construction of a "third world" of illusionistic objects is plausible, then religious development hinges on a set of functions that could collectively be called *illusion processing* (Pruyser 1979). This processing is obviously an exercising of the imagination with the help of certain cultural resources and guided by certain tutors. It leaves room for innovation and creativity, for personal variation of collectively held ideas, just as it can be stifled by pressure for slavish conformity to public models.

In regard to the latter situation a strong caveat is in order, one that takes into account a perversion of the illusionistic sphere that occurs all too frequently: the staging of illusionistic ideas or entities as if they were realistic. Many religious debates are emeshed in this fallacy. For instance, if the doctrine of scriptural inerrancy (which is properly an illusionistic proposition) is literalized in the realistic sphere, one is saddled with having to deny evidence for the theory of evolution. Along with relocating illusionistic propositions from their proper sphere into the realistic sphere, one also has to switch from one language game to another or else—as frequently happens in arguments of this kind—engage in double-talk that makes no sense at all. While one may attribute the example just cited to poor or undisciplined thinking, it is apparent that other perversions of illusionistic ideas are a product of institutionalization. In the process of institutionalization the original illusionistic idea may eventually become unrecognizable, and playful attitudes, let alone innovative proclivities, will be overtaken by a grim pseudorealism, with sanctions for deviancy. The acme of perversion by institutionalization was the Inquisition.

Barring such perversions, the constant threat of which requires unrelenting vigilance, how does or should the religious imagination develop? As everyone knows, the infant's original transitional object is sooner or later given up and replaced by new ones. But the practice of attachments to symbols goes on, continually allowing the growing person to experience the fascination, excitement, and solace they offer. Though transitional objects are characteristically held in high esteem, a degree of unresolved ambivalence may produce an occasional outburst of anger against them. This anger may, at a later age, amount to doubt about, or disbelief in, the very object of one's faith. But even apart from affective lability and ambivalence, the inevitable ambiguities of life are likely to give the illusionistic sphere and its objects always a somewhat delicate, if not precarious, status. Proof of this delicate quality of illusions (in religion, art, and science) lies in the historical fact that civilizations can decline and regress to barbarism, if not savagery. In that case autism and realism prevail, one barely checked by the other.

Such historical collapses of a people's illusionistic sphere highlight an important feature of illusionism: the opportunity it offers for sublimation of erotic urges and the neutralization of aggression. Civilized persons have modified their impulses by focusing them on well-chosen objects with which they can engage in harmless and possibly even constructive activities. It is the imagination, especially the culturally tutored fantasy, that fashions the symbols, stylizes the modes of dealing with symbols, and sets the rewards for engagement in symbolic activity. Through the trained imagination, the illusionistic sphere promotes that optimal fusion of erotic and aggressive energies whereby the former has the edge over the latter and transforms it into healthy and constructive activity. The transformation occurs not just in one's head, as in a daydream, but in the civil arena.

As an example of such constructiveness, nay of creative innovation, I cite Martin Luther King, Jr.'s work, culminating in his glorious "I have a dream" speech. That speech straddled both the world of ideas and the world of facts; it introduced a new paradigm (Kuhn 1970) after showing the bankruptcy of an older one; and it combined Jahvistic wrath with the benevolence of a God-in-Christ. But for all his patent creativity, King showed great reliance on the great illusionistic traditions of the Bible, black preaching, and Gandhian nonviolence! Absorption in these traditions had become to him a sacred playing—with one sidewise glance at the brutal facts of the realistic world, and another keen glance at the ever-present explosive turbulence of the autistic world.

If I may turn again to autobiography, I recall the great affection I and my brothers had for a transitional object that served us for many years: an illustrated children's Bible. It was read to us in an atmosphere, staged daily after dinner, of motherly concern and warmth complete with body contact as we huddled up to her, listening and looking at the pictures. The experience was punctuated by moments in which we boys took turn reading passages aloud and holding the book by ourselves. The book stood ready day and night in a corner of the mantel, always visible, close to a large portrait of our deceased father. I mention this latter fact in order to allow for the likelihood that emotive aspects of personal (autistic) imagos became intermingled with the illusionistic personages encountered in the biblical stories, with whom transitional or enduring identifications could be made.

I will add another experience that had no mean effect, then and later, on my appropriation of religious ideas: the fortuitous circumstance that I attended a denominational school from kindergarten through the ninth grade that espoused much greater Calvinist orthodoxy than did my family. Home and school were two different religious and emotional worlds: the first was mellow, optimistic, and forgiving; the second strict, somber, and punitive—both equally taking recourse to Scripture and the Institutes of the Christian Religion. There is nothing like it to convince a young boy that religion is what you make it, that all of it is what I now call illusionistic. Fortunately, the choice was not difficult to make: home won over school, undoubtedly because the former had deeper roots in my childhood practicing of the transitional sphere. The Hand of God, much talked about in school, seemed closer to my mother's tender-and-firm hand than to the threatening slaps of my teachers. Small wonder, then, that I have always found the highlight of the liturgy in the benevolently outstretched hands of a fulsome pastoral blessing (Pruyser 1969), and that one of my dearest pictures is Rembrandt's etching of the father blessing the prodigal son upon his return home.

In my ongoing practicing of religion, it also began to dawn on me, in part due to the intellectual demands that the school made for rote memorization of psalms, catechism, and biblical passages as well as Palestinian geography and lore (with grades that were to be taken as seriously as those for reading, writing, and arithmetic), that learning religion is not unlike learning a craft. One has to know a lot, and one has to master certain procedures and skills. Religion makes demands upon the intellect and linguistic performance in addition to the work it does on feelings. In my case the religious imagination had to follow canons of excellence and live up to high aims. One had to read, study, and engage in intelligent debate so as to hone one's skill in thought and argument. No human talent should be sacrificed in acquiring religious savvy; we were told that man was, after all, only a dash lower than the angels.

In this precept lies, of course, the ever-present danger of arrogance. To put this in psychodynamic terminology, religious education must address the autistic givens of primary narcissism and omnipotent thinking. I do remember vaguely that religious practices and instruction made me feel, at times, a bit small, and admonished me to feel and act humbly—much as this went against the grain of my natural inclinations. Yet these experiences must have stuck; they did prepare me for the emphatically affirmative response I was to make, many years later, when I came across the following statement by Sidney Mead (1970):

> No man is God. This is what I understand to be the functional meaning of "God" in human experience. Whatever "God" may be—if indeed being is applicable to "God"—a concept of the infinite seems to be necessary if we are to state the all-important fact about man: that he is finite.

Marvelous! The function of the infinite, the universe, or any god is not merely to be there, but to teach us *that man is unlike this*. Voltaire, the skeptic, proceeded from an Enlightenment image of man as a rational and capable being; Schleiermacher felt that man needed to recapture a lost feeling of reverence. Mead, living in the twentieth century, recognizes that man is naturally given to grandiosity, with dire results shown in such calamities as the Nazi and the Hiroshima holocausts.

I must admit that, despite all these antecedent religious lessons, I had a hard time making, in my late teenage years, the mandatory "profession of faith" that would formalize my membership in the Dutch

Reformed Church. My philosophical bent, coupled with a degree of neurotic resistance to anything externally imposed, made me feel uneasy with "convictional language" (Zuurdeeg 1958) and the confessional mode of speaking. I partly despised, partly envied my classmates who rattled off their answers to the questions of the examining committee and went through the rituals of induction with ease, which included receiving communion for the first time. Enlightened as I felt I was, I would not participate in a bloody "cannibalistic feast," and least of all under pressure. Did not Christianity preach emancipation from legislated rituals of atonement? Many years later, two insights made me change my mind on this issue. The first evolved from a series of earnest conversations I had with a clergyman that led me to realize the narcissistic component in my opposition to the communion ceremony. I had imagined myself omnipotently not only to be above regression, but beyond any need for even a temporary regression, after I had grandly diagnosed other people's communion celebration as a primitive, regressive act. The second insight came when I attended an Easter service in Calvin's St. Peter's Church in Geneva, in which the people (myself included) were served *white, sparkling* wine. This proved what I had long surmised, namely that the "blood and broken body" imagery and parlance of typical Protestant communion services had somehow gone awry, completely ignoring the other meaning of blood as "vital juice" and of bread as "staff of life." I cite these incidents as examples of the workings—for better or for worse—of the imagination.

The symbolism of ritual can become skewed in destructive directions by all participating parties, not least the Church itself. Ritual is dislodged from its playful functioning in the illusionistic sphere and displaced into the realistic one when it is grimly legislated as a necessary act by the institution. Precisely then, it has no imaginative element but becomes only a token of realistically advocated conformity to somebody's Kafkaesque rules.

A WARNING:
THREATS TO THE IMAGINATION
FROM TWO SIDES

At several places in this essay I alluded to the precariousness of the illusionistic sphere and the delicacy of its objects. The imagination is constantly threatened from two sides: from the side of autism by hallucinatory entities or events, and from the side of realism by actual entities or events. Much of what follows is meant to alert pastors and religious educators to danger situations they are wont to encounter in their work with people.

As some of my autobiographical citations have shown, neurotic needs and defenses may encroach upon the orderly imagination and tutored fantasy in illusion processing. These symptomatic intrusions from the side of the autistic sphere produce, as Winnicott (1971) observed, a morbid quality in some children's play: oral and anal, sadistic and maso-chistic preoccupations make their playing compulsive, repetitive, and stereotyped, and cast a pall of grimness over their activities. This kind of playing is not joyous and imaginative, least of all creative. It stands in sharp contrast to the *happy* playing of a healthy child who "is satis-fied with the game" without undue intrusion of excited Id impulses. In Winnicott's opinion, happy playing depends on the child's *capacity to be alone* (Winnicott 1958).

This capacity to be alone is rooted in early childhood experiences of "being alone, as an infant and small child, in the presence of mother." Winnicott was well aware of the paradoxical nature of his statement; it stems from the fact that the individuation-separation process (see LeBlanc's contributions to this book) occurs at the transition from one matrix to another. In the first matrix, mother and child are mutually dependent, even symbiotic, and the child neither feels nor is regarded as an autonomous self; in the subsequent matrix the child's separate-ness from the mother is practiced, with increasing independence, "aloneness," and autonomy generating a palpable selfhood. What makes for this crucial "capacity to be alone"?[2]

Most theorists today answer that one must have within oneself, with trust and reliance, a dynamic image of the benevolent mother, which not only sees one through in times when she must be physically absent, but functions as an auxiliary ego that enhances the child's mastery of his or her impulses. Other clinicians have accentuated different features of this growth dynamic, which is both intrapsychic and interpersonal: Erikson (1966) sees "numinosity" in the greeting rituals between mother and in-fant and stresses the quality of trust as an indispensable preparation for wholesome development; Schafer (1960) speaks of the "loving and beloved superego" that benevolently guides the growth process.

I believe that children's induction into the illusionistic world and their chances for a wholesome practicing of its procedures and skills are greatly influenced by the vicissitudes of the internal and external ob-ject relations I have just described. "Impingements" (Winnicott's term) from any side, ranging from bad mothering and situational depriva-tions to mental or physical handicaps within the child, thwart the for-mation of a good internal object and a trusting relation to the world outside. Such impingements generally stimulate the autistic fantasy and thus produce distortions in the appropriation of illusionistic entities and procedures. Gods become monsters, the self is held to be despicable or unworthy, curiosity becomes dangerous, thinking becomes beset by ap-prehensiveness, playing becomes grim and repetitious. In a recent book

---

[2]The capacity to be alone may be that condition in which the "I" and the "me" form a synthetic unity. See J. Ryu's chapter in this book. This capacity also in-volves a subtle, healthy combination of self and other.

Rizzuto (1979) has described the rather awkward God representations of some troubled adults, plausibly reconstructing the dynamic origins of these representations from the impingements that had occurred in their early lives.

The imagination can also be threatened by the realistic world. In fact, I think it fair to say that there is a constant pressure from the realistic sphere to curtail the novelty producing, potentially creative imagination that is nurtured in the illusionistic sphere. From the angle of realism, illusions are dangerous or else frivolous. Single-minded dedication to reality forces the arts to be reproductive or representational; it forces science to be utilitarian or technological; and it forces religion to be the warp and weft of the social fabric (Durkheim 1912) that should not be disturbed. In the realistic sphere symbols are turned into mere emblems or signs; the Cross becomes a piece of costume jewelry.

Realism has a distaste for the mysterious. It wants its objects to be tangible and unambiguously denotable: a rose is a rose is a rose. Without denying the virtues of common sense or minimizing the need for adequate reality testing, I must say that single-minded dedication to the realistic world leads all too easily to the intellectual narrowness of positivism, the essence of which is captured in the early (1922) Wittgenstein's phrase: "Whereof one cannot speak, thereof one must be silent." Or else, it leads to a "thingification" of ideas and propositions. In some cases of marked brain damage, the patient is reduced to concretism (Goldstein 1947) due to failure of concept formation; more tellingly for our concern here, such a patient can no longer engage in "as if" thinking and lacks playfulness.

We cannot take the realistic world lightly if we want to survive. Realism is badly needed, as psychoanalysis has always held, to curb and counteract the dangerous impulsivity of the autistic world. These two worlds stand in a dialectical and dynamic relation to each other, mediated by the ego, which derives its autonomy precisely from being given a double input of stimuli from the Id and from the world (Rapaport 1958). The religious imagination can indeed go haywire, concocting incubi, witches, or unicorns. Given such demonstrations of the ever-present specter of whimsical, autistic fantasy, and the destructive impact it has at times clearly had on the social order, realists have a point when they appear to be fearful of the imagination.

Moreover, we should acknowledge that perceptions of the realistic world—people, animals, plants, mountains, seas, the firmament, as well as human artifacts such as buildings, tools, works of art, laboratoria, temples, graves, and so forth—are necessary stimuli for setting the process of imagination in motion. Here we see the positive side of institutionalization: without libraries we could hardly have theology; without churches we could not have corporate worship or liturgy. Without organized tradition we have no ritual, no sense even of origins and destinies. And without some assembled doctrines, we could not have any illuminating reinterpretation of doctrines (of which Runyon's chapter in this book is an example).

Realism has, however, a momentum of its own that can smother the imagination. When realists are too fearful of the autistic fantasy going rampant, their fear may spread to the illusionistic sphere as well, so that they end up forbidding the reading of fairy tales to children. One only has to browse through Bettelheim's (1976) *The Uses of Enchantment* to see what psychological and cultural deprivations such purism imposes. Indeed, an all-too-stark realism may delegate religion to the "fairy tale" category, thereby denigrating both.

By "institutionalization" I mean not only ecclesiastical organization with its visible trappings; I include the invisible structuring of the mind that Kierkegaard (1854-1855) called "Christendom." Piously trained minds tend to develop habits of thought and language that confuse illusionistic with realistic ideas. Wittingly or unwittingly, a displacement occurs in which the products of the imagination are pried loose from their place in the illusionistic sphere and relocated in the realistic world where they are transformed into so-called plain truths and hard facts. Entertainable religious propositions become presented eventually as unarguable doctrines. Religious development becomes thwarted by doctrinaire teachers who insist on intellectual and behavioral conformity to enforced norms that leave nothing to the imagination. They teach docility rather than venturesome explorations. And so we get arguments for the existence of God and the correctness of certain church doctrines that use the logic of natural phenomena and empirical verification methods, thus taking away all mystery from the religious object.[3] Along with this displacement, transcendence becomes scaled down to a mere intensification of the intergenerational power differences between teachers and pupils, parents and children, the state and its citizens.

In Christendom piously trained people signal not their religious struggles but their "finds": their car bumpers carry stickers with "I found it." Their commercially packaged tours to Israel are anachronistically labeled "visits to the Holy Land" as if they were pilgrimages. They pretend to know "what God says" and will tell you so, unasked. They present their convictions as churchly beliefs that are so self-evident that there is no place for doubt.

In regard to this slippage from the illusionistic into the realistic sphere, the need for renewal becomes clear and trenchant. The slippage is so constant that attempts at renewal must be made with equal constancy and vigor on two fronts. To recapture a sense of mystery and transcendence, people must be called back from "thingish" and factual thought to imaginative thought. The second front for efforts at renewal

---

[3]The churchly form of this displacement has been acidly stated by John R. Fry in *The Great Apostolic Blunder Machine* (1978).

is ethical thought and action. The realistic sphere in which we dwell with an attitude of "that's the way things are" is always badly in need of infusions from the illusionistic sphere, which alone is capable of creating the ideals that may and should improve the conditions of our lives.

REFERENCES

—————————————— • ● • ——————————————

Bettelheim, B. 1976. *The Uses of Enchantment*. New York: A. A. Knopf.

Durkheim, E. 1912. *The Elementary Forms of the Religious Life*. London: George Allen & Unwin.

Erikson, E. H. 1966. "Ontogeny of Ritualization." In *Psychoanalysis—a General Psychology: Essays in Honor of Heinz Hartmann*, 601-21. Edited by R. M. Loewenstein, L. M. Newman, M. Schur, and A. J. Solnit. New York: International Universities Press.

Freud, S. 1911. *Formulations on the Two Principles of Mental Functioning*. Standard ed., vol. 12. London: Hogarth Press, 1958.

——————————. 1927. *The Future of an Illusion*. Standard ed., vol. 21. London: Hogarth Press, 1961.

Fry, J. R. 1978. *The Great Apostolic Blunder Machine*. New York: Harper & Row.

Goldstein, K. 1940. *Human Nature in the Light of Psychopathology*. Cambridge MA: Harvard University Press.

Gombrich, E. 1960. *Art and Illusion*. Bollingen Series 34:5. Princeton NJ: Princeton University Press.

Jaspers, K. 1949. *The Perennial Scope of Philosophy*. Translated by R. Mannheim. Hamden CT: Shoe String Press, 1968.

Kierkegaard, S. 1854-1855. *Attack upon Christendom*. Translated by W. Lowrie. Princeton NJ: Princeton University Press, 1944.

Kuhn, T. A. 1970. *The Structure of Scientific Revolutions*. Second ed., International Encyclopedia of Unified Science: Foundations of the Unity of Science, 1:2. Chicago: University of Chicago Press.

Mahler, M., F. Pine, and A. Bergman. 1975. *The Psychological Birth of the Human Infant*. New York: Basic Books.

Mead, S. E. 1970. "In Quest of America's Religion." *The Christian Century* 87:752-56.

Otto, R. 1917. *The Idea of the Holy*. Translated by J. W. Harvey. London: Humphrey Milford-Oxford University Press, 1928.

Polanyi, M. 1958. *Personal Knowledge: Towards a Post-Critical Philosophy*. Chicago: University of Chicago Press.

Pruyser, P. W. 1968. *A Dynamic Psychology of Religion*. New York: Harper & Row.

——————————. 1969. "The Master Hand: Psychological Notes on Pastoral Blessing." In *The New Shape of Pastoral Theology: Essays in Honor of Seward Hiltner*, 352-65. Edited by W. B. Oglesby. Nashville: Abingdon Press.

——————————. 1974. *Between Belief and Unbelief*. New York: Harper & Row.

_____. 1976. "Lessons from Art Theory for the Psychology of Religion." *Journal for the Scientific Study of Religion* 15:1-14.

_____. 1979. "An Essay on Creativity." *Bulletin of the Menninger Clinic* 43:294-353.

_____. 1983. *The Play of the Imagination: Toward a Psychoanalysis of Culture.* New York: International Universities Press.

Rapaport, D. 1958. "The Theory of Ego Autonomy: A Generalization," In *The Collected Papers of David Rapaport,* 722-44. Edited by Merton M. Gill. New York: Basic Books, 1967.

Rizzuto, A-M. 1979. *The Birth of the Living God: A Psychoanalytic Study.* Chicago: University of Chicago Press.

Schafer, R. 1960. "The Loving and Beloved Superego in Freud's Structural Theory." *The Psychoanalytic Study of the Child,* 15:163-88. New York: International Universities Press.

Tillich, P. 1959. *Systematic Theology,* vol. 1. Chicago: University of Chicago Press.

Tracy, D. 1975. *Blessed Rage for Order: The New Pluralism in Theology.* New York: Seabury Press.

Wiggins, J. B., ed. 1975. *Religion as Story.* New York: Harper & Row.

Winnicott, D. 1951. "Transitional Objects and Transitional Phenomena." In his *Collected Papers,* 229-42. London: Tavistock Publication, 1958.

_____. 1958. "The Capacity to Be Alone." *International Journal of Psychoanalysis* 39:416-20.

_____. 1971. *Playing and Reality.* New York: Basic Books.

Wittgenstein, L. J. J. 1922. *Tractatus Logico-Philosophicus.* Translated by D. F. Pears and B. F. McGuinness. Atlantic Heights NJ: Humanities Press, 1974.

Woodger, J. H. 1956. *Physics, Psychology and Medicine.* London: Cambridge University Press.

Zuurdeeg, W. F. 1958. *An Analytical Philosophy of Religion.* Nashville: Abingdon Press.

CHAPTER EIGHT

Alienation and the Human Self

• ● •

JAI POONG RYU

Sociological theory has approached the human self on two fronts: (1) by studying how individuals emerge within their social matrix and how they become molded, labeled, shaped, conditioned, or differentiated by various social forces and procedures; (2) by considering the nature of the bonds that develop between society and individuals, including the condition typically described as alienation. Nearly all sociologists recognize that there is a dynamic tension between individual self-fulfillment or self-expression and societal demands for conformity. By means of the concept of alienation, much sociological theorizing is devoted to accounting for this tension and the conflicts it engenders.

Jai Ryu gives a concise overview of the dominant sociological theories of selfhood and alienation with a view toward attempting a synthesis. Where LeBlanc, in a previous chapter, accentuates the differentiation of a nascent individual child from his or her mother, Ryu stresses another differentiation process: the I and the Me emerging from an inchoate primitive self. The I is the more holistic, unified, and synthesizing aspect of the self, and it is typically spoken of in the singular; the Me's tend to be many, often fragmented, and sometimes mutually conflicting aspects of the self, typically staged in the plural. Ryu relates the I-Me differentiation processes to the various social and economic conditions in the modern world, and pays attention to a kind of pathological differentiation in which the I and the Me are actually disjointed.

One of the most persistent and pervasive criticisms of contemporary society is that individuals are largely alienated. Most social critics point out loneliness in crowded population centers, erosion of normative structures in mass society, powerlessness in the face of massive and complex systems, and inability to project the future in increasingly unpredictable times.

This paper examines various sociological traditions for better illumination and clearer understanding of human alienation. The principal orientation may be summed up as follows:

(1) Alienation is rooted in social structure. The structural conditions producing alienation stem chiefly from industrialization. Thus, unless our industrial way of life is fundamentally restructured, it is not possible to eliminate alienation. Instead, we should search for ways to cope with it.

(2) Widespread alienation becomes a social problem. Alienated individuals, as opposed to committed ones, impede the efficient operations of social organizations and undercut the democratic functioning of society (Faunce 1981, ch. 5). The first-line victims of alienation are, however, individuals. Thus, the causal sequence proposed here is: a structural cause (i.e., industrialization) ——→alienation of individuals (victimization of individuals) ——→structural consequences (social problems). The first focus, though, must be on the meaning of alienation for individuals. We should first ask how alienation registers in the makeup of individuals. Other important questions will come subsequent to this quest for the internal meaning of alienation.

(3) For a clear understanding of alienation in the self, it is useful to draw from both the structuralist and social-psychological (mostly the symbolic interactionist) traditions in sociology. Structuralists tend to underplay psychological dynamics in the human self, while advancing understanding of the structural causes and consequences of alienation in modern society. The symbolic interactionists have articulated the emergence and growth of the self, but they have failed to link the structural attributes of the society with the internal happenings in the self.

(4) Symbolic interactionists have made a revealing distinction between the "I" and the "Me" in the human self. One of my principal postulates is that alienation takes place when the self is differentiated between the "I" (a modified version of the symbolic interactionists' "I") and the "Me" in such a way that the "Me's" overpower the "I".

I will proceed in four steps: (1) Sociological Literature on Alienation: Exposition and Critique; (2) Social-Psychological Literature on the Human Self: Exposition and Critique; (3) A New Meaning of Alienation: A Synthesis of the Two Sociological Traditions; and (4) Coping with Alienation: Today and Tomorrow.

SOCIOLOGICAL LITERATURE ON ALIENATION: EXPOSITION AND CRITIQUE

I will briefly review here three sociological views that generated fairly comprehensive analyses of the alienation phenomenon: those of Marx, Durkheim and Thomas, and Faunce.

Karl Marx

Marx shared Hegel's view that there is a "universal essence of man" which, when realized, constitutes the "self-fulfillment of mankind." According to Marx, this process of self-fulfillment can take place only through free and creative labor. Labor is the "existential activity of man, his free conscious activity—not a means for maintaining his life but for developing his universal nature" (Marcuse 1941, 275). The mechanization of labor under capitalism, however, makes it impossible for the labor to be free and creative and, consequently, one cannot realize one's own "universal nature."

From the viewpoint of Marx, alienation takes a number of forms. Laborers are, first, alienated from the products of their labor. They have no control over the disposition of the commodities they produce. "The object which labor produces, its product, is encountered as an alien entity, a force that has become independent of its producer" (ibid., 276). Second, workers are alienated from the means of production. In the typical modern factory system of production, laborers no longer own the tools or the machinery with which they work. Actually, it is observed that the workers themselves become a tool of production, no longer distinguishable from other means of production.

While these two forms of alienation held a prominent place in Marx's writings, there is a third type prominent in his earlier writings: self-estrangement. Marx described this form of alienation as follows:

> What constitutes alienation of labor? First, the work is "external" to the worker, that it is not part of his nature; and that, consequently, he does not fulfill himself in his work but denies himself, has a feeling of misery rather than well being, does not develop freely his mental and physical energies but is physically exhausted and mentally debased. The worker therefore feels himself at home only during his leisure time, whereas at work he feels homeless. His work is not voluntary but imposed, "forced labor." It is not the satisfaction of a need, but only a means for satisfying other needs. (quoted in Fromm 1966, 98)

What gives the work its alienating character is the modern factory system where hired work is a means rather than an end and is an instrumental rather than consummatory activity. The meaning of alienation, especially of Marx's third type, is distortion of the basic (free and creative) character of work and the consequent denial of man's basic (universal) nature. The cause of alienation is capitalism and its chief victims are industrial workers.

Emile Durkheim and W. I. Thomas

Another body of sociological literature on human alienation can be found in a host of publications focused on "anomie." While Durkheim coined the word and developed the concept, Thomas's notion of the "individualization of behavior" parallels it closely.

The principal subject of interest for both Thomas and Durkheim was how effectively a society can put human desires under control. Durkheim assumed that there was nothing in man's organic nature to limit his desires. Thus, the essential question for sociologists is who determines "the quality of well-being, comfort or luxury legitimately to be craved by a human being"? (Durkheim 1951, 247) Durkheim's answer is that only society can "set the point beyond which the passions must not go." According to Thomas, if individuals are unchecked by society, they become hedonistic, seeking "pleasure first." Society seeks "safety first," an orientation embodied in the moral codes of a culture.

Both Durkheim and Thomas were sensitive to tension between society and individuals, which they held to be generally minimal in preindustrial, small peasant communities. Community was then an all-pervasive and effective agent. Repression of the wishes "was demanded of all . . . and . . . pleasure was not countenanced as an end in itself" (Thomas 1967, 71-72). In modern societies, however, the community's power to regulate individual behavior is typically weakened. As a result, individuals today are likely to redefine situations in unique ways, continuously shaking social stability and ceaselessly introducing change and disorganization. Thomas characterized this process as "the individualization of behavior."

Durkheim's term was "anomie," meaning the absence of norms resulting from a state of weakened social control and the erosion of shared beliefs and values. After studying suicide as the physical demonstration of human alienation, he concluded that "anomic" conditions tend to promote tendencies for suicide (Durkheim 1897). Thus for these two thinkers, alienation means "individualization of behavior" or "anomie"; its cause is the disappearance of small peasant communities and the emergence of complex and unstable societies.

William Faunce

To Faunce, alienation refers to a disjuncture between self-esteem maintenance and the status-assignment process: "We are alienated from others or from any organization in which we are a member to the extent that the criteria we use to evaluate ourselves are different from the criteria used by others in evaluating us" (Faunce 1981, 138).

Self-esteem maintenance is a social process. To be certain that we are what we think we are, we need periodic confirmation from others. An individual's quest for such verification typically takes place in society's "status structure," a hierarchy of persons arranged according to their social honor and status. If the criteria used for status assignment within the status structure of the groups, formal organizations, community, and society in which we are members are the same criteria that we use in evaluating ourselves, we have a "commitment to, or an identification with these social organizations." Should there be a significant "disjuncture," alienation tends to be the result (Faunce 1981, 135-41).

Occurrences of such disjunctures are quite common in modern industrial societies and are most visible among those of lower socio-economic status. The principal cause of modern alienation is industrialization.

Critique

My overall criticism of these views is that they pay insufficient attention to the internal dynamics of the human self. The human self is presupposed to be an autonomous entity, a person whose basic nature might be denied or affirmed (Marx), who might be lost or secure in anomic situations (Durkheim), who is destined to define his situation with little help from the society's moral codes (Thomas), or who sees little relevance between his self-definitions and society's views of his worth (Faunce).

In general, sociologists treat individuals much like physicists consider atoms, that is, as entities whose substances cannot be reduced any further. Sociologists tend to focus their attention on the relations between individuals, the structures underlying such relations, the functions of these structures, or conflicts between individuals and groups. The task of knowing what happens *in* the individuals, as a result of what happens *to* them, has been assigned to the psychological disciplines.

Marx, for example, identified the conditions that lead to self-estrangement: when work becomes devoid of any intrinsic value, the human self is repelled by it and the result is often alienation. When Marx spoke of self-estrangement, however, he was concerned not only with the estrangement of a person from work or commodities, but with estrangement of the human self from itself. If alienation of an individual from things external to himself had been Marx's exclusive concern, his concept of self-estrangement would have been superfluous.

Durkheim and Thomas also provided eloquent analysis of how anomic conditions tend to promote deviant or suicidal behavior. They, too, seemed to have assumed that internal happenings in the deviants' selves were not a proper query for sociologists. Similarly, Faunce (1981, 135) began by stating: "When we speak of alienation or estrangement, we need to specify first what it is that the person is alienated or estranged from (things or people other than himself)."

Our concern here is, however, with the human side of alienation—with the victims who are individual selves. There are no doubt external structural causes and consequences of alienation. But human alienation or estrangement is, by definition, the estrangement of a certain element or aspect of a human self from other elements or aspects of that self. It is a phenomenon where the self is at odds with itself, and that phenomenon has been lost in the necessity of drawing boundaries between sociology and psychology.

Fortunately, there exists in sociology a body of social-psychological knowledge that bridges the gap to some extent. I allude to the symbolic interactionists' distinction between the "I" and the "Me." Self-estrangement is, in my analysis, estrangement of the "I" from the "Me," a process engendered by the structural attributes of industrial society.

SOCIAL-PSYCHOLOGICAL LITERATURE ON THE HUMAN SELF: EXPOSITION AND CRITIQUE

The literature on the human self in sociology is mostly the work of the symbolic interactionists. Although one may infer from other sociological writings how their authors might interpret the self, this particular school has most explicitly focused its attention on the human self. Influenced by the pragmatic philosophy of William James, the psychophysical parallelism of Wilhelm Wundt, and the behavioristic tradition of J. B. Watson, this school has generated a number of important insights for inquiries about the self.

Self and Others

Social life is created, maintained, and changed through interactions between creatures of the same kind. Social interaction implies that the actions of one creature are in part the basis for the actions of another. Prior to physical attack, for example, a wolf bares its teeth and the other animal responds to it as a sign that an attack is about to begin. These sorts of gestures are taken by the others as signs of a particular action. If one could identify and isolate a class of gestures that serve as common signs both to their maker and receiver, one would have a rudiment of language. Certain gestures or words are called "significant symbols" if they have the same meaning to both maker and receiver. For the most part, human social life is made possible and carried on through such significant symbols, which comprise nonverbal signs and language.

According to G. H. Mead, whenever significant symbols are used, a process called "role-taking" is present. In role taking one "puts himself in the attitude of the other." A speaker checks consciously and unconsciously whether what he says is being conveyed to the other person as he intended it. Moreover, when we interact, we see what we do and we hear what we say by feedback from the attitudes of the other party. Thus, in role taking we become in some sense objects to ourselves. As Mead (1934, 68-69) put it,

> We are more or less unconsciously seeing ourselves as others see us. We are consciously addressing ourselves as others address us. . . . We are calling out in the other person something we are calling out in ourselves, so that unconsciously we take over these attitudes. We are unconsciously putting ourselves in the place of others and acting as others act.

Thus, one paramount fact of the human self is that it can become an object to itself. This capacity for self-objectification produces two major elements in the human self: the objectifier and the objectified, the "I" and the "Me." The internal landscape of the self is thus arranged by various juxtapositions of these two major elements.

Internal Dynamics of the Human Self

Most sociologists of symbolic interactionists' persuasion accept James's distinction between the "I" and the "Me" in accounting for the structure of the self. James (1890, 176) stated that a person appears in thought in two ways: "Partly known and partly knower, partly object and partly subject. . . . For shortness we may call one the 'Me' and the other the 'I.' . . . I shall therefore treat successively of (A) the self as known, or the 'Me,' the empirical ego as it is sometimes called; and of (B) the self as knower, or the 'I,' the pure ego of certain authors."

The "Me" is, in its broadest sense, the sum total of all that a person can call his or hers. The "Me" typically arouses feelings and emotions of self-appreciation and prompts actions of self-seeking and self-pre-serving (ibid., 195).

The "I," the knower of the "Me," is more difficult to conceptualize. It is that which at any moment is conscious. The "Me" is only one of the many things of which it is conscious. One generally considers the "I" to be the same at all times throughout a life span. "This has led most phi-losophers to postulate behind the passing state of consciousness a per-manent Substance or Agent. This Agent is the thinker; the 'state' is only its instrument or means. 'Soul,' 'Transcendental Ego,' 'Spirit' are so many names for this permanent sort of Thinker" (ibid., 196). According to James, however, the "I" is not a substance like soul or spirit; rather, it refers to certain comparable characteristics of experience from time to time. On this subject, he observed:

> The consciousness of Self involves a stream of thought, each part of which as "I" can remember those which went before, know the things they knew, and care for certain ones among them as "Me" and appropriate to these the rest. This "Me" is an empirical aggregate of things objectively known. The "I" which knows them cannot itself be an aggregate; neither for psy-chological purposes need it be an unchanging metaphysical entity like the soul. . . . It is a thought, at each moment different from that of the last moment. (ibid., 215)

The "I" and "Me" are, to James, no substantive entities, but distin-guishable sets of *thoughts* arising out of experiences. Most symbolic in-teractionists appear to accept James's notions that these two are distinctions arising out of actual experiences. Mead states:

> The "I" is always something different from what the situation itself calls for. So there is always that distinction, if you like, between the "I" and the "Me." The "I" both calls out the "Me" and responds to it. Taken to-gether they constitute a personality as it appears in social experience. The self is essentially a social process going on with these two distin-guishable phases. (1934, 4)

Summary

The self is, in symbolic interactionism, a social process made possi-ble by man's unique capacity for symbolic communication. The use of symbols necessitates objectification of the self. The self thus comes to contain two distinguishable aspects: the objectifier and the objectified, or the "I" and the "Me." While these two are always present in the self, they are not substantive entities but phenomenological or functional distinctions stemming from pure experience (James), from ongoing social processes (Mead), or from symbolic thinking (Cassirer).

Critique

My criticism of this framework for understanding the self is twofold. According to this approach, the process through which the human self comes into being is eminently social. To understand the human self, one has to look into the social processes through which the self emerges. Here one would have hoped that the symbolic interactionists might be interested in studying how the self would fare differently in varying types of society, today and in history. This school has, however, paid little attention to this problem. Its point of emphasis is the opposite of the structuralist school reviewed before: it considers what happens *in* the self, while the latter considers what happens *to* the self. Regarding the question of what happens *to* the self in a contemporary world in which social conditions have spawned widespread alienation, the symbolic interactionists have little to offer.

My second criticism concerns the symbolic interactionists' treatment of the self as a phenomenon *in awareness*. The "I" and the "Me" are phases in thoughts about oneself. While the "I" and the "Me" are conceptualized as the knower and the known *in* the person, both are known *to* the self: the *I* of the moment is present in the memory of the *me* of the next (Mead 1934, 178) and becomes incorporated into the *Me*. Viewed in this light, the "I" results from the processing of the "Me's," or vice versa. Both are objects of *human awareness*.

This preoccupation with the elements of the self that are revealed in awareness is understandable, if we know Western civilization. The West has insisted, both in metaphysics and in science, that everything is doubtable and thus objectifiable. (See Nachbahr's chapter in this volume.) There is, however, in the self something that asserts itself *in life* and in action, though not necessarily in awareness. We will thus have to reconceptualize the "I" and the "Me," and will do so in the next section.

A NEW MEANING OF ALIENATION: A SYNTHESIS OF THE TWO SOCIOLOGICAL TRADITIONS

When we bring the topic of the human self under investigation, we may first wish to know what the self is. Otherwise, how can we identify something as either the true self or as its alienated version? But another, more fundamental question must precede this one: Who wants to know? And after that is answered, the next question is: How do they plan to know? In my view, these two questions have stirred some deeply biased presuppositions in Western thought.

Biased Presuppositions

Many people—theologians, philosophers, psychologists, anthropologists, sociologists, and others—wish to know what the human self is. These are professionals whose interest in the subject of the self is conditioned and controlled by their training and disciplinary concerns. The modes of operation in their inquiries have been molded in accordance with the dictates of reason or science, depending on the discipline.

In general, whether the discipline is one of the humanities or one of the sciences, or for that matter a hybrid, leading Western thinkers have shown a great penchant for theorization and concept formation. So much so, indeed, that it took a Husserl around the turn of the century to call attention to the splendors of the directly observable world to which the overworked theoreticians had all but lost access. Husserl's phenomenology called thinkers and observers "back to the things themselves" by teaching them a special form of intellectual and perceptual self-discipline. Alas, pretty soon Husserl's own phenomenology became an overworked conceptual system that lost track of its original assignment.

Inasmuch as all theories are forms of objectifying some chosen subject matter, theories of the self may be criticized for not dealing adequately with one outstanding feature of the self in human experience: *its spontaneity and liveliness as an existential given*. In fact, one could say that the chief victim of objectification theories has been the human self. The symbolic interactionists' view of the self suffers also from overtheorization. Their "I" and "Me" have become *objects for thought*.

Redefining the I-Me Distinction

Full objectification of the human self is an impossible intellectual undertaking. This is due almost entirely to the nature of the human self: it insists on being a total, integrated, dynamic entity and to be so regarded in any theory as well.

Basically, every self demands, often unknowingly, that it be treated as a whole. Various features of the self may be good or bad, dynamic or static, effective or defective. The human self wishes above all, however, to stay alive as a totality. No scientific undertaking can render full justice to this totality. This insistence on total self defies the conventional distinctions between the personal and the interactional, between experience and the conceptualization of it, and between the empirical and the normative that typically characterize our inquiries about man.

The hope is, of course, that after the human self has been dissected analytically and its components dealt with separately, the separated parts would be conceptually so resynthesized that the totality of the human self would not be compromised. But achieving this synthesis appears to be more a delusion than a realizable hope, for the results of any such synthesis are unpredictable and will vary from individual to individual. A conceptual synthesis is just that: an abstraction, devoid of concrete, individuating characteristics. Marx describes this totality in the abstract when he argues that, under capitalism, "the whole (self) has been broken up into numerous parts whose interrelations can no longer be ascertained." In fact, he defined alienation itself as "the splintering of human nature into a number of misbegotten parts" (Ollman 1958, 135).

It should be noted that no definition of the full self is possible. The moment a self is defined, even if adequately, it will change by the very fact of absorbing its latest definition. Once any self-definition is constructed, the self finds itself continuing to question and redefine it. Reflective man puts his self-definitions to test in actual or imagined situations, to see if the definition holds up. Thomas (1923) implied these continual redefinitions of the self by the self when he considered the "desire for new experiences" as one of four basic human wishes.

What, then, is this dynamic in the self that insists on its totality and resists being fully defined? What is it in the self that likes or dislikes its self-definitions, wishes to be free, or longs for new experiences? Let us call this dynamic the *I*, and consider all the parts of the self that are revealed in awareness, and thereby become known and objectified, the *Me*.

The "I" of symbolic interactionism evolves from social interaction and is a "thought." I would insist, however, that we do not and cannot know where the "I" ultimately comes from. Social interaction is definitely one major contributor to the "I," but there may be other contributors. The "I" is in part a thought in awareness, but there are also noncognitive and nonobjectifiable aspects in our experience of the "I," that is, experiences that are spontaneous, affective, or volitional.

We retain, however, the symbolic interactionists' concept of the "Me" as the organized set of others' attitudes that one assumes for oneself. It is in the dynamic relation between this "Me" and the reconceptualized "I" that we will attempt to see how alienation is felt or comes about *in* the human self.

New Meaning of Alienation

According to Ollman (1971, 132), Marx grasped the meaning of alienation dialectically as "the absence of unalienation." Marx believed further that there is no standard from which to judge what constitutes "unalienation." As will be seen below, however, it is possible to articulate the state of "unalienation" in particular relationships between the "I" and the "Me." Human infants and illiterate peasants in small villages in primitive societies are good starting examples.

Newborn infants have an awareness of neither the "Me" nor the "I," nor of the world surrounding them. They are fused and undifferentiated. As the child later moves about, he begins to perceive himself as an entity distinguishable from others. After the child can make such a distinction, he undergoes a long process that leads to a sharper and more comprehensive differentiation between his "I" and "Me." At first, a child comes to the awareness of the "Me" and appropriates it to his "I." The fact, say, "My mom loves me" is registered in the self as "I am lovable." Continued appropriation of the "Me" to the "I" becomes increasingly difficult, because the situations in which the child finds himself vary greatly with growing age. In different situations the self finds itself defined differently. The world is, in short, inconsistent in its definition of the child's self and beleaguers the child with many diverse senses of the "Me." A child who has been led to believe himself to be smart may find, for example, that he is only an average student at school.

Until these inconsistencies are perceived by the child (and this perception may result in an identity crisis), we may say that the child is "unalienated." There can be no feeling of alienation, in other words, unless there is first a differentiation between the "I" and the "Me."

Also, to illiterate people in peasant villages in preindustrial societies, differentiation between the "I" and the "Me" in their selves was seldom occasioned. Their world order was generally fixed and stable, and change was minimal. One generally saw one's self-images to be consistent in life's many situations. In small peasant communities, Thomas (1967, 71-72) noted, the community was an all-pervasive and effective regulating agent. The community reaches, he quoted a Polish peasant, "as far as a man is talked about." Self-images of most people were set by the community and the question of "who am I?" was rarely asked because the answer was only too apparent.

In very primitive societies the case was apparently more dramatic. According to E. Cassirer (1925, 157), in the earlier stages of human history, the feeling of "self" was immediately fused with a definite mythical-religious feeling of the "community." The "I" felt and knew itself only as a member of a community, grouped with others into a family, a tribe, or a village. "Only in and through these (groups) does one possess oneself; every manifestation of its own personal existence and life is lined, as though by invisible magic ties, with the life of the totality around it." As in the case of the infants, the "I" and the "Me" of the individuals in primitive village societies were fused and they did not experience alienation as we understand it today.

Differentiation between the "I" and the "Me" is a necessary but not a sufficient meaning of alienation, however, for even among the adults (noninfants) in industrial societies (nonprimitive), there are certain individuals who seem largely unalienated. Research by industrial sociologists and psychologists has identified three occupational groups "in which behavior and attitudes suggesting alienation were seldom found" (Faunce 1981, 162-64). These were the professions (medicine, law, university teaching, clergy, etc.), skilled trades, and farming. The researchers noted widespread alienation among workers in unskilled and semiskilled jobs. Here a question arises as to what may account for these differences between occupations within the same societal structure.

Modern societies are characterized by a high degree of industrialization, urbanization, rationalization, and bureaucratization, which radically transformed the social landscape into which generations of human selves came to live. These powerful processes promoted ever-finer divisions of labor, life-styles, beliefs, values, norms, and symbols. In modern societies, therefore, individuals typically find themselves in a multitude of situations in which their selves are defined differently and often inconsistently. This proliferation of the "Me's" in the self results in a segmentation of life that was largely unknown in preindustrial societies. This proliferation also tends to arouse the "I" in the self to act as the knower, integrator, and accommodator of the now-proliferated "Me's."

But while the modern industrial milieu has occasioned the rise of the explicit "I" and its differentiation from the many "Me's," it has largely left the "I" helpless, powerless, meaningless, and often isolated. For the differentiation of the self in modern societies often means the triumph of the "Me" over the "I." This is so because the "Me's" in the self are firmly anchored in the social structure and the economic necessities on which the modern self rests. One cannot ignore the "Me" at work if one does not want to lose one's livelihood, nor can one be indifferent to the "Me" in the family without risking personal traumas, and so on. In most situations the only realistic choice for the "I" is subservience to some aspect of "Me." While modernization has promoted the rise of the "I" in the self as the knower, integrator, and accommodator of the "Me's," it has given the "I" little with which to do its newly assigned tasks.

By breaking up small-group societies, the industrialization process has removed and freed individuals from the fixity of traditional community constraints. In actuality, however, this freedom generally meant a freedom of the "I" to be subservient to the "Me's" that are deeply entrenched in a largely immutable social structure. This is perhaps what Sartre meant when he said that man is not blessed with, but rather "condemned to," freedom.

To some people, the freedom from traditional community constraints apparently means something more genuine. Cases in point are the above-mentioned professionals and skilled tradesmen. For these people, who constituted almost 30% of the employed civilian labor force in America in 1978, their "I's" may not be as subservient to their "Me's" as they are for non- or semiskilled workers. In these privileged occupations, the workers are generally free from others' supervisions, interferences, and control. Persons in these occupations tend to come into contact with other people who need their services and skills. Hence they are not likely to be approached with unfavorable images and negative labels that may create conflicting self-images in them. Even if they are faced with critical or unpleasant evaluations, these professionals and skilled workers can retain their favorable self-images by attributing those negative perceptions to ignorance or jealousies.

In sum, then, human alienation is the felt estrangement of the "I" from the "Me" within the self. The internal meaning of alienation is that (1) the self is so situated that an accentuated differentiation between the "I" and the "Me" becomes felt; and (2) the "Me's" play such an overpowering role as to render little or no experiential significance to the "I." These two are the necessary and sufficient factors in human alienation. Where one of these factors is absent—as in the cases of infants, illiterates in primitive villages, professionals, skilled workers, and farmers—one's life may be "unalienated" or less alienated. I submit that this definition is generally consistent with the views of Marx, Durkheim, and Faunce although my definition of the internal meaning of alienation is not the same as theirs.

COPING WITH ALIENATION: TODAY AND TOMORROW

I assume that most people wish to live in a society in which man "experiences himself as the center of his world, as the creator of his own acts, . . . as active bearer of his own powers and richness." We would doubtlessly deplore those conditions where man's "actions are not his own; . . . or while he is under the illusion of doing what he wants, he is driven by forces which are separated from his 'self'; . . . or man experiences himself as an impoverished thing, dependent on powers outside him" (Fromm 1965, 111, 114). In short, we prefer unalienation to alienation.

As we saw above, however, "unalienation" is only a relative condition. The cases of the unalienated observed among infants, professionals, and the like are not examples of boundless freedom or exquisite happiness. What, then, can be hoped for? How can we cope with the aggravating conditions that result in alienation?

One of the fundamental quests in this book is for "transformational knowledge" (Pruyser) that speaks to the processes of change from one condition to another: for example, from sickness to health, and in this case from alienation to unalienation. If the analogy between alienation and illness is a valid one, we can think of our coping strategies in terms of cure and treatment. I will argue that radical cure is not possible, although treatment is necessary, desirable, and may lead to some improvement of the untoward conditions.

Cure—Elimination of the Cause of Alienation

While the chief victims of alienation are individuals, its main causes are: (1) structural attributes of an industrial society (Faunce 1981, 130-81); (2) capitalistic mechanization of labor (Marx); and (3) emergence of large and complex societies (Durkheim). Individual and personal problems found in a modern society are often caused by social-structural conditions (Mills 1959, 165-76). For example, the main victims of poverty are individuals, but this condition is also largely caused by the social structure. Moreover, while divorces generate many personal and emotional traumas, they too are caused mainly by social and economic structures of a society.

The key structural attributes of modern industrial societies are: a highly advanced technology, complex forms of social organization, rapid social change, a strong orientation to economic growth, and so on. From the standpoint of an individual, all these features promote segmentation of life; foster proliferations of the "Me's" that typically result in role conflicts; impose deprivation of spontaneity, liveliness, and creativity in the "I"; and entail other signs of alienation. Thus, elimination of the causes of alienation would be served only by a total and radical restructuring of our industrial way of life.

Although there remains some nostalgia for preindustrial society, which is thought to have been stable and secure, it is apparently not strong enough to attempt reversing history; the latter would be both unrealistic and undesirable anyway. Fromm (1941, 99) comments,

> With the breakdown of the medieval system of feudal society. . . . man was deprived of the security he enjoyed, of the unquestionable feeling of belonging, and he was torn loose from the world which had satisfied his quest for security both economically and spiritually. He felt alone and anxious. But he was also free to act and to think independently, to become his own master and do with his life as he could—not as he was told to do.

That many individuals did not become their "own masters" at all and are profoundly alienated is the concern here, but the possibility of their ever becoming their own masters lies in today's world and not in longing for a return to yesterday's world.

Also, in spite of numerous accounts of utopias in which life is portrayed as unalienated, practical applications of utopian ideas have rarely, if ever, worked. Ollman (1958, 252) observes that Soviet writers are "simply wrong when they claim that nationalization of the means of production and the abolition of the capitalistic class have done away with all forms of alienation." Marcuse (1958, 238, 258) also implies that alienation is common to all industrial societies whether there exists "the featured values of 'bourgeois' or 'Soviet' . . . work mentality." This judgment is also shared by A. Schaff (1965, 240), a Polish philosopher and member of the Central Committee of the Polish Communist party.

Therefore, I conclude that attempting to restructure radically our present industrial society in order to eliminate the known cause of alienation would be in vain and would likely bring about other undesirable consequences. But this conclusion implies an admission that we are pretty well locked into our present industrial milieu, and that the human alienation caused by it is, alas, modern man's general fate.

Treatment—Alleviation of the Symptoms of Alienation

I have presented alienation as a kind of "illness" of the self in which the "I" is differentiated from and subservient to various discordant "Me's." It would be very rare for an alienated person to complain that his "I" is subservient to his "Me." Rather, one is more likely to feel symptoms than the sickness itself. What are the symptoms of this differentiation and subservience? A review of sociological literature on the types of behavior and attitudes associated with alienation indicates that three main symptoms can be identified: (1) a feeling of powerlessness, leading to apathetic behavior; (2) a feeling of meaninglessness and overly conforming behavior; and (3) a state of normlessness and low aspirations for oneself.

The structural complexity of industrial societies coupled with a typically impersonal and rational way of life tends to generate a feeling that "I can't beat the system," or "I am only a cog in a wheel." One's "I" succumbs to this sort of self-definition ("Me's") of powerlessness and impotence, and often becomes apathetic.

Extensive structural differentiation in industrial societies tends to segmentalize the course and pattern of human life. As a result, each individual comes to play ever-more roles and consequently to have ever-more self-definitions ("Me's") that are often quite conflictual. Also, rapid social and technological changes happening during one's lifetime further destabilize these already proliferated "Me's." The result is frequently the feeling of meaninglessness or bewilderment over what is appropriate, fair, or reasonable in any situation. The easiest and most widely employed course of action in these circumstances is simply doing what others do—overconforming. One's "I" here simply gives up its role of integrating, directing, and accommodating its own various "Me's," and the person becomes what Riesman (1953) calls an "other-directed" type of individual. In this case, the subservience of the "I" to the "Me's" has gone rampant.

While the term *normlessness* is based on Durkheim's concept of anomie, it has come to mean in contemporary sociology a situation in which there are no legitimate means to achieve socially prescribed goals (Seeman 1959). Like powerlessness, this condition is more common in the lower and working classes than in the middle or upper classes. The less-educated and underprivileged tend to define themselves ("Me's") in terms of stereotypes given them by others—for example, "I am ignorant, lazy, and have no skills necessary for any notable achievements." Instead of attempting to overcome the presumed deficiencies, the persons lower their aspirations by placing their "I's" on a level with their "Me's." The result is often defeatism, self-degradation, withdrawal, and retreatism.

What can be done to treat these symptoms of alienation? Is there any ground for hoping that at least some palliative treatment is possible? I definitely see some possibility for alleviation, for I contend *that people are not as powerless as they think they are, that situations are not as meaningless as they appear to be, and that the cultural ethos of our times is not as normless as it is alleged to be.* The "I" of modern man has succumbed to the "Me" for understandable reasons, but it appears to have done so excessively, exaggeratedly, and too readily. Its excessive subservience has largely been due to the self's defensiveness. Persons do not want to look ridiculous; they fear being shunned, and they are protective of their current self-images ("Me's"). Ironically, however, what they do for self-defense often results in self-defeat.

Yet alienation is more than a defeat of individual and personal selves, and can have far-reaching consequences. As Faunce (188) puts it, "Alienation . . . necessitates a bureaucratic control structure, which engenders further alienation . . . , which encourages stricter bureaucratic controls." Alienation thus breeds further alienation by strengthening the causes of alienation. It is a terrible, tragic, and vicious cycle.

We can begin breaking this cycle only by attacking the excessive subservience of the "I" to the "Me's" in the human self. Attempts to treat the symptoms of alienation may operate at the following levels of approach.

The Individual Level

Nietzsche's (1966, 81) sardonic remark, "Whoever despises himself still respects himself as one who despises," seems true to me. Even when the "I" is subservient to the "Me's," the "I" is there working, though elusively. The elusive working of the "I" may drive some to deny its existence, as it has led others to hypothesize a metaphysical entity such as the Soul, or to argue that the "I" needs to be objectified.

I suggest that we emphasize the "I's" functional reality, without presuming to know much about its mode of operation. We should not belittle the self by equating it with our social roles ("Me's"). There is more to the human self than all the statuses and roles that one occupies, and this fact must be acknowledged in myself and in others.

In most social situations, it is the "Me's" of a person that are interacting. I suggest, however, that we foster the agenda of existentialists such as Marcel, who holds that one's "I" should interact with others' "I's." For a true encounter to occur, for example, a husband's "I" should be in communication with his wife's "I." In such encounters an untold variety of mysteries of human life can be experienced. Such a life cannot be dull, and such selves cannot be defeated. Counselors, pastors, teachers, parents, and moral leaders should foster "I-I" relations to replace the prevailing and alienating "Me-Me" relations.

The Organizational Level

Sociological research has demonstrated repeatedly that alienation is widespread in organizations and occupations that allow little opportunity for workers to participate in any form of decision-making processes. Blauner (1964) found alienation higher in textile and automobile industries than in chemical and printing industries. As mentioned before, alienation is less likely among the workers in professions, skilled trades, and farming.

The type of work one is engaged in offers the human self a "Me." If this "Me" is too narrowly and rigidly defined, though, and if one's very existence is made to hinge on it, the only choice for the "I" is to be subservient to that "Me," and this is often expressed in behavior patterns of apathy, low aspiration, and overconformity—in a word, alienation. People who assign work to others—teachers, personnel officers, business executives, foremen, bosses, and so forth—should find ways of enlarging the opportunities for decision making by workers. In fact, such personnel policies have proven profitable to companies. Bureaucratic controls then become less necessary, the work situation becomes more lively and gratifying, and individual talents become better utilized.

The Societal and Global Level

In a broad sense, *alienation* is an individual's response to certain dehumanizing conditions in the modern world: the threat of thermonuclear destruction, poverty in the midst of material affluence, the blatant inequalities between classes and groups, the mammoth size and immense complexities of social structures, the rapid pace of change, and so forth. In coping with these conditions, some persons' "I's" can only offer submission to small, powerless, meaningless, normless "Me's." Here is where religion, ethics, and other great value systems can help stem the tide by making people feel as Dostoyevski emphasized in *The Brothers Karamazov,* that I am personally responsible for all these dehumanizing conditions and thus also in some sense accountable for my own alienation. Tireless education coupled with daring attempts to empower the powerless is the way for society to alleviate the symptoms of alienation.

Although different levels of approaches have been suggested here, the overall recommendation is a direct one: Let us work to restore the "I" to its rightful place in the self. May the future of mankind be so fortunate that our "I's" can be free, creative, spontaneous, and responsible instead of becoming some objectified, theorized, belittled cogs in society's wheels.

REFERENCES

•●•

Blauner, R. 1964. *Alienation and Freedom*. Chicago: University of Chicago Press.

Braverman, H. 1974. *Labor and Monopoly Capital*. New York: Monthly Report.

Cassirer, E. 1925. *Mythical Thought* (Volume two of *The Philosophy of Symbolic Forms*). Berlin: B. Cassirer.

Cooley, C. H. 1902. *Human Nature and Social Order*. New York: Scribner's.

Durkheim, E. 1947. *The Division of Labor in Society*. Translated by George Simpson. Glencoe IL: Free Press. (Originally published in 1893.)

_____. 1951. *Suicide*. New York: Free Press. (Originally published in 1897).

Faunce, W. A. 1981. *Problems of an Industrial Society*. 2d edition. New York: McGraw-Hill.

Fromm, E. 1941. *Escape from Freedom*. New York: Holt.

_____. 1965. *The Sane Society*. Greenwich CT: Fawcett.

_____. 1966. *Marx's Concept of Man*. New York: Ungar.

Husserl, E. 1970. *The Crisis of European Sciences and Transcendental Phenomenology*. Translated by David Carr. Evanston IL: Northwestern University Press.

James, W. 1890. *Principles of Psychology*. Volume two. New York: Henry Holt.

Marcuse, H. 1941. *Reason and Revolution*. Fairlawn NJ: Oxford University Press.

_____. 1958. *Soviet Marxism*. New York: Columbia University Press.

Mead, G. H. 1934. *Mind, Self and Society*. Chicago: University of Chicago Press.

Mills, C. W. 1959. *The Sociological Imagination*. London: Oxford University Press.

Nietzsche, F. 1966. *Beyond Good and Evil: Prelude to a Philosophy of the Future*. Translated by W. Kaufmann. New York: Random House.

Ollman, B. 1958. *Alienation: Marx's Conception of Man in Capitalistic Society*. Cambridge MA: Cambridge University Press.

Schaff, A. 1965. *Marxism and Human Individual*. Vienna: Europa Verlag.

Seeman, M. 1959. "On the Meaning of Alienation." *American Sociological Review* 24 (December).

Thomas, W. I. 1967. *The Unadjusted Girl*. New York: Harper & Row. (Originally published in 1923.)

Watson, J. B. and W. McDougall. 1928. *The Battle of Behaviorism: An Exposition and Exposure*. London: Routledge.

Wolff, K. H. 1950. *The Sociology of Georg Simmel*. New York: Free Press.

CHAPTER NINE

The Relational Self in the Black Church: from Bondage to Challenge

—————————• ● •—————————

ARCHIE SMITH, JR.

For the writer of the next chapter, the black church in America is an impressive illustration of the formative influence of community on self-hood. A man of many professions (minister, counselor, social worker, and social activist) who leans on several disciplines (theology, psychology, sociology), Archie Smith, Jr. is both product and leader of black church life and knows it in its nooks and crannies. He obviously loves this tradition for its own sake, for what it has done in the past, and for what it continues to do in the present.

But he also sees the black church as a paradigm for the church in general, recognizing that its dynamic tradition of healing the wounded and liberating the oppressed, whether individually or communally, is a potent challenge to all who profess to love the Gospel but fall so short of living it.

By describing in detail the therapeutic and moral aspects of pastoral care in this tradition, Smith demonstrates that it always took selfhood as a relational process rather than as the individualistic substance the Enlightenment proclaimed it to be. Hence, his chapter is both a sharp critique of prevailing trends in modern societies and a constructive offer of an alternative vision that could reshape a world gone awry.

This essay identifies relational selfhood[1] as a key concept in black culture that links and undergirds the moral and pastoral care ministry

---

[1]The concept of the relational self is derived from the work and thought of George Herbert Mead, who understood mind, self, and society to be inseparably linked and dialectically interwoven. It was Mead who emphasized communi-

of the black church.[2] The black church is a microcosm of the Christian church and has been identified as the most powerful institution in the "Negro's world."[3] "American Blacks participate in a form of Christianity that was created and developed in the communal life of Blacks as a people."[4]

I will establish the idea of the relational character of selfhood as the ground for joining the therapeutic concerns of pastoral care and liberation ethics in ministry. My purpose is to heighten awareness of the interwoven character of personal and systemic oppression and make clear the need to join internal liberation and external transformation in the praxis of ministry. I want to emphasize the importance of keeping an analysis of inner and outer transformation together in liberation ministries. It is my contention that a relational view of ministry, one that

---

cative interaction as the primary basis for the emergence of the social self and for the rise of new social structures within society. Yet, any discussion of the human self may begin with a confession, namely that the self cannot be grasped or known in its totality, but only in its fragments. The self is always fragmented in its roles, functions, and appearances. All such roles and appearances express the self's relational character. People are eminently relational beings. In order to be selves, people must *ex*-press or *ob*-jectify themselves in order to come to know themselves through others. Hence, the social and relational nature of the self will be emphasized.

[2]In this essay the black church is treated as a microcosm of the Christian church. Selected literature on the history of the black church includes: Carter G. Woodson, *The History of the Negro Church* (Washington D.C.: Associated Publishers, 1921); Benjamin E. Mays and Joseph W. Nicholson, *The Negro's Church* (New York: Institute of Social and Religious Research, 1933); Arthur H. Fauset, *Black Gods of the Metropolis* (Philadelphia: University of Pennsylvania Press, 1944); C. Eric Lincoln, *The Black Muslims in America* (Boston: Beacon Press, 1961); Donald G. Mathews, *Slavery and Methodism* (Princeton NJ: Princeton University Press, 1965); H. M. Nelsen et al., *The Black Church in America* (New York: Basic Books, 1971); Joseph R. Washington, Jr., *Black Sects and Cults* (New York: Doubleday, 1972); E. Franklin Frazier, *The Negro Church in America,* and C. Eric Lincoln, *The Black Church since Frazier* (New York: Schocken Books, 1974); Melvin D. Williams, *Community in a Black Pentecostal Church: An Anthropological Study* (Pittsburgh PA: University of Pittsburgh Press, 1974); Hart M. Nelsen and Anne Nelsen, *Black Church in the Sixties* (Lexington KY: University of Kentucky Press, 1975); Olin P. Moyd, *Redemption in Black Theology* (Valley Forge: Judson Press, 1979); Randal K. Burkett, *Black Redemption* (Philadelphia: Temple University Press, 1978); James Deotis Roberts, *Roots of a Black Future: Family and Church* (Philadelphia: Westminster Press, 1980).

[3]John Hope Franklin, *From Slavery to Freedom: A History of Negro Americans* (New York: Random House, 1969) 561-62.

[4]Henry H. Mitchell, *Black Belief* (San Francisco: Harper & Row, 1975) 13.

joined inner liberation with outward social transformation, found expression in the ministry of the historical black church.

Relationality means that people are constituted through their relations with other people. Our humanity (or human-ness) is derived from and inseparably linked with other people. The reality of self is in its relations. The self is communal and dialogic in character. A relational view of selfhood permeated African cultures, and it was retained and developed on this side of the Atlantic in the communal and church life of black Americans.[5]

The relational selfhood rooted in African sensibilities is summarized by the ancient proverb: "One is only human because of others, with others, for others." The New Testament speaks in similar terms with reference to the whole Christian community as the Body of Christ: "You are members one of another." The black church was the place where this relational understanding of selfhood was practiced in solidarity with other victims of oppression.

The notion of God as creator and liberator of the oppressed underlies relational selfhood. Here God is understood as the supreme socius, the transcendent and incarnate one who frees oppressed and innocent victims from an enslaving past, calls them to purposeful transformation in history, and directs them toward unrealized possibilities.[6] This God is transcendent and immanent in that He struggles in and through all living things everywhere to break the yoke of oppression and to call people forward to new communal potentialities for power, justice, and love. As creator, God is not only transcendent but also fully incarnate in the freedom struggles of the oppressed.

I will interpret the mission of the black church from a particular relational and liberation perspective. The historic black church was born in bondage. From its inception it was a servant church embedded and engaged in the anguish and freedom struggles of an oppressed people. Unlike most immigrants who came to these shores to flee religious per-

---

[5]Ibid. Also see Eugene D. Genovese, *Roll, Jordan, Roll: The World the Slaves Made* (New York: Vintage Books, 1972); Gayraud S. Wilmore, *Black Religion and Black Radicalism* (New York: Doubleday, 1973); Albert Raboteau, *Slave Religion* (New York: Oxford University Press, 1978).

[6]This Whiteheadian idea of God is developed in the works of John B. Cobb, Jr. See especially his *A Christian Natural Theology* (Philadelphia: Westminster Press, 1965); *God and the World* (Philadelphia: Westminster Press, 1965); and *Theology and Pastoral Care* (Philadelphia: Fortress Press, 1977). This idea of God has strong affinities with the African High God, the supreme socius who underwrites, guarantees, and values existence as good. This supreme being is a moral God who is intimately involved with the created order. See Mitchell, *Black Belief*, 58-94; and John Mbiti, *African Religions and Philosophy* (New York: Praeger, 1969); and *Concepts of God in Africa* (New York: Praeger, 1970).

secution or poverty, Afro-Americans came involuntarily. They were brought in chains and sold as chattel on the auction block in the land of freedom. From their beginnings Afro-Americans were denied acceptance as human beings and barred from full participation in the mainstream of social, economic, and political life in America, including church life.[7]

The ministry of the black church emerged *from* and *within* the moral context of violent oppression. It was a ministry that identified the oppressed condition of black slaves with that of ancient Israel. The liberating gospel and mission of Jesus was embraced, for Jesus was understood as the Elder Brother whose ministry was one of setting captives free. The black church identified with Jesus, the salvation bringer. Slavery was the evil to overcome. Deliverance was the deep yearning of black people in bondage.

The history of the black church in the United States has been complex. Protest and rebellion, along with moderation, passivity, and resignation have characterized the life of the black church.[8] Protest and passivity have existed side by side throughout its history. It has often been a church that has kept together spiritual awareness and social political activism as it sought to be faithful to its Lord. It is a servant church that strives to meet the spiritual and material needs of black people. Fundamentally, it is an expression of the black community itself.[9]

The black church in slavery did not seek to separate its mission and experience of suffering from the sufferings of the whole black community. It was the spiritual face of the black community and expressed the inner moral life of a people in bondage. It provided spiritual guidance and direction while it sustained and nurtured the sufferer and his or her family. As W. E. B. DuBois noted, the black church predates "the Negro home."[10] It was the extended family form, the conserver of values that mediated hope and gave a sense of belonging to strangers, weary travelers, troubled, lonely, and lost souls, the sick and bereaved. Traditions of care and moral discernment in the black church not only made possible the survival of blacks under brutal conditions of slavery in the

---

[7]Eldon G. Ernst, *Without Help or Hindrance* (Philadelphia: Westminster Press, 1977) 72-78.

[8]Ronald L. Johnstone, "Negro Preachers Take Sides," in Nelsen et al., *The Black Church in America,* 274-86; also see Peter J. Paris, *Black Leaders in Conflict* (New York: Pilgrim Press, 1978).

[9]Joseph R. Washington, Jr., "How Black Is Black Religion?" in James J. Gardiner, S.J. and J. Deotis Roberts, Sr., eds., *Quest for a Black Theology* (Philadelphia: Pilgrim Press, 1970) 22-43.

[10]W. E. B. DuBois, *The Souls of Black Folk* (Greenwich CT: Fawcett Premier, 1961) 146.

United States; it also made possible some quite dynamic and creative responses to the most brutal form of human oppression known. Black slaves transformed the meaning of Christianity in the Americas by performing the greater miracle of revealing the limits of white power and arrogance, and giving to an oppressed people hope for a new humanity. Black people came to see and know the providence of God amidst their deepest suffering and sorrow.[11] They believed that God condemned slavery and that Christian freedom meant political emancipation.[12] Black Christianity spoke for all humanity when it proclaimed the freedom and inviolability of the human soul.[13]

For this reason the concept of relationality will be emphasized instead of the Western substantialist view of selfhood so prevalent in modern industrial societies.[14] The Western substantialist view holds that I am a bounded, singular, uniquely self-made, more-or-less integrated, autonomous center of awareness and power vis-à-vis other selves.[15] This substantialist view of selfhood is the antithesis of the view of the human self that informed the sensibilities of the black church in bondage; and it must be rejected if the black church is to be a servant and communal church today.

A relational view of selfhood is made difficult, however, in a society that has encouraged an individualistic and nuclear model of the human person—"Look out for Number One," or "Me first." The relational self builds on the idea that there is an underlying relatedness of reality, a web that is the primary constitutive condition out of which social and personal reality emerge. The important point is that all reality is dialectical, fundamentally interrelated, and evolving.

This idea of relationality as the web of life found concrete expression in the history of the black church and is crucial for the freedom struggles of black people today. It was their view of God, as the mighty deliverer who indwells history, that underlay this relational view of reality. It became the hope and basis for moral discernment, critical reflection, and emancipatory activity in the historic black church.

---

[11]See Mitchell, *Black Belief,* 152.

[12]James H. Cone, "The Sources and Norm of Black Theology," in Lincoln, *The Black Experience in Religion,* 122.

[13]Genovese, *Roll, Jordan, Roll,* 167.

[14]Michael A. Cowan, "Emerging in Love: Everyday Acts in Ultimate Contexts," this vol., ch. 4.

[15]Clifford Geertz, "From the Natives' Point of View: On the Nature of Anthropological Understandings," in Paul Rabinow and William M. Sullivan, eds., *Interpretive Social Science* (Berkeley: University of California Press, 1979) 225-41.

The nineteenth- and early-twentieth-century black church shared this relational vision, which enabled it to link personal faith with responsibility for social justice. Its relational vision embraced the liberation struggles of the whole black community, religious and secular. Figures such as Jeremiah B. Sanderson, George Washington Woodbey, Frederick Douglass, and many others made the social and political advancement of black people the burden of their life's commitment. Their sense of mission courageously confronted conditions of segregation as they sought to humanize the social order.[16]

> It is that though the Black church was effective in the nineteenth century partially because of the circumstance of history, it was effective mainly because it never was free to separate its interior institutional life from its mission in and on behalf of the world. From the perspective of seventy years later, if the Black church had a diminishing impact it is because it had turned more and more in upon itself, and faced less and less outwards the world.[17]

Today the black church struggles to survive as a servant church amidst new and complex forms of repression. Now, as then, its task is still to feed, clothe, and shelter the masses of rejected blacks who remain marginal to this society, while at the same time sustaining them spiritually and giving them the courage to be as they work for the transformation of this society.

Contemporary society poses as formidable a challenge to the liberation ministry of the black church as did the system of slavery. The challenge to the black church and its ministry comes from the workings of a modern, technological society that threatens the dignity, freedom, and existence of all human subjects. The black church has a mission of liberation and humanization to realize in this society.

> Born of the intransigent faith of an oppressed people and nurtured in their determination to make a distinctive witness for God in spite of their distress, the Black church has thus far weathered the historic conventions which called it into being. Unlike its counterparts in the American mainstream, it seems relatively unconfused about its spiritual commitments and its moral responsibilities. The Black church has its problems, but they do not appear to be problems of the faith, or in the interpretation of the faith in the context of social change.[18]

---

[16]Larry George Murphy Lee, "Equality before the Law: The Struggle of Nineteenth-Century Black Californians for Social and Political Justice" (Ph.D. dissertation, Graduate Theological Union, 1973).

[17]Lawrence N. Jones, "They Sought a City: The Black Church and Churchmen in the Nineteenth Century," in Martin E. Marty and Dean G. Peerman, eds., *New Theology No. 9* (New York: Macmillan Co., 1972) 172-73.

[18]C. Eric Lincoln, "The Black Church in the American Society: A New Responsibility?" *Journal of the Interdenominational Theological Center* 6:2 (Spring 1979): 88.

The black church in America has nurtured a distinctive ambience that has been unique to its own tradition.[19] Survival and deepening spiritual commitments in the face of social injustice, suffering, and change have been characteristic of the black church in the black experience. Despite acute historical contradictions, and the presence of moral and systemic evil, the black church has maintained a tenacious belief in the goodness of God. Outreach and solidarity with the victims of oppression have marked the ministry of the black church in the black experience. James Weldon Johnson captured this experience in song.

> *Stony the road we trod,*
> *Bitter the chastening rod,*
> *Felt in the days when hope unborn had died;*
> *Yet with a steady beat,*
> *Have not our weary feet*
> *Come to the place for which our fathers sighed?*
> *We have come over a way that with tears has been watered,*
> *We have come, treading our path through the blood of the*
> *   slaughtered,*
> *Out from the gloomy past,*
> *Till now we stand at last*
> *Where the white gleam of our bright star is cast.*[20]

The question facing the black church today is whether its spiritual resources and traditions can minister to our secular, highly differentiated, pluralistic, and technological society.

It has been argued by many scholars that modern secular and scientific culture, under the domination of technology, has diminished the human capacity for critical reflection and freedom. It has made people its captive. The main goal of modernity is to perpetuate itself. "Culture, rather than constituting consciousness, stands as the denial of consciousness."[21] Hence, modern culture has increased alienation while it has actually narrowed people's capacity to envision alternative forms of liberation from it. Objectively, modern culture has alienated people from nature and from one another and from their own creations in art, religion, ethics, science, and society. Marcuse stated the problem: "A comfortable, smooth, reasonable, democratic unfreedom prevails in advanced industrial civilization. . . . Independence of thought, autonomy, and the

---

[19]Ibid., 91.

[20]James Weldon Johnson, "Lift Every Voice and Sing," in Langston Hughes and Arna Bontemps, eds., *The Poetry of the Negro* (New York: Doubleday, 1970) 32.

[21]George Friedman, *The Political Philosophy of the Frankfurt School* (Ithaca: Cornell University Press, 1981) 167.

right to political opposition are being deprived of their basic critical function in a society which seems increasingly incapable of satisfying the needs of the individuals through the way in which it is organized."[22] Subjectively, modern culture has contributed to a sense of disequilibrium, anxiety, despair, or hopelessness.[23] "The root of the crisis is in the Enlightenment itself; the end point is in the human mind. And with this crisis, the general crisis of history—its failure to move beyond itself—becomes all the more urgent."[24] It is this society in which the black church and its ministry are situated and from which they cannot be separated. The black church is not an island unto itself; it is emphatically a part of the mainland. This is also a larger moral context in which the pastoral care and spiritual ministry of the black church are to be realized.

While it is true that the masses of black Americans have remained marginal to this society, they are not entirely outside of it. They have membership in this society and are deeply affected by its workings. Therefore, black people in America cannot solve their own problems of oppression without helping to transform the very society that enslaved them and has kept them at a disadvantage. "Such a double life, with double thoughts, double duties, and double social classes, must give rise to double words and double ideals, and tempt the mind to pretense or revolt, to hypocrisy or radicalism."[25] How free, then, is the black church to respond to its new challenge and responsibility? The peculiar ethical paradox facing black Americans is that, as an oppressed people, they must creatively struggle against the internal and external effects of white racism and white power, while at the same time they must seek the transformation of the system that exploits them. Their selfhood is constituted by these double duties: to transform an oppressive system that has denied them full humanity, and to creatively struggle against the internal effects of white racism and white power. This challenge to black America is reminiscent of a theme in Jeremiah's letter to the captives of his time:

> *Seek the welfare of the city where I have sent*
> *you into exile, and pray to the Lord on its behalf,*
> *for in its welfare you will have welfare.*
> (Jeremiah 29:7 [NAS])

In the main, pastoral care and therapy as well as traditional Christian social ethics have not made modern secular society, particularly its ex-

---

[22]Herbert Marcuse, *One-Dimensional Man* (Boston: Beacon Press, 1964).

[23]F. H. Heinemann, *Existentialism and the Modern Predicament* (New York: Harper & Brothers, 1953) 9.

[24]Friedman, *Political Philosophy of the Frankfurt School*, 185.

[25]DuBois, *The Souls of Black Folk*, 149.

ploitive economic organization and racial oppression, the object of critical reflection and change. Pastoral care and therapy, in the white tradition, have sought to help the individual adjust to the existing framework of the larger society, thereby legitimating existing social arrangements.

> Most pastoral care in the mainline churches is practiced without a great deal of sensitivity to the relation between personal problems and larger social-ethical questions. On the other hand, the reverse is probably also true. Social-ethical problems are often addressed without much knowledge of or sympathy for the more intimate and personal dimensions of human suffering.[26]

The practice of joining the personal and communal-ethical dimension of ministry was characteristic of the black church in bondage. Its task has been to comfort the suffering and bereaved ones, feed, clothe, and shelter the hungry and destitute, as well as to break the yoke of oppression. Making the connection between personal problems and public issues has been characteristic of the black church's ministry, while the separation of personal problems from the larger social-ethical questions has been more characteristic of mainline white churches. The social-gospel tradition has been a minority movement within mainline white Protestantism; instead personal salvation has been the dominant theme. During the civil rights movement of the 1960s, white churches first resisted and then mainly followed the lead of black churches in the struggle against white racism and the oppression of blacks. They were never in the forefront of the movement to combat white racism.

Liberation from oppression today requires that the praxis of ministry be joined with critical biblical and theological reflection and linked with recollection of a forgotten past. The task of a critical theology and ministry of liberation is to recognize and to confess the partial and provisional nature of our theologies, and to seek the continued and unfolding pattern of God's justice and emancipating activity in the concrete history of the innocent, suffering victims of our time. A ministry of liberation may undertake to discern God's self-disclosure and to assist members of the church of Jesus Christ to fashion their moral and ethical life in a manner that is consistent with the manifestation of God's unfolding movement of liberation in history.

NEW CHALLENGES

The raison d'être of the black church today is the same as it has always been in the past, although it now functions under different and more complex conditions than it faced in its earlier history. Its goal is to witness to God's emancipatory and reconciling and healing activity in history. Liberation from oppression today requires that theological

---

[26]Don S. Browning, *The Moral Context of Pastoral Care* (Philadelphia: Westminster Press, 1976) 17.

praxis and ministry be inseparable from critical reflection upon a society that seems fatefully committed to unfreedom (under the guise of freedom) and hopelessly victim to an attitude that has domesticated the radical and potentially transforming edge of Christian religion—"My country, right or wrong!" Civil religion has often supported race denomination and the exploitation of women. It has frequently served to justify military involvement abroad, which has led to the death of many of the world's innocent victims and defenseless people of color.

Today, questions about the black church need to be raised afresh in its continued struggle for emancipation, reconciliation, discipleship, peoplehood, and redemption in the United States and elsewhere. Social science information can be an indispensable resource for the black church and for any contemporary church whose consciousness and direction are not only formed by biblical faith, but whose appropriation of the Gospel is also shaped in subtle ways by the society in which it ministers. Hence, social theory and analysis must be taken seriously; and the relevance of social and psychological information for struggles of the Christian church in a sexist, racist, capitalist, and bourgeois Western society must be sought.

Today, the black church is challenged to keep the outer and inner dimensions of reality together in emancipatory struggle, and within a critical theological framework wherein the forgotten past is remembered. This implies a critique of social-science theories that claim to be value-neutral but nevertheless function in the service of the status quo. Such theories are not cognizant of their own ideological roots. Thus they serve to reproduce limited images of social reality and to further entrench oppressed people in the very structure that needs to be criticized and transformed.

Ideally, the black family, church, and community exist in a mutually supportive relationship and together may articulate alternative values that affirm the material and the spiritual, the social and psychic life of the person in the community. The issue is survival of the human subject in the present society and the possibility of transformation in a new and liberating society yet to be achieved. Survival as black people is a formidable challenge in a society that continues to deny them authentic freedom, along with the material and spiritual basis for dignity and self-conscious selfhood. The survival and welfare of black people in this society are inseparable from that of all people.

The black church and its ministry have often been charged that they serve only to dull the potentially critical and emancipatory, reconciling and healing task to which they have been called. This charge has been especially relevant when the black church has supported, uncritically, the status quo of race relations, or else has withdrawn. It has sometimes been viewed as an opiate to militant action.[27] The black church, as a

---

[27]Gary T. Marx, "Religion: Opiate or Inspiration of Civil Rights Militancy?" in *Protest and Prejudice: A Study of Belief in the Black Community* (New York:

therapeutic[28] and prophetic community, has a vital yet difficult role to play in today's complex society as the Church of Jesus Christ. Its task is to identify with innocent victims of oppression, to promote a sense of anamnestic solidarity,[29] and to help diagnose, interpret, and transform oppressive structures and conditions. It can undergird liberation struggles and proclaim in what concrete and universal sense God is on the side of the oppressed and innocent victims, and indeed on the side of every man, woman, and child, and every race.

Today, the black church is further challenged by these complex issues of prophetic faith to chart the linkage between outer and inner transformation within a theological perspective that has relevance for the Christian church and its practice of ministry in modern society.

The black church and every contemporary church in Western culture is in some manner faced with the crisis of modernity. Modern culture, rather than liberating people for self-determination and responsible communal existence, has increased a sense of moral malaise, alienation, and despair. It has diminished the chief human capacities (namely, freedom, reason, and love) for critically reflecting upon our situation and transforming a repressive social order. In Herbert Marcuse's terms, modern technological culture has created a one-dimensional society in consciousness and practice.[30] Hence, the crisis of modernity is not only sociological and historical; it is psychological as well. There is the crisis of the human psyche, the diminished capacity for critical consciousness in modern culture. Critical consciousness here means the capacity to perceive the dynamic interplay between the per-

---

Harper & Row, 1969) 94-105; C. Eric Lincoln, "White Christianity and Black Commitment: A Comment on the Power of Faith and Socialization," *Journal of the Interdenominational Theological Center* 6:1 (Fall 1978): 21-31; William H. Grier and Price M. Cobbs, *The Jesus Bag* (San Francisco: McGraw-Hill, 1971).

[28]See Cheryl Townsend Gilkes, "The Black Church as a Therapeutic Community," *Journal of the Interdenominational Theological Center* 8:1 (Fall 1980): 29-44. Also, Archie Smith, Jr., "Religion and Mental Health among Blacks," *Journal of Religion and Health* 20:4 (Winter 1981): 264-87.

[29]The term *amnesis* means to forget the past or to block the past from memory. *Anamnesis* has the opposite meaning. *Anamnesis* means remembrance of things past. It is to recollect the forgotten past and to participate in a common memory and a common hope. Anamnesis, or remembering, is a way of keeping alive the dangerous memory of those who lost their lives while struggling for the freedom of others. See Eric Voegelin, *Anamnesis* (London: University of Notre Dame Press, 1978); Russell Jacoby, *Social Amnesia* (Boston: Beacon Press, 1975); Rudolf J. Siebert, *From Critical Theory of Society to Theology of Communicative Praxis* (Washington D.C.: University Press of America, 1979).

[30]Marcuse, *One-Dimensional Man.*

sonal, social, political, and economic contradictions, and to take action against the oppressive elements of reality.[31] The hegemony of modern mass culture has actually narrowed the range of psychic possibilities available to people. It has even been difficult for the marginalized persons in contemporary culture to develop and sustain a form of prophetic consciousness that remains critical of the basic value assumptions and workings of modern culture. Hence, "The crisis of modernity is not so much the lack of principles as the lack of consciousness of principles and the further inability to actualize those principles."[32]

However, among Afro-American slaves in the early black church, there was a radical consciousness of the gospel of Jesus, a critical social vision that enabled them to resist being completely demoralized by slavery.

> The doctrine, "Render therefore unto Caesar the things which are Caesar's, and unto God the things that are God's," is deceptively two-edged. If it calls for political submission to the powers that be, it also calls for militant defense of the freedom of the spirit and the autonomy of the personality. But the master-slave relationship rests, psychologically as well as ideologically, on the transformation of the will of the slave into an extension of the will of the master. Thus, no matter how obedient—how Uncle Tomish—Christianity made a slave, it also drove deep into his soul an awareness of the moral limits of submission, for it placed a master above his own master and thereby dissolved the moral and ideological ground on which the very principle of absolute human lordship may rest. It was much more than malice that drove so many Southern masters to whip slaves for praying to God for this or that and to demand that they address all grievances and wishes to their earthly masters.[33]

It was their relatively autonomous culture that provided a defense against the negative effects of slavery, nurtured a sense of communal solidarity, and kept them from being seduced by white interpretations of Scripture.

The urgent need today is for the black church to continue its own traditions of caring ministries to modern-day victims of oppression. This includes sustaining, nurturance, guidance, healing, and confrontation. It must be joined with the development of a consciousness capable of critical reflection upon the workings of our mass society. In this regard, the roles of both church and family life are crucial for the development of a critical consciousness. The family life of black people must be recognized as the basic social unit responsible for the early formation of personality and values, the acquisition of male-female role relations, the

---

[31]Paulo Freire, *Pedagogy of the Oppressed* (New York: Seabury Press, 1968) 19.

[32]Friedman, *Political Philosophy of the Frankfurt School,* 263.

[33]Genovese, *Roll, Jordan, Roll,* 165.

psycho-emotional-moral grounding of nurturing relational patterns in community, and the development of adaptive capacities. The mother's role in the extended family, in both home and church, is crucial for the development of self-identity and for the creation and maintenance of patterns of care and social vision.[34]

The black family is also the place where strong kinship bonds are nurtured and a strong work, religious, and moral orientation is developed.[35] The development of inner qualities must be viewed against oppressive systemic forces such as racism and sexism, chronic unemployment, substandard living conditions, and poor educational opportunities. These forces have exerted unusual strains upon black family systems, and yet black families have contributed to the ongoing creation of important adaptive cultural mechanisms and have survived great odds. The resiliency of black family systems may prove to be an instructive resource for family survival in the wider society. It must also be recognized that systemic oppression has contributed to pathogenic processes within black families, resulting in black-on-black crime, alcohol and drug abuse, and other destructive relational patterns within family life. In this regard, the resources of the black church may be a stimulus for curative relational patterns that can enrich family life and buttress spiritual and moral development.[36]

The black church is referred to as a durable institution because it outlasts the normal evolution of individual family units. When children grow up and marry, they often return to the church as a new family unit. The fact that at least ninety-eight percent of all black Americans confess some religious affiliation suggests that the black church remains a vital force in the lives of most blacks.[37] It is the spiritual embodiment of the black experience.[38] It now functions in a society of rapid and complex changes. Therefore, it must now fashion its ministry so as to address the sprritual needs of the larger society and humanize a social order that seems intent upon its own demise.[39]

---

[34]See Nancy Chodorow, *The Reproduction of Mothering: Psychoanalysis and the Sociology of Gender* (Berkeley: University of California Press, 1978); Edith Jacobson, *The Self and the Object World* (New York: International Universities Press, 1969); Ronald D. Laing, *The Politics of the Family* (New York: Random House, 1971).

[35]Robert B. Hill, *The Strengths of Black Families* (New York: Emerson Hall Publishers, 1972).

[36]Roberts, *Roots of a Black Future.*

[37]Lincoln, "White Christianity and Black Commitment," 22.

[38]Lincoln, "The Black Church in the American Society," 88.

[39]Ibid., 92.

The remainder of this chapter identifies a way for the church to envision a relationship between the therapeutic and liberating functions of pastoral-care ministries (transformations in *personal* existence) and liberation ethics (transformation in *social* existence). In this way the black church, or any contemporary church, may be able to link in awareness and praxis the dialectical relationship between internal liberation and external transformation.

The liberation struggles of black people in the United States have entailed the need for freedom from interior forces of enslavement as well as freedom from external forms of oppression. In this light therapy—which has emphasized self-other regard—and liberation ethics—which has emphasized the transformation of the social order—may be kept together in the practice of ministry.

The primary function of therapy is to combat demoralization that may result from certain relational patterns.[40] Therapeutic relationships attempt to address internally or externally induced stress such as feelings of impotence, isolation, despair, damaged self-esteem, failure, or a loss of meaning in life. The task of the therapeutic relationship is to bring about self-understanding and to help effect change so that individuals and groups may be empowered for self-determination. It seeks also to establish or to reestablish a sense of connectedness or integration with self and within one's own group. Moreover, the therapeutic relationship may strengthen or enlarge the individual's and group's capacity for self-critical discernment, imagination, warmth, empathy, and sense of justice and vitality, and it can help deepen the capacity for hope and love.

Clyde J. Steckel argues that faith transformation is sometimes enhanced through social-action programs in the church. In some churches participation in therapeutic relationships such as prayer meetings (where church members share their sufferings and pray for one another[41]), revivals, Marriage Encounter, or Alcoholics Anonymous may contribute to spiritual growth and faith transformation. But the therapeutic relationship alone may not be sufficient to bring about the mature moral discernment and Christian perfection called for in biblical faith.[42] Ethical discernment and critical theological reflection are essential dynamics in spiritual growth and faith transformation.

Both liberation ethics and therapy may be concerned with strengthening awareness of new possibilities and direction in the relational pat-

---

[40]See Jerome D. Frank, "Psychotherapy: The Restoration of Morale," *American Journal of Psychiatry* 131:3 (March 1974).

[41]See Gilkes, "The Black Church as Therapeutic Community." Also, Mitchell, *Black Belief.*

[42]See Clyde J. Steckel's ch. 10 in this volume.

terns of both individuals and groups. The various forms of liberation ethics and therapy may be placed on a continuum, as shown below:

THERAPEUTIC RELATIONAL PATTERNS			
SCALE OF ACTION	INDIVIDUAL	COUPLE	FAMILY
SPECIFIC RELATIONAL PATTERN	One-to-one talk therapy or pastoral counseling; spiritual direction, meditation, consultation, or advice.	Marital, couple therapy or pastoral marital counseling, relationship therapy, consultation, or advice.	Family systems therapy, pastoral family systems, therapy with nuclear or extended family, consultation or advice.
SCALE OF ACTION	SMALL GROUP		COLLECTIVE STRUGGLE
SPECIFIC RELATIONAL PATTERN	*Therapeutic communities:* church, sect, cult, revivals, hospice, prayer meetings, peer self-help group, religious community, Alanon, Marriage Encounter, Alcoholics Anonymous, small sharing group in the church, deacons, elders, basic Christian community, etc.		Revolutionary struggle, social movements, peace movements, participation in and with national and international groups for social and political justice.

SOCIAL ETHICS			
SCALE OF ACTION	SMALL GROUP	COMMUNITY ACTION (LOCAL LEVEL)	LARGE GROUP
SPECIFIC RELATIONAL PATTERN	church social action-reflection groups	boycott, strike, etc.	mass protest, mass forms of resistance, reform movements, revolutionary struggles.

The term *therapeutic relationship* refers to the link established between two or more people with the aim of effecting a change or furthering a curative process that relieves suffering. Usually, the "therapeutic relationship" shall refer to a change in oppressive relational patterns that relieves the suffering of the oppressed and may result in constructive and supportive relations in society. This implies that people are agents who can participate cooperatively in socially redemptive processes. By serving a fellow sufferer, or by helping to change the systemic character of injustice, one can further the redemptive work of Christ in the world (Matt. 25:39-40).

Therapy may take the form of psychotherapy[43] or one-to-one talk therapy (as in the dialogue of therapy) with a professional or a friend;

---

[43]See Barbara Lerner, *Therapy in the Ghetto: Political Impotence and Per-*

often a family member, especially mother or grandmother, is called upon. It may take the form of marital, or couple, therapy or family-systems therapy. It may come through participation in a therapeutic community (i.e., a church, fraternity, sorority, basic Christian community, or religious order); or it may come through revolutionary struggle as oppressed people unite in solidarity and collectively confront an issue—such as colonialism, sexism, or racism—that one person alone could not change.

These points on the continuum are not mutually exclusive; rather, they are interrelated. For example, many who have engaged in mass protest, such as the civil rights movement of the 1960s, often find it necessary to engage in one-to-one or small group therapeutic relations as they integrate meaning and work through the more personal dimensions of their involvement at the level of collective change. As one participant put it: "I needed to face inside of me the changes I was pushing for on the outside . . . what it means for my family." Therapeutic relational patterns can mediate between the personal and the larger social dimension of change. They help to support and sustain individual involvement in large-scale change. Hence, it is not surprising that prayer, spiritual and gospel singing, and testimonials often preceded direct involvement in the civil rights movement.[44]

> Don' let nobody turn you aroun'
> Turn you roun', turn you roun'.
> Don' let nobody turn you roun'
> Walking up the King's Highway.

The church as therapeutic community is perhaps the most prevalent social form of therapy in black communities. W. E. B. DuBois referred to black worship and revival as "intense excitement."[45] Some of the key therapeutic elements he saw were strong preaching, singing spirituals, gospels, and jubilee songs, dancing, shouting, and fervent prayer. He described shouting as the one element that was most devoutly regarded:

---

sonal Disintegration (Baltimore: Johns Hopkins University Press, 1972). Lerner's research heightens awareness of the connection between political impotence and a sense of personal or psychic disintegration. Her finding is that psychotherapy, when linked with strategies of social change, can strengthen self-affirmation. "From the perspective detailed here, the conflict over individual versus group methods in community mental health rests on a false dichotomy because the essential nature of constructive psychotherapy and social action is the same. So too are the goals of both: to promote effective action in one's own behalf, in the former case by removing internal psychological obstacles to such action, and in the latter by removing external obstacles to it" (11).

[44]See Watt Tee Walker, "Somebody's Calling My Name," in *Black Sacred Music and Social Change* (Valley Forge: Judson Press, 1979).

[45]DuBois, *The Souls of Black Folk,* 140.

Finally the Frenzy or "Shouting," when the Spirit of the Lord passed by, and, seizing the devotee, made him mad with supernatural joy, was the last essential of Negro religion and the one more devoutly believed in than all the rest. It varied in expression from the silent rapt countenance or the low murmur and moan to the mad abandon of physical fervor, and the stamping, shrieking, and shouting, the rushing to and fro and wild waving of arms, the weeping and laughing, the vision and the trance. All this is nothing new in the world, but old as religion, as Delphi and Endor. And so firm a hold did it have on the Negro, that many generations firmly believed that without this visible manifestation of the God there could be no true communion with the Invisible.[46]

Revivals were social and psychological therapy for the participants. They *are* a form of psychic release (and healing) and social cohesion. Plainly, too, revivals provided a sense of communion with the Divine. "Back of this more formal religion, the church often stands as a real conserver of morals, a strengthener of family life, and the final authority on what is Good and Right."[47] Worship and revival in the black church tradition were the most trenchant assertions of African character, linking therapeutic expressions with the moral life.

Traditionally, the black preacher was the community therapist par excellence.[48] He or she continues to be a bringer of glad tidings, a doctor of souls, a spiritual and psychological healer, an interpreter of the Unknown, a comforter in times of sorrow, and one who expresses the longings, disappointments, and resentments of a stolen and oppressed people.[49]

This form of therapy may be linked with liberation ethics, which seeks to involve people in changing a society that has systematically excluded and denied full humanity to the poor and people of color, especially blacks and Native Americans. The civil rights movement and the ministry of Martin Luther King, Jr. may be viewed as an attempt to link the therapeutic resources of the black church and the gospel of Jesus with liberation ethics.

Liberation ethics may take place at the level of the local church, as in a church-sponsored social action-reflection group; or at the community level, as in a local demonstration such as a boycott or strike; or at

---

[46]Ibid., 141.

[47]Ibid., 143.

[48]For an explication of the administrative function of the black church as "therapeutic," see Floyd Massey, Jr. and Samuel Berry McKinney, *Church Administration in the Black Perspective* (Valley Forge: Judson Press, 1976); also Henry H. Mitchell, *Black Preaching* (Philadelphia: J. B. Lippincott, 1970); and H. Beecher Hicks, Jr., *Images of the Black Preacher* (Valley Forge: Judson Press, 1977).

[49]DuBois, *The Souls of Black Folk,* 144.

the societal level, as in a mass demonstration such as the 1963 March on Washington, or the Vietnam Veterans' March on Washington, or the Native Americans' walk from the West Coast to the White House. The task of liberation ethics is to expose the systemic character of human exploitation and seek the transformation of society and community life. This idea of exposing the systemic character of human exploitation was dramatically used by Martin Luther King, Jr. in the civil rights movement by singling out the castelike system of racial segregation.[50]

At all of these levels (small group, local, societal), people may engage in action and then step back to reflect critically upon what they have done; or they may engage in rational analysis, as a prelude to direct action, in order to clarify the nature of their obligations to society. From the perspective of black communities struggling to be free from external and internal forms of race and gender exploitation and class oppression, ethical reflection must emerge out of the day-to-day struggle for freedom and embrace the values of communal responsibility and solidarity. In this view, the responsible self is a relational self that understands that God is the one ultimate actor who addresses us in our many self-expressions and through His many actions that touch us.

Liberation ethics, in the black church tradition, takes Scripture seriously. It cannot ignore the Scriptures, nor the folk traditions and practices of the faith communities of the oppressed who sought, in their time, to be faithful to God in the face of cruel suffering and injustice. Reflection done from this standpoint, and in the light of God's self-disclosure in Jesus and His continued liberating activity "to set captives free," may be termed liberation ethics and viewed as a way to discipleship. Forms of freedom, justice, power, and love are rightly focal concerns for liberation ethics. The Scriptures and the faith of our predecessors live on in memory and in contemporary expressions as the communities of oppressed peoples today evolve their understanding of what it means to be a faithful people reconstituting themselves in the promise of a redeeming social order.[51]

Sharing and nurturing are essential elements that help to sustain meaningful activity in small groups within church and society. Apart from group support, the building of trust, and the experience of reconciliation, it may be impossible for groups or individual Christians to sustain effective action and critical reflection or to see clearly their mis-

---

[50]John M. Swomly, Jr., *Liberation Ethics* (New York: Macmillan Company, 1972) 184; J. Deotis Roberts, "Christian Liberation Ethics: The Black Experience," in *Religion and Life,* vol. 48 (Nashville: Abingdon Press, 1979); Enoch H. Oglesby, *Ethics and Theology from the Other Side: Sounds of Moral Struggle* (Washington D.C.: University Press of America, 1979).

[51]See Speed Leas and Paul Kittlaus, *The Pastoral Counselor in Social Action* (Philadelphia: Fortress Press, 1981).

sion as God's agents of renewal and redemption in the midst of change.[52] "The local church can be a source of preparation and support to enable the laity to be the people of God at work in the world."[53] In the black church tradition the work of the Holy Spirit is identified with a love that "flows from heart to heart and from breast to breast," establishing group support and solidarity.[54]

Therapy aims at self-understanding and emancipation, whether through psychotherapy or pastoral counseling, family therapy, or through participation in a therapeutic community, or in struggles for social justice. When individuals, families, or groups are politically impotent and also members of oppressed communities, then therapeutic relationships may be means for empowerment to promote effective action and personal integration as a resource for transforming communal life.

By itself therapy cannot transform social reality; nor can liberation ethics do it alone. Neither strategy is the ultimate truth. They are provisional strategies that must undergo critical reflection and may be judged in light of God's liberating activity on behalf of the oppressed and all people.

Michael Cowan, a therapist, has challenged us to place our everyday acts in face-to-face relations within the ultimate context of love. When we speak to one another and hear one another in the spirit of deep mutuality, we are engaged in reciprocally transformative activity.[55] Then we have moved spiritually and morally from modes and models of domination to modes of mutuality and transformation. The deep structures of transformation are located in God's self-disclosure in the life, death, and resurrection of Jesus, who is the representative of a new and liberated humanity. "The spirituality now required is one of shaping an open future in accordance with relevant possibilities given by God."[56]

We are challenged by a comprehensive vision of the aim that is present in all things derived from God. Liberation ethics and therapy may be informed by the unity of three interdependent and interwoven strands: (1) the *personal;* (2) the *communal;* and (3) the *resurrection/ transformative.* The *personal* strand refers to the individual's respond-

---

[52]Thomas R. Bennett, "Project Laity: Groups and Social Action," in John L. Casteel, ed., *The Creative Role of Interpersonal Groups in the Church Today* (New York: Association Press, 1968) 53-72; and Robert C. Leslie, "The Uniqueness of Small Groups in the Church," *Pastoral Psychology* 15:145 (June 1964): 33-40; idem, *Sharing Groups in the Church* (Nashville: Abingdon, 1970).

[53]Bennett, "Project Laity," 72.

[54]Mitchell, *Black Belief,* 152.

[55]Cowan, "Emerging in Love."

[56]Cobb, *Theology and Pastoral Care,* 54.

ing to and shaping his environment even as he is shaped by it.[57] The *communal* strand is individuals in relations with each other, the corporate body. This is the church or community of selves with its many forms and structures of social life. This second strand suggests that the individual form (1) is constituted in its relations with others (2). The communal indwells the personal and the personal dwells in community. The communal, as a dialogical unit, is crucial for the transformation of relational structures in politics, work, and other realms of activity.[58] Together, people shape a common history and destiny. For this reason, the communal requires the narrative form for its exposition. "So the demand to love, exemplified by God's own self-giving love, issues an agapic self-sacrifice, in living out the story of the cross. Accordingly, there now appear the communal virtues we so frequently demarcate as 'Christian'—patience, meekness, faithfulness."[59] The *resurrection-transformative* is revelatory, morally creative, and transformative because it is spun from the power and creative freedom of God that both indwells and transcends the private lives of individuals and the authority of specific communities. The third strand is characterized by the strange eschatological language of the New Testament—the Risen Christ—and by the freedom of God's electing love in the Hebrew Scriptures.[60] This third strand is the basis of a new covenant and awareness in which God's goodness and fidelity indwell the personal and communal strands, infusing them with new power, freedom, wholeness, moral vision, and direction. In the resurrection-transformative view, God's goodness is that which irrupts from beyond all human calculations—the resurrection of Christ.[61]

The *personal, communal,* and *resurrection-transformative* strands are interwoven to form a whole, the web of life. They are mingled in the Christian story and found concrete expression in the black church tradition. The resurrection-transformative strand gives direction to all things; it is an aim or urge toward unrealized freedom and new possibilities. The three strands, taken as a whole, constitute a challenge for affirming the emancipatory potential in liberation ethics, therapy, and pastoral care. Ethics may attempt to meet this challenge by clarifying our commitments and calling people forward to envision new possibilities for human becoming and to reconstitute themselves in a moral

---

[57]James William McClendon, Jr., "Three Strands of Christian Ethics," *Journal of Religious Ethics* 6:1 (1978): 54-80.

[58]Gibson Winter, *Liberating Creation: Foundations of Religious Social Ethics* (New York: Crossroads, 1972) 49-50.

[59]McClendon, "Three Strands of Christian Ethics," 58.

[60]Ibid.

[61]Ibid., 59.

community characterized by respect, justice, and agapic love. Therapy may attempt to meet this challenge by freeing persons from internal forms of oppression, empowering them to grow and to participate as mature, responsible, and self-regarding selves in community.

The norm that guides both ethics and therapy is agape. It is morally creative, redemptive, and emancipatory in that it is not self-seeking, but is motivated by neighbor-regarding concern for others. Agape ultimately derives from God. It assumes that all people are of intrinsic value; that all life is interrelated; and that every person is a potential medium of God's grace and care. This particular norm of agape meets its greatest challenge in a secularized, materialistic, and mechanistic culture where unilateral power relationships dominate. Unilateral power is expressed as power over others. Self-interest guides this form of power. "It operates so as to make the other a function of one's ends, even when one's aims include what is thought to be the good of the other."[62] Superiority is the central symbol of unilateral power in technological society. In such a society, the essentially religious impulse has been trivialized and qualities of personhood (i.e., sexuality, love) are reduced to commodity forms. People become means to serve the ends of technology. Today all of life is threatened by the real possibility of nuclear, global annihilation. These destructive possibilities form a part of the spiritual scenario of this technological age. But it is not the only scenario.

The Christian church points to an alternative story. The cross and resurrection are Christian symbols of the coming triumph of good over the powers of evil and destruction. These symbols may be seen in the emancipatory potential of liberation ethics and therapy when the goodness of life is called forth and the creative powers of people are set free for the work of liberation, healing, and justice in the global community. However, this situation does not yet exist.

The challenge to the black church, and to every church, is to help nurture the responsible and relational self, to promote relational patterns of love and justice, and to witness to God's emancipatory, reconciling, and healing activity in history.

Historically, the idea of the relational self found expression in such figures as Sojourner Truth, Harriet Tubman, Martin Luther King, Jr., and many others who linked faith with emancipatory activity. Today, the black church is challenged once again as a therapeutic and relational community to be prophetic in a modern technological society, a mechanistic age. Its task today is the same as it has been in the past: to witness to the risen Christ in the face of seemingly insurmountable odds. It may identify with innocent victims, promote a sense of anamnestic solidarity, help to diagnose, interpret, and transform exploitative relationships or structures, and expose conditions of human oppression.

---

[62]Bernard M. Loomer, "Two Kinds of Power," *Criterion* 15:1 (Winter 1976): 14.

The black church is not alone in this struggle. God is present as the supreme socius and inexhaustible ground of existence who shares the struggles of daily life, gives us freedom to overcome brokenness, and calls us forward to new horizons. Martin Luther King, Jr. witnessed to this living presence in his own life and thought. "I am convinced of the reality of a personal God. . . . it is a living reality that has been validated in the experiences of everyday life. . . . God is a living God. In Him there is feeling and will, responsive to the deepest yearnings of the human spirit: *this* God both evokes and answers prayer."[63]

The relational self suggests that social reality and psychic life, like public and personal existence, are interwoven in the unfolding web of existence. Liberation ethics and therapy are challenged to call attention to this relational structure of existence as the ultimate source of meaning and valuation. The emancipatory interests of liberation ethics and therapy may be kept together as part of an effort that seeks the ultimate source of meaning in the social processes that constitute us. "The emphasis here is on discerning God's offer and call forward in every situation."[64]

In this light, the ethical and therapeutic emancipation of the relational self derives its ultimate source of meaning and valuation from the primordial transformative process of creativity and wholeness that calls Christians forward to reconstitute themselves in responsible freedom, justice, agape, and a new and open future—the reign of God.

Is this implied challenge to the black church unrealistic? Some have already concluded that it is an unrealistic challenge and therefore too much to ask. Others may hold out the possibility of such a role for the black church in today's society.

> Perhaps it was not incidental that when God raised up a man to lead America through the racial crisis that had troubled us for more than a century, He did not turn to the wealth and power, the tradition and experience, the prestige and the glory of the establishment churches in America. They had had their chance, and they had defaulted. But God raised up a leader from the Black church, and now the problem is behind us. Perhaps God was trying to say something to America in general, and to the Black church in particular.[65]

The problem is not entirely "behind us." It continues as part of a larger complex pattern of repression and domination.[66] It is to the present, with

---

[63]Martin Luther King, Jr., *Strength to Love,* 1st ed. (New York: Harper & Row, 1963) 141-42.

[64]Cobb, *Theology and Pastoral Care,* 55.

[65]Lincoln, "The Black Church in the American Society," 93.

[66]Faustine C. Jones, "External Crosscurrents and Internal Diversity: An Assessment of Black Progress, 1960-1980," in *Daedalus* 110:2 (Spring 1981): 71-101. The rest of this volume is dedicated to a similar assessment of the progress, or lack of progress, of American Indians, Chicanos, and Puerto Ricans. The problems of race are never a simple problem of "black" and "white." The racial picture in America is increasingly pluralistic, complex, and stratified.

its complex problems of repression and domination, that the black church must now respond. The black church, as the spiritual face of the black community and as a durable institution, should not be underestimated. The black church, as a therapeutic and prophetic institution, is crucial to the moral struggle for outer and inner transformation in the United States. In solidarity with victims, it can play an important role in the realization of a new and liberating society.

CHAPTER TEN

The Emergence of Morality and Faith in Stages: A Theological Critique of Developmental Theories

—————•●•—————

CLYDE J. STECKEL

As a Protestant pastor and theologian who holds a doctoral degree in religion and personality and is now functioning as dean of a theological seminary, Clyde Steckel combines several domains of scholarly and professional knowledge. He wants pastors and theologians to make use of the social sciences in order to gain a rich and empirical idea of the human condition. But he also raises some sharp questions about certain propositions and themes that run through those sciences, wondering how compatible they are with the overriding tenor of Christian faith. He does not go into trivia, and his chapter is no diatribe against science; it is, rather, an appeal to theologians, thoughtful believers, and the church to use critical discernment in appreciating the crucial differences between the accounts that science and faith give of the human condition, and to deal adequately with the diverse pedagogical implications of these differences.

Steckel's focus is the Christian idea of *metanoia:* radical transformation of, in, and toward faith. He compares its emphasis on discontinuity with the strain of developmental psychological thought known as stage theory, which appears to absorb the successive stage-specific differences of growth into a continuity model, and often chooses prescription over description in defining the "final" or "highest" stage. Taking as paradigms of the developmental model the theories of Kohlberg on the development of moral reasoning and of Fowler on the development of faith, Steckel finds their final or highest stages at odds with the *metanoia* theme. His critical comparisons and the constructive conclusions

he reaches bring to mind some venerable earlier attempts at a specifically Christian "stage theory" made by Bunyan in *Pilgrim's Progress* and
by Kierkegaard in *Stages on Life's Way*. What, indeed, is the final stage
or the highest attainment in morality and faith, not only descriptively,
but normatively?

INTRODUCTION

The question initially addressed to our task force of theologians and
social scientists, whether Christian belief is more compatible with a
particular theory of human nature, would seem to require, on first consideration, an affirmative answer. A theory of human nature compatible with Christian faith would surely affirm the value of a belief in God,
prayer, some kind of divine spirit in human nature, good works, service,
hope, and other such virtues.

On second thought, however, this initial answer becomes less appealing. A descriptive theory of human nature *need not,* and indeed *cannot,* make judgments about the existence or nature of God, or about the
purpose of human enterprise. If descriptive theories of human nature do
indeed make such judgments, they have transgressed their proper
boundaries and have become philosophy or theology. Besides, Christian
faith has taken root in a variety of cultures at different times, each one
with its own theories of human nature. There is an exchange of mutual
influence, of course, in which Christian thought and cultural understandings of human nature are both altered. But it would be exceedingly difficult to demonstrate a particular cultural affinity for Christian
faith at a given time, or cultural incompatibility, for that matter. One
could conceivably argue that some cultures have been initially more favorable to Christian influence than others. But no major world culture
has been shown to be either impervious to such influence or already
"Christianized" because of some remarkable coincident harmony between its previous views on human nature and those emerging from
Christian faith.

These second thoughts seem to call for a negative answer to our initial question about Christian belief and a particular theory of human
nature. But new questions arise. Did not Christian belief emerge out of
Judaism into the Greco-Roman world of antiquity? Has not the history
of Christianity been so entwined with that of Western culture that we
would expect Western theories of personality (even the most self-consciously scientific and "secular") to reveal their Judaic and Christian
roots in some obvious ways, especially when compared with Eastern or
African viewpoints?

While pondering those questions, let us consider a further one: what
really is the importance of the first question anyway? What difference

does it make whether a particular theory of personality is more compatible with Christian belief than some other theory?

For individuals and the community of Christian believers in the modern world, it is a terribly important question, if Christian belief is to be more than a private or esoteric set of ideas unaffected by modern scientific and philosophical thought. If Christian belief requires a constant effort to understand all things from a faith perspective in an integrated fashion, and to make informed moral judgments, then it is very important how the accumulating knowledge about human nature from all branches of modern thought is to be related to Christian belief. And if Paul Pruyser is correct that we are dealing here with *transformational* knowledge rather than objective, detached, descriptive statements about human nature, then it is very important for all members of faith communities, their professional leaders, and other workers in the "helping professions" to explore this question afresh.

These initial reflections point to a potentially vast domain for exploration. Even an attempt to catalogue modern uses of the social sciences by theologians and ethicists would be a major undertaking. Tracing the whole history of theological uses of cultural images of human nature would be impossibly immense.

THE QUESTION OF DEVELOPMENT

The scope of this essay will be quite modest when compared with such limitless possibilities. I will be examining certain modern developmental theories of human personality from the vantage point of this question: Is there a Christian theological viewpoint on human development that can be related to modern scientific theories, to the possible enrichment of each kind of viewpoint?

In one respect this is not a new undertaking. Since the rise of Freudian psychology at the turn of the century, Catholic and Protestant theologians of diverse leanings have taken up Freudian psychology for its positive uses in religious life and thought, as well as to challenge its limitations. This essay stands in that same tradition of inquiry.

But in another sense this is a new question, because the more recent theories of moral development (Kohlberg) and faith development (Fowler)—based on Piaget's work in cognitive development and Erikson's stages of epigenetic development—have attracted wide attention among religious leaders for clues to such mysteries as spirituality, the religious education of children and adults, confirmation education, the relationship between rational and emotional elements in religion, and much more. These new theoretical maps of moral and faith development have seemed both to "fit" the experience of parents, teachers, and clergy, and also to illumine persisting problems they face. These theories have been so helpful, in fact, that in their brief and popularized forms they have often been taken up with such zeal that the research foundations and all the usual cautions and qualifications have been paid slight heed.

There is a further reason for exploring this developmental question: Pruyser has argued in the introductory chapter that traditional theology has neglected childhood development while emphasizing adult transformation according to some ideal of religious or moral virtue. If that is so, traditional theology needs exposure to the enrichment that modern developmental research can provide. However, theology must also be cautious about cultural enrichments that may carry alien deities.

THE BACKGROUND OF DEVELOPMENTALISM

Before taking up Kohlberg and Fowler, we need to recall something of the history of developmentalism as an interpretive concept. Nineteenth-century evolutionary thinking in biology, pioneered by Lamarck and given fuller theoretical elaboration by Darwin, held that all living species, along with each individual member in every specie, evolved or developed according to an observable and predictable plan, from small numbers of relatively undifferentiated cells into large and complex systems of interdependent and highly differentiated cells and organs. These "plans" were not viewed as genetically fixed, of course, since environmental influences played a large role in determining which kinds of living things would survive and flourish, and which would become extinct. Such changes, though, take many generations. And even where parts of the genetic plan are no longer necessary (the human appendix, for example), the developmental pattern is repeated from generation to generation.

Darwin held that human beings had evolved according to the same principles that governed all living things, and for that he was vilified by certain theologians and other defenders of human uniqueness. But Darwin did not press the implications of evolution for understanding the development of the human personality.

It was Sigmund Freud who formulated a theory of psychosexual development based upon his discoveries in the practice of psychoanalysis. Freud was educated as a biological scientist and considered himself a research worker in that field throughout his career. His stages of psychosexual development (oral, anal, Oedipal, latent, heterosexual) evolved from his observations in the practice of psychoanalysis. He regarded these stages to be as characteristic of the development of the human personality as the stages of passage from the caterpillar to the moth. He believed that his new science, like all science, must be deterministic, and that all events in the human mind are therefore, in principle, understandable and predictable.

The breadth of Freud's interests and his powers of intuition and speculation repeatedly broke through the narrow confines of a deterministic evolutionary theory, however. Not only did he try to deal with the limitless complexities of the human mind, but he also pressed his interpretive investigations into anthropology, history, culture, and art. The richness of his discoveries and insights attests more to his genius than to the explanatory adequacy of a deterministic developmental theory.

One such discovery of particular importance for this essay is Freud's concept of the ego. Personality developed and emerged in the clash of instinctual drives with the prohibitions of civilized society. As a part of growth, the personality developed a set of internal administrative mechanisms, the ego, which mediated between these conflicting claims. Yet that was never an easy achievement, according to Freud. Critical stages of development, especially the Oedipal, might be poorly navigated, thus creating repressed instinctual needs that might break out into neuroses or psychoses later on. Even a well-adjusted ("sublimated") adult is still maintaining a compromise with his instincts.

So far, it might not seem that the concept of the ego takes us outside a deterministic developmental scheme. But if we examine the practice of psychoanalytic therapy, it becomes clear that Freud was not just engaging in scientific analysis and readjusting damaged psyches, but that he was also a Socratic teacher. He really did believe—with all the strength of his genius and the Enlightenment philosophy of his age— that therapy involved the acquisition of insight, and that with greater insight into one's psychic history, one could live less neurotically, devoting more of one's energies to love and work. In other words, Freud was indeed engaged in the pursuit and application of transformational knowledge, in the service of human melioration.

This giant step that Freud took outside the framework of deterministic science immensely enlarged the concept of the ego. No longer just the beleaguered administrator between the warring powers of instinct and civilized society, the ego also became the mental agency of reflection and decision, using new insights to modify thinking and action toward more positive attainments.

It is not surprising that this enlarged understanding of the ego in Freud's thought has a familiar ring; it is the reason of classical philosophy returning in a new guise—that of a modern psychological theory of personality in which an agency of reflection and decision is still present.

Freud did not ever resolve the logical contradiction between his deterministic science of personality and his belief in the power of insight to free a person from the crippling effects of neurosis. Erik Erikson, in his eight-stage theory of epigenetic development (trust, autonomy, initiative, industry, identity, intimacy, generativity, integrity), enlarges and transforms Freudian developmental theory in three important ways.[1]

---

[1]Erik Erikson, *Childhood and Society* (New York: W. W. Norton & Company, 1963) 247-74.

First, Erikson elaborates his developmental theory with a far more adequate inclusion of interpersonal, familial, social, and cultural dynamics than Freud was able to do. Historical events, social conditions, and family histories really count for something in the emergence of personality, as Erikson amply demonstrated in *Young Man Luther* or *Gandhi's Truth.*

Second, Erikson's eight stages describe a lifelong series of growth dynamics, each with its own opportunities, challenges, times of crisis, and possible failures. Apart from any questions of their adequacy, Erikson's eight stages are more comprehensive and inclusive than Freud's psychosexual stages, in which the last stage, heterosexuality, runs from adolescence to the end of life.

Third, Erikson, even more than Freud, discusses the emergence of the ego in its functions of reflection and choice, and the consequences of key choices for the rest of a personality's development. He has abandoned determinism in any formal sense and replaced it with a theory in which many real dimensions of freedom are to be found in the process of development, along with all the biological and cultural determinants that shape personality.

One of the prices to be paid for a rich, complex, and inclusive theory, of course, is a certain loss of focus and clarity. We cannot really tell how much either freedom or determinism really counts (or genes, or child-rearing practices) when placed within the whole network of influences. Another price has been criticism from historians who find his work still too psychological when fundamental explanations are offered; from cultural anthropologists who are dubious about his contention that personality development is structurally alike in all cultures; and from classical psychoanalysts who oppose the degree to which Erikson has adopted a social understanding of personality development.

These important questions about the adequacy of Erikson's epigenetic developmentalism have not, however, appreciably dimmed the wide appreciation for Erikson among those seeking a more adequate understanding of religious development. Indeed Erikson himself frequently speaks about the importance of religious beliefs and participation in communal religious life at key developmental stages, especially in adolescence and old age.

Jean Piaget, who along with Erikson is a formative influence in the moral- and faith-stage theories of Kohlberg and Fowler, comes to his four "eras" (stages) by a different route than that taken by Freud and Erikson. Piaget has conducted extensive research in the cognitive development of children. He wants to know how they think and reason, and how and when children pass from one stage to the next. While not unmindful of unconscious and instinctual dynamics in the life of the child, Piaget is interested in the formation of the conscious mind, not the unconscious. He does not offer a psychodynamic theory of personality, as do Freud and Erikson.

But in a cultural and philosophical sense, Piaget shares the same world of thought as Freud and Erikson (as indeed do all developmentalists), a world profoundly shaped by Kantian philosophy, in which conceptual structures "given" in the mind are the organizers of the data of sense experience. Therefore an understanding of these structures is of the utmost importance in understanding the character of human knowledge.

The developmental theories share another set of common notions— not derived directly from Kant, but from nineteenth-century biology— that are framed in the concepts of deterministic science: namely, that the stages of development are *sequential, hierarchical,* and *universal.* They follow a determined sequence in the same order. Each stage carries forward the operations of the previous stages. And such stages can be observed in all members of the specie, including the human specie.[2]

MORAL AND FAITH DEVELOPMENT

The forgoing review and summary of developmentalism set the stage for our consideration of Kohlberg's stages of moral development and Fowler's stages of faith development. We may now return to the theological question raised at the beginning of this essay, to wit, whether such modern developmental theories can be placed in a mutually enriching relationship with Christian thinking about human nature.

Lawrence Kohlberg and his associates have done extensive research on the development of moral reasoning in children. Out of that research Kohlberg has discerned *six stages* of moral development, grouped into *three levels* with two stages in each:

Level I Preconventional
        stage 1 —Heteronomous morality
        stage 2 —Individualism, instrumental purpose, and
               exchange
Level II Conventional
        stage 3 —Mutual interpersonal expectations, relationships,
               and interpersonal conformity
        stage 4 —social system and conscience
Level III Postconventional or Principled
        stage 5 —social contract or utility and individual rights
        stage 6 —universal ethical principles

At the preconventional level, moral influence comes primarily from outside the individual, in the fear of punishment or the growing recognition of the give-and-take required in relationships. At the conventional level moral influence is a mix of social pressure and internalized

---

[2]Thomas Lickona, ed., *Moral Development and Behavior: Theory, Research, and Social Issues* (New York: Holt, Rinehart & Winston, 1976) 34-35.

values, but the values held are those of a particular social system. At the postconventional or principled level, moral influence is centered in universal understandings of society, individual rights, and transcendent values.

Kohlberg's immensely insightful, useful research and theoretical framework on moral development seem to depart from the usual criteria of developmental theories, however. The postconventional level, and particularly stage six, is *not* an attainment that can be observed in all adult members of the human specie, but only in a very few, and so is no longer a truly *universal* developmental stage. All developmental theories account for blocked or distorted development at each stage, of course, but these negative outcomes can be traced to genetic malfunction or to environmental hazards, not to failures in the social system or some moral defect in vast numbers of people that would keep them in a state of permanently arrested development. Kohlberg's curious departure from developmental thinking is a clue to the other part of Kohlberg's program, his effort to discover and state universal moral principles. At level six we no longer find the moral human being simply described, but rather imagined in a normative sense.

Kohlberg's work as a moral visionary and teacher in no way discredits his research on moral development in children. Still, it is a distinct and separate undertaking, and should not be quite so smoothly blended into his outline of moral development since it raises questions about the degree to which Kohlberg's normative moral vision may also have shaped the earlier stages.

James Fowler, a student and associate of Kohlberg at Harvard (now at the Candler School of Theology, Emory University), conducted research with children in an attempt to discover stages of faith development that might complement the stages of moral development. His six stages are not grouped into levels, but nevertheless roughly parallel Kohlberg's:

1. Intuitive—projective
2. Mythic—literal
3. Synthetic-conventional
4. Individuative—reflexive
5. Paradoxical—consolidative
6. Universalizing

In organizing his research findings into these six stages, Fowler employs seven dimensions of experience to illustrate and explain the significance of each stage. The first dimension is the *form of logic,* which follows Piaget from preoperational through concrete to formal operations at the last stages. The second dimension is *form of world coherence* in which the movement is from episodic through narrative, symbolic, and conceptual to "unitive actuality." The third dimension is *role taking* in which the movement is from rudimentary empathy through mutual role taking to mutuality with all of Being. The fourth dimension is the *locus of authority,* which begins with parents and moves through valued persons and communities to "judgment purified of egoistic striving and attentive to the requirements of Being."[3] The fifth dimension is *bounds of social awareness,* where the movement is from family through social class to transclass awareness. The sixth dimension is *form of moral judgment,* where Fowler modified Kohlberg and begins with punishment and reward, moving through law and order to a "higher law" and "loyalty to Being." The seventh and last dimension is *the role of symbols,* in which the progression begins with magical-numinous and moves through literal to conventional, conceptual, a blend of symbol and idea, and finally a "transparency of symbols."

Fowler's provocative and intriguing research deserves further testing by other scholars and religious educators. Even more than in Kohlberg's stages, however, the normative character of Fowler's final stages is so clear that we must once again ask whether it is really a theoretical framework for interpreting the stages through which *every human being* passes in the emergence of faith.

A closer examination of the content of Fowler's last two stages reveals the normative character of his scheme. Stage five, the paradoxical-consolidative, is still flawed according to Fowler, "because one is caught between these universalizing apprehensions and the need to preserve one's own being. . . . At that stage one acts out of conflicting loyalties. A readiness to spend and be spent on behalf of others is limited by concern for one's own, or one's family, or one's survival. Perceptions of justice outreach the readiness to sacrifice self for the sake of justice and in the spirit of love."[4]

In stage six, the universalizing stage, these paradoxes are overcome "through a moral and ascetic *actualization* of the universalizing apprehensions. . . . In penetrating through the usual human obsession with survival, security, and significance, they threaten measured standards of righteousness, goodness, and prudence. . . . It is little wonder, then, that persons best described by stage 6 frequently become martyrs to the visions they incarnate."[5]

As with Kohlberg, this sixth stage is attained only by a few saintly individuals (Fowler lists Martin Luther King, Jr., Gandhi, Mother Theresa, Dag Hammarskjöld), so it is *not* truly a universally human stage of development, but is actualized by very few. Carol Gilligan's crucial work on the stages of moral development in women, and her identification of rule (male) and relationship (female) emphasis, which

---

[3]Jim Fowler and Sam Keen, *Life Maps: Conversations on the Journey of Faith* (Waco TX: Word Books, 1978) 96-99.

[4]Ibid., 88.

[5]Ibid., 88-89.

seems gender-specific, raise critical issues about all modern developmental theories, from Freud to Fowler.[6] Gilligan's research demonstrates that girls and boys develop differently, and that they think and feel differently about moral decisions and social norms. Most studies appear to favor the male method of moral reasoning (rules and their transcendence) and turn the male norms into "humanly universal" characteristics. The norms of maintaining relationships, characteristic of girls and women, are thus viewed as morally immature.

THEOLOGICAL "PERSONALITY THEORIES" AND STAGES

In our brief survey of developmentalism and its current expressions in the moral and faith development theories of Kohlberg and Fowler, two key questions have emerged. First, how do developmental theories arising from a deterministic understanding of science provide for human freedom, and how far can the exercise of freedom qualify the inexorable march of the stages? Second, how are we to assess the normative discussions of the final stages in Kohlberg and Fowler?[7] One could deal with each question separately, but I will attempt a theological analysis that will assist in the discovery of answers to both questions at the same time.

A single personality theory and a single set of developmental stages cannot be derived from scriptural and theological writings in the Christian heritage, so it is not a matter of parallel columns or charts. The Judeo-Greek sources of the biblical writings, along with developments in the classical, medieval, and modern periods of thought, contain so many images of human nature that a singular "Christian" personality theory or set of developmental stages would be out of the question.

But there is a focal image of human personality in the Christian tradition that embraces the varieties of emphases in particular cultures and epochs, and that is the affirmation that humanity is distinct in bearing the very *image of God*. One widely held interpretation of that belief is that the human soul or spirit is a special divine creation, joined indissolubly with the human body. Another commonly favored view is that the image of God refers to the unique powers of the human mind or reason. Some theological traditions have held that the human will, free both in choice and in the power to create, is that part of human nature that best expresses the divine image. Other traditions argue for moral consciousness and conscience as the most Godlike dimensions of human nature.

---

[6]Carol Gilligan, *In a Different Voice* (Cambridge MA: Harvard University Press, 1982).

[7]Fowler acknowledges this normative character of developmental progress in both his and Kohlberg's work in ch. 24 of his *Stages of Faith* (New York: Harper & Row, 1981). He also acknowledges the "more mysterious and unpredictable vector of extraordinary grace," under which he includes conversion (303).

Each of these traditions represents something of value. Nonetheless, I believe that the most inclusive concept for all these dimensions of the image of God is that of *spirit*. Spirit does not represent a disembodied divine soul that has become trapped in human flesh; indeed it is no separate substance or thing at all. Spirit depends upon the biochemical processes and structures that comprise the human person, and when these are seriously limited, as in brain damage, spirit is also diminished. But the human spirit goes beyond the usual preoccupations with security and growth that characterize living species, and creates transcendent meanings embodied in cultures and religions, seeking to express a divine order and make sense of the flux of experience.

If human beings bear the image of God by virtue of their spiritual being, the key dimension of spirit for this essay is *freedom*. Freedom is self-determination (as Nachbahr agrees in his essay on mystery and insisted in our group discussion). Freedom is not the absence or suspension of causes, as in voluntarism. The human self reflects, chooses, and acts in the midst of the network of determinations (genetic, historical, environmental) that shapes its destiny. Freedom is expressed in imagination (as Pruyser persuasively argues in his chapter on imagination in religion). The human self is capable of memory and imagination, and thus can conceive alternative courses of action to create an imagined reality. Hence, the choosing self becomes one determinant of what the person is to become, in the midst of other determinants.

Judaic and Christian theological reflections on human freedom have accented the paradox of the loss of true freedom in the Fall and the restoration of freedom by God's grace, not by human effort. These are more *psycho*-logical than logical propositions, however, reflecting the human experience of divine liberation from conditions of bondage that did not yield to the most heroic striving. Whatever the Fall may mean in the Book of Genesis, in mythology, or in theology, it cannot mean the total loss of freedom or else human selfhood would be lost as well. (Runyon's suggestion in our group discussion that my outlook here is more Wesleyan than Calvinist may reflect a mixing of logical and *psycho*-logical propositions that I tried to distinguish above.)

If we bring these reflections on human spirit and freedom to bear on the moral and faith developmental theories of Kohlberg and Fowler, we find both a correspondence and a challenge.

The correspondence is to be found in the way in which increasing freedom and the creative expression of human spirit are indeed affirmed in the more advanced stages of each theory, and thus stand as the inner aim of earlier stages.

The challenge is directed to the sequential, hierarchical, and universal claims made about the developmental stages. The free exercise of the human spirit requires caution about such claims. It would be better to speak of degrees of probability. The fact that many people go through certain stages in predictable ways does not warrant universalization. Indeed the fact that others may pass through other stages, or familiar stages in a different order, says nothing about which way is better or worse in any normative sense. Alas, once the statistical norms have been established, it is all too tempting to use them diagnostically and "remedially" on deviant cases. To affirm the reality of the creative human spirit and the fact of freedom should in no way diminish our interest in research on whatever predictable regularities can be discovered in human behavior. But it does mean that we cannot make them laws or norms in a moral or religious sense.

"THEOLOGICAL STAGES"

Earlier I suggested that there are also "stages" of faith development in the Christian tradition that might be fruitfully compared with modern developmental theories. Let me propose the following list:

creation
fall into sin
justification
repentance and confession
sanctification
perfection

These categories are not, of course, gathered in any one place in Scripture, creeds, or theological writing as a set of "stages" in Christian development. Yet they are central themes in any discussion of the Christian life, so they might help us to identify some distinctly Christian elements in faith development to place alongside the stages of Kohlberg and Fowler.

One immediate and obvious difficulty arises. These proposed categories do not fit a developmental view of the process. The fall into sin, and salvation through justification and repentance seem better to describe the sudden conversion of the scoundrel than the gradual unfolding of moral and religious maturity in a child reared in the faith; or they better express the continuing, daily struggle of the Christian believer with faithfulness and continuing disobedience, but these are *not* the stages that most Christians move through in a lifetime.

It is, of course, an imprecise and unfair comparison. The "stages" that run from creation through fall to redemption and perfection are not a roadmap of "the way it happens" in real life. Rather they constitute a symbolic and conceptual framework for the whole life of faith, not the unfolding development of the life of faithfulness.

But before we leave it at that, let us reflect just a bit more on the striking differences between the list I am proposing and all the developmental theories we have examined. It is the difference between *discontinuity* and *continuity*. The transitions from creation to fall, and from sin to salvation, do not reflect continuity but rather discontinuity. Developmentalism of any kind requires a fundamental orientation to *con-*

tinuity, in which changes and key turning points are found, to be sure, but where the unfolding processes of development reflect the underlying continuity of human experience. The more radical discontinuity presupposed in my list of theological categories is not without its own underlying continuity, however, and that is the abiding faithfulness of God, no matter how far humanity becomes estranged from Him. No matter how wide and deep the separation, God continues faithfully and patiently to bridge the chasm, offering restoration through justifying love that defies every human effort to achieve a permanent separation.

That is an important kind of continuity after all, and the two kinds of theories may not be so far apart as supposed. But differences remain that should not be overlooked. For the developmentalists, the structures of continuity are built into the fabric of human experience, while in the theological viewpoint articulated here the fundamental continuity of experience is the abiding faithfulness of God. Although the practical evolution of human faithfulness may look about the same regardless of which theory is employed, to discern and name God rightly is of immense urgency if we are to know truly how to judge the flow of continuity and discontinuity in which we move each day. For if we locate continuity in some presumed "given" structure of human experience, we forever will be trying to discover and then legislate that structure, which leads to human sciences that overreach themselves and to human societies that become tyrannies. But if we locate that continuity in God, we are then better able to arrange our scientific knowledge and the ordering of societies in ways that truly liberate the power of discovery and faithfulness.

I have been trying to show that the difficulties in comparing my list of theological categories with the developmental theories of Kohlberg and Fowler are not so formidable as they might first seem; and I have tried to suggest a way to make that comparison using the concepts of continuity and discontinuity. Difficulties still remain, though, of the kind that have plagued the Christian movement from its beginning. There *is* something fundamentally discontinuous in a faith that begins (Mark 2) with a call to repent, to turn away from an old life and to enter a new life. Christian faith *is* a way of repentance and salvation. And so it has always been difficult to account for the status of children born *into* a believing family and Christian community. Ways have been found, of course, through infant baptism, religious education, confirmation, and Christian family-life programs to foster gradual growth and development into the life of faith. But whenever Christian theological inquiry is pursued in these areas, such discontinuities always emerge and thus press every gradualist or developmental viewpoint to acknowledge the radical discontinuities at the heart of Christian faithfulness.

A second area in which our list of theological categories requires us to raise questions about the stages of Kohlberg and Fowler is in their final stages, where Kohlberg speaks of universal ethical principles and

Fowler speaks of a universalizing religious orientation. Earlier I suggested that these final stages are not true developmental stages but stand as normative visions that reach back into the outer stages, drawing people toward perfection. In my own list of theological categories, I identified *sanctification* and *perfection* as the latter movements of the journey of faith, so we now must ask whether Kohlberg and Fowler are talking about essentially the same characteristics of faith.

Sanctification has historically referred to that process of becoming holy that is to characterize the Christian life after justification, repentance, and confession. "Holy" does not primarily refer here to "sacred" as distinct from "secular," but rather to an increasing *wholeness* of one's life through faithful trust in God, in which all aspects of life are increasingly brought together in loyalty to God.

Perfection has historically referred to the completion of the process of restoring all that has fallen in sin to the fullness that God originally intended. Most of the symbols of this perfection, such as the Kingdom of God, will only be evident at the end of history itself.

Christian history is filled with examples of movements, sects, and denominations that have arisen in protest against faith and morals in existing churches, and those movements have attempted to practice a fuller sanctification or perfection in the present. The preponderant weight of the Christian tradition, however, is on the side of caution about the degree of sanctification or perfection that can ever be actualized in any present moment. The Catholic traditions have expressed this caution in the system of confession and penance, and in a pragmatic approach to church order. Lutheran traditions have emphasized the distinctions between the earthly and heavenly kingdoms, and Luther's statement of *simul justus et peccator* (at the same time righteous and sinful) as evidence of the daily reality of an incompleted Christian life. And the Calvinist traditions have warned against human pride in the good works that are supposed to be a grateful response to God's providential grace.

It is precisely this cautionary word about the degree of sanctification or perfection that we must bring to the final stages of Kohlberg and Fowler. Every religious tradition has its saints and heroes, of course, and we should never invoke caution to detract from their truly miraculous achievements. In a cynical and suspicious age we especially need their inspiration. But in theories of moral or faith development, we should make a better place for the countless "saints" whose lives may be far from public acclaim, but whose commitment to universal values is just as steady, whose lives are just as transparent as those few who become public figures. Moreover, we should find some better way, on the theological grounds being argued here, to acknowledge the "not yet," the imperfected sides of their lives, without having those imperfections cast any doubt at all on the saintly or heroic aspects of their character.

Regarding this latter point, Fowler's characterization of the final stage of universalizing religion is particularly one-sided. Fowler's resolution of the paradox of self and others, of security and service, is more representative of an otherworldly mysticism than of a faith in which this world's complexities and dilemmas are *all* claimed as the arena of God's grace and human response. Only at the end of all things, including history, can such a resolution of paradox be imagined. And Fowler's speculation that so many stage-six types suffer martyrdom because they threaten conventional security is more like the romantic view of the lonely visionary as a martyr to the truth than it is a general account of martyrdom. Many people and movements threaten conventional security, and some of course are killed, but many more are either put away or simply ignored. Chance and circumstance have much more to do with who gets martyred than the purity of a universalizing religious vision.

IMPLICATIONS FOR RELIGIOUS LIFE

So far I have tried to show that faith development in predictable stages does not easily blend with some biblical and theological descriptions of faith. In particular, the radical transformation required in faithfulness and the equally radical critique of perfectionistic tendencies do not seem to fit a developmental pattern in religious life.

In this concluding section I will outline two implications of this theological critique for religious life today. These implications will be viewed in light of the positive value of developmental theories discussed earlier; but for the sake of economy and clarity, this discussion will emphasize the differences with developmentalism rather than the large area of common ground they share. The first implication has to do with the restoration of transformation in the "developmentalist churches." The second implication has to do with defining a self-critical religious life that at the same time affirms the "final stage" possibilities in Kohlberg and Fowler.

Radical Transformation in the "Developmentalist Churches"

It follows from the scriptural and theological themes presented earlier that there must be something decisive and transforming about entering into the life of faith. Weighty decisions must be considered. Values in conflict must be assessed, gains and losses counted. There is a necessary turning away from an old life, understood as bondage to alien deities, no matter how secure and alluring, and a turning toward a new life that is blessedness and peace while also containing struggle and suffering.

Since Christian life is intrinsically communal (no matter how diverse the individual forms this faith pilgrimage may take), churches have always created communal forms to guide this faith transformation. These communal forms have generally represented two types: radical conversion and gradual growth. Conversionist forms have predominated in the earliest periods of new movements (early Christianity, the first generation of breakaway groups); in perfectionist groups (ascetics, monastics, holiness groups, and the like); and in groups where the normative religious experience is one of radical personal transformation (e.g., modern revivalism).

"Gradual growth" forms of transformation have predominated in the later periods of established church bodies, especially those with a certain degree of latitude about worldly life and its values (e.g., Catholic, Orthodox, and major Protestant denominational groups), where infant baptism, religious instruction, rituals for confirmation, and other major life experiences have framed an orderly progression through the religious life from birth to death.

It is this latter group of churches I am calling the "developmentalist churches." These are the churches that will claim my attention here. The conversionist movements are of concern as well, because everything claiming to be authentic religious conversion is likely to be far more complex and mixed than their advocates would allow (as psychologists of religion have amply demonstrated). But here I must limit my attention to the kind of developmentalist church tradition in which I stand, and the kind of church that needs to reexamine its forms of transformation.

"Developmentalist churches" need to pay far more attention than they usually give to the experience of radical turning that is at the heart of the faith experience. The reasons for this neglect are serious and merit full consideration: the religious nurture of the child from birth, the desire to avoid the extremes of emotional conversion, the need to negotiate the subtle and complex difficulties of moral choice, and the strength of tradition itself. But finally all these reasons should not allow such churches to neglect the transforming power of faith.

In many such churches the sacrament of confirmation is expected to provide the instruction in the tradition and the public profession of personal faith that is first made by the parents at baptism. But in most such churches their candidates for confirmation are too young to be making adult decisions. And in many churches confirmation marks the completion of religious instruction and a departure from active church life that may not be resumed until the young adult is settled into a community, a job, and a family. Confirmation simply does not come at the right time, and it often does not place the radical transformation of faith at the center of its otherwise legitimate concerns.

In other churches it may be that vocational questions are intended to put the radical challenge of faith before all people, particularly the young. The challenge to consider the pastorate, priesthood, religious orders, or missionary service may be the medium for presenting the transforming power of faith. Even where specific religious professions are not central, the vocation of all Christian people in the world may be emphasized as the true test of transformation—vocation as suffering, sacrificial, transforming work in the world through one's daily employment, politics, volunteer activities, and personal relations.

In some churches it may be the social-action programs that attempt to shape a faith transformation that is both deeply personal and politically transforming. Also, in some churches therapeutic relationships and communities such as Marriage Encounter or Alcoholics Anonymous become the medium of a more searching faith transformation.

I am not questioning the value of any of these or other similar forms of faith transformation in the "developmentalist churches." But I am advocating a more thorough and focused process of instruction and personal decision so that even in the most diverse and tolerant congregation and denomination there may still be a clear presentation of the transformation that faith both gives and requires.

This process might best be centered on adult faith decisions around the thirtieth year of life. Following Erikson, this is typically the period in which the person is moving from consolidating identity and establishing intimate relationships into the time of generativity, where one is formulating a life vocation centered on the care of the coming generation. This can be a time of searching and probing exploration of the direction and purpose of life. It is also a time when sophisticated ethical and theological reflections are more appropriate than the ideological dogmatism that predominates during adolescent identity formation.

A period of biblical, theological, and ethical study for all church members in their thirtieth year, leading to a public declaration of one's personal faith and a specific plan for illustrating one's faith transformation, might be a way in which the "developmentalist churches" could more aptly express that faith is a process of radical transformation.

Such a new kind of "adult transformation" program would not in any way change the fact that there are differences of time and season in which a given person hears the call and responds. As with confirmation, some people would participate perfunctorily and some not at all. But at least the churches would be saying more clearly than at present that adult faith is meant to be an experience of "turning around," of transformation. Confirmation could still be a time of saying, "This is my church." Now there would be a way to say: "This is how I mean to live my faith as an adult."

Defining a Self-Critical Religious Life
That Simultaneously Affirms a Final Stage

My critique of Kohlberg and Fowler in the previous section concluded with misgivings about their "final stages" on the grounds of confusion about norms and description, and a needed caution about the degree of sanctification or perfection possible in this life. Here I want to suggest some ways to envision the spiritual perfection to which one is called without losing self-critical awareness, paradox, or a sense of ambiguity.

Kohlberg's sixth stage of universal ethical principles and Fowler's universalizing religious stage can certainly be theologically affirmed in their general outlines. A mature moral and religious outlook should embrace the universe of diverse experiences, cultures, and religions. Where Kohlberg and Fowler both go astray is in the attribution of such universalizing morality or religion to few actual people, thus revealing this stage as a normative description of the good life rather than the final stage of development. Part of their mistake, as I suggested earlier, was in naming a few saintly and heroic people as proof that only a few people actually make it to the final stage. In fact, many people achieve this final stage, lacking only public attention, which is quite unreliable as a test of sainthood anyway.

I propose that there is indeed a process of "going on to perfection" that is both a gift and goal in Christian life. It is universalizing in its scope, but never far removed from the agonies and paradoxes of specific moral dilemmas and actions undertaken out of faith. Moreover, in this process of perfection, the peace of overcoming separation is never far from a probing critique of all such achievements.

This understanding of Christian perfection is both circular and progressive. It is circular in its awareness that every day in the life of the Christian is filled with the distorted perceptions, missed opportunities, blind spots, good intentions gone astray, and the willing or thoughtless perpetuation of irresistible evils—and that these matters must all be acknowledged, confessed, repented, and made good where possible, relying only on the sufficiency of God's forgiving grace to provide new beginnings free of despair and guilt. Each day this miniature drama of death and resurrection is reenacted in Christian life, even though on the larger stage there was a decisive passage through death to life in Christ that does not ever need to be repeated. Any spirituality that neglects this daily miniature drama will fall into either a prideful perfectionism or guilty despair, both of which miss the mark.

This understanding of Christian perfection is also progressive. The circular or repetitive character of Christian faithfulness is always set in the larger context of the movement of history from creation through the Fall to restoration and the promise of fulfillment. Practically, this means that each new day is a new step towards that fulfillment. The Christian person and community can count on that progress as a part of their hope, and can trust that God is bringing these things to pass. That is not to say that such progress is automatic, even though it is guaranteed. Each person is responsible for prayers that can enable progress; responsible for renewing personal efforts to express the justice and love of God in daily life; responsible for examining previous goals and setting new goals; responsible for engaging with the whole church in the struggle to express the will of God *for this moment, in this place;* responsible for the ministries of the liberating word among the oppressed and alienated. The exercise of all these responsibilities really counts in the movement toward fulfillment in history. It is not just a matter of God doing it all, sometime in the indefinite future, or God simply working through us. Our work matters greatly if there is to be movement toward perfection.

These reflections on the character of Christian perfection sharpen our sense of where there is agreement with Kohlberg and Fowler (and with developmentalism generally), and where there are irreconcilable differences. Christian perfection is indeed universal. It includes all people, all cultures, all religions, even though its symbolic expression represents a particular set of historic events. Christian perfection does grow and develop, often in predictable ways. In these senses there is general agreement with Kohlberg and Fowler.

Yet this kind of Christian perfection is never far from its own sense of insufficiency in light of evils around and within. It is characterized by a heightened sense of paradox and ambiguity. Such spirituality thrives on vigorous self-examination and criticism. It is not abstract or transcendent. It does not dwell in realms beyond the daily struggle for life in the face of death. In these ways Christian perfection, as presented here, is not easily reconciled with Kohlberg or Fowler.

In the life of the churches, this understanding of Christian perfection would suggest disciplines of daily personal prayer and communal worship that attend to both the repeated miniature drama of death and new life but also affirm genuine progress in the life of faith. Both failures and forgiveness, goals and movement towards goals over time, would characterize such spiritualities. In many churches of my acquaintance, spirituality has become so privatized and goal setting has become so secularized that it is difficult to suggest workable models for assisting such movement toward perfection. Such models need urgently to be developed, however, if we are to move beyond the present tendency in many developmentalist churches to avoid spiritual discipline altogether, or to reach out for Eastern and psychologically based methods.

CHAPTER ELEVEN

The Mystery
of the Embodied Self:
A Metaphysical Perspective

———————— • ● • ————————

BERNARD A. NACHBAHR

Since the next chapter is close to this book's end and its author is a philosopher, it is ill advised to attempt a précis of Bernard Nachbahr's concluding reflections. Suffice it to say that the author places the self—about
which all other contributors to this volume have written—in a metaphysical perspective and thus attempts to define its essence. He also examines the premises from which some of the other authors have
proceeded and does some evaluation of their theses.
The fact that the metaphysician's contribution is placed at the end rather
than at the beginning of this volume reflects the spirit of the task force
that produced this book. That spirit was one of free, venturesome exploration followed by critical reflection, rather than cautious adherence
to a prescribed route mapped out in advance by unshakable convictions.

In order to clarify what the metaphysician may have to contribute
to an understanding of the human condition, it is useful to recall briefly
(1) the traditional claims metaphysicians make about their trade. (2)
Next the question will be raised how a metaphysician today (since Kant)
develops some fundamental statements about the self in the world and
(3) how he applies them to questions of freedom and determinism. (4)
Finally, in view of the readership this book addresses itself to, some implications for the religious experience will be drawn out.

A FEW NOTES ON METAPHYSICS

Ever since David Hume advised his readers to burn all books on
metaphysics as nonsensical, a profound skepticism has increasingly become characteristic of our civilization. Hume claimed that reasoning by
itself, that is, minus any observation, cannot yield any verifiable infor-

mation about reality. Lacking sense data, reason may know certain necessities about its own activity (as in mathematics and logic), but it cannot yield, in Hume's terms, matters of fact. With claims such as these, Hume effectively removed the whole area of "absoluteness," of "absolute necessity," the traditional realm of "meta-physics," from reasoning. Absolute reality (which includes among its categories God, ultimate standards of right and wrong, of truth and falsehood, of beauty and ugliness) is no longer accessible to rational knowledge. Reason is only valid and useful within the limits of science, of mathematics and logic; it has a legitimate function in analyzing our ideas and assumptions (as in political philosophy, the philosophy of science, and so forth), but regarding the ultimate questions of religion, morality, and art reason can offer no more than "sophistry and illusion."

This skepticism regarding reason is not merely a challenging theory of an isolated eighteenth-century thinker, but is very much part of our civilization. It has entered into the social consciousness, the mind of our times. We are all heirs to Enlightenment skepticism, even—or rather especially—those of us who have never heard of Hume or who have never read any other philosopher for that matter. The implications and consequences of this skepticism are too numerous and too serious to be treated in a few pages. They are varied and far reaching, and they have an impact on a variety of areas, from religious beliefs to sociopolitical and economic arrangements. It has even been suggested that this form of skepticism lies at the root of many of our problems, be they religious, moral, political, educational, or economic.

However, one implication should be mentioned and is easily discovered even by superficial observation. If science alone yields information about what is real and reason on its own cannot unlock any reality, then the whole metaphysical realm of ultimacy and absoluteness either becomes unreal (as it is for an increasing number of people) or it becomes the object of private and individual choice without any rhyme or reason. A little probing uncovers this latter, widespread bias quite easily. When asked about the whys of their religious beliefs, their moral convictions and aesthetic tastes, many people customarily will try to justify their positions in these matters by appealing to tradition, social authority, desire or feeling, but not to reason. "This is the way I feel, the way I was brought up." In this regard religious fundamentalism is fed by the same skepticism as the most radical moral relativism: the powerlessness of reason to lead us outside Plato's cave of ever-relative appearances and ever-changing opinions.

Combined with that other fundamental characteristic of our civilization, individualism, this antimetaphysical skepticism has produced a veritable supermarket of religious beliefs, of moral codes and life-styles, of aesthetic standards. And every choice one makes in this market is on principle as good (or bad) as any other, as long as it respects the rights of others to make their choices. There are no other absolute standards, known by reason, that can guide us as to the rightness or wrongness of our choices.

Of course, there have always been critics of this individualism and skepticism who represent many different persuasions, including the social sciences. But many of these critiques remain theoretical, without entering into the general social consciousness, into the spirit of our civilization. Criticism has come from religion, specifically those denominations in Christianity that assign reason a role in religious faith. But religion has lost much of its impact on the social consciousness of our civilization; it has become one's private option. Social consciousness is intimately linked to the social order and for any theory, however true, to penetrate the spirit of a civilization, certain conditions in the social order must be fulfilled. For instance, the classical libertarian notion of freedom as individual and particular choice without foundation in universal reasons is embodied in our political, juridical, and economic order. One may show in theory (for instance, in a course in metaphysics) the inadequacy of this concept and elaborate a theoretically much more solid concept of freedom. Nevertheless, the latter remains theoretical, not incorporated in the praxis of the social order and social consciousness.

This fact constitutes a certain limitation to the essays in this book, including the present one. The crucial question, How should the social order be arranged so that, for instance, Dr. Cowan's ideas on love could become part of the social ethos? is not explicitly raised in this book. The transformational knowledge it offers aims primarily at the transformation of individuals, not of society. Perhaps a Marxist on the panel would have been a useful participant in this regard.

Also, many of the critiques of this individualistic skepticism never regard it in its totality and in its roots or radical principles. Some of the essays in this book offer vivid examples of this partial criticism. Especially those written from the perspectives of social theory (Ryu, Smith, Cowan) are sharply critical of traditional, libertarian individualism. Yet at the same time there are several instances in which it becomes clear that the authors (unwittingly) share some of the skeptical assumptions of our era about the "nature" of the human condition, individuality, freedom of choice, the privacy and subjectivity of values, the limits of human knowledge, and so forth. A total or radical critique of individualistic skepticism would first raise the question whether humankind has any rational knowledge of what is ultimate and absolute and, if so, then explore what we can say about humankind from such a metaphysical perspective.[1]

---

[1]For a brilliant attempt at total criticism of individualistic skepticism, see R. Mangabeira Unger, *Knowledge and Politics* (New York: Free Press, 1975) esp. chs. 1-3.

Obviously this is not the place to deal with these questions in any detail. We presuppose here an affirmative answer to the first question and propose a few reflections on the second, without the necessary proofs and detailed arguments. Philosophy, and especially metaphysics, is a laborious, often tortuous enterprise. What follows in the next pages is simply some evidence of this often slow and difficult process without the process itself. The interdisciplinary character of this book might be a sufficient justification for this rather unphilosophical and somewhat dogmatic procedure.

Before I begin some further clarification of the nature of metaphysics seems in order. In our relativistic time the claim may seem preposterous, but from the earliest days of philosophizing in Greece, metaphysics has claimed that one can offer statements about human reality that make no assumptions whatsoever and that express something that is inescapable, absolutely necessary, unavoidable, or unconditional in that reality. Of course, the statements themselves, the concepts used, are revisable, alterable, historically bound; however, what they try to articulate is not alterable, but rather belongs with strict necessity to the very constitution ("nature") of being human—in whatever civilization one lives, in whatever period of history or prehistory, whatever one's race, color, sex, mental, and physical makeup.

To clarify what is meant by unconditional necessity, let us contrast it with conditional necessity. All scientific and even mathematical statements do not give us more than conditional necessities, that is, they depend on an "if" clause. Two important "if" clauses of science, for instance, are: "If we continue to interpret reality according to present-day scientific models (e.g., the Freudian model), then statement X (every human being is subject to the Oedipus complex) is necessary"; and "If things continue to behave as we have observed them so far, then statement X (all that lives must die) is necessary." The necessities of mathematics obviously depend on the axioms of the various mathematical systems. "Two parallel lines can never meet" is true on condition that one accepts the Euclidean axioms. It is not true if one assumes non-Euclidean axioms.

"Meta"-physics claims to go "beyond" such scientific or mathematical necessities. A classic example is the principle of causality: everything that happens must have a cause, a reason why it happens the way it does. This principle claims that under no condition, under no circumstances, can anything happen that is not the effect of something else. Obviously we *assume* the validity of this principle in daily life and in our scientific research: we cannot seriously look for the causes of cancer unless we assume that there are such, even if we never find them. The principle does not claim that we know the cause of everything nor that we can always find it. It is up to the metaphysician to *justify* and *prove* such a principle.

What a metaphysical proof is follows from the above. A metaphysical statement can never be proven by pointing to a fact, all facts being conditional, contingent, and relative to our ways of organizing experience. "All people must die, because until now we have observed that everybody does" is not a metaphysical but rather a physical scientific statement. A metaphysical statement is proven by showing that the very act of denying it implies as condition of its possibility the affirmation of what is denied—or, what is denied is so inescapable that in the very effort of escaping it reasserts itself. For example: "I refuse to make a choice." In the very act of refusing, one is making a choice (Sartre: man is doomed to freedom; it is inescapable). Such a statement is not a logical contradiction, (a contradiction within a statement or between two statements), but a transcendental contradiction, or also a self-contradiction—that is, a contradiction between what one says and the act of saying it. A few more examples will clarify this. When I say (with all skeptics), "Nothing is true, all is relative," I claim in my very activity of stating these propositions a truth and an absoluteness that is denied by what I say (the contents of my statement). What makes these statements possible is my inescapable search for what is true and absolute. Similarly, if I assert (with old-fashioned Behaviorists) that *all* human behavior can, on principle, be understood according to the model of observable stimulus and response, I am contradicting myself and destroying my own theory. In claiming that my statement is *true*, I assert that there is more to my activity of making that statement than that it is merely caused by a stimulus, and hence that not *all* human behavior can be understood on this model.

There is no assertion here that human behavior cannot be studied and interpreted as a response to stimuli. The contradiction only arises when the behaviorist claims to give us an exhaustive and exclusive account of all human behavior, that is, when he stops making a scientific statement and engages in philosophical or even metaphysical statements. He errs by maintaining that his account is not simply *a* valid, though relative, point of view on human behavior; it is the *only* point of view. By so doing, he overlooks his allegiance to the stimulus-response account, and in the contents of his statement he denies his own activity.

The reader might well ask: what difference does it make whether a statement such as "all people are mortal" is physical, and so based on observation, or metaphysical, and so based on reflection on the human experience? Obviously all people are going to die no matter what. There are, however, very important differences. If I take the statement as physical or scientific, mortality appears as a fact, and various sciences investigate that fact and explain it from observable causes. It becomes a fact that all living people share. When I take the statement as metaphysical, I establish human mortality not merely as a *fact,* but as an inescapable *necessity.* I am no longer interested in the *observable causes* of the fact of mortality, but rather in the *unobservable meaning* of its necessity: what does it mean to be mortal, not merely for me, but for all humans, universally, absolutely? There might even be a practical consequence to the difference between these statements. If the statement "all people are mortal" is no more than scientific, people who have their bodies frozen after death might have a point! If the statement is also metaphysical, they are involved in a self-contradiction, a denial of their humanity.

THE EMBODIED SELF
FROM A METAPHYSICAL VIEWPOINT

What is going to be said in this and the following section is a reinterpretation of traditional body-soul discussions that have come to us from our Greek heritage. This reinterpretation is inspired by Kant's radical critique of all traditional metaphysics, by Hegel and Heidegger, and can be found in a number of contemporary authors (Blondel, Rahner, Maréchal, Lonergan). The following pages are a mere skeleton summary of such a metaphysics. Hence the unavoidable abstractness, the lack of detail and of adequate demonstration, and the brevity of the subsequent assertions.

Metaphysics starts with the most radical doubt that is humanly possible, in order to arrive at a starting point in which nothing is assumed or taken for granted. It calls into doubt the validity and reliability of whatever we sense, of all that the sciences tell us, of all that tradition (including the philosophical tradition) and authority (including religious authority) hold for certain. No *content* of our knowledge is taken for granted and the only certainty left is the very *activity* of doubting and questioning. In an effort to question everything, the metaphysician (that is, every human being, although most often only implicitly) questions his own activity. He asks not merely, "What is the meaning of life?" but more radically: "Is there any meaning to my activity of asking such questions?" This means that the activity of questioning is reflexive, or questions itself. The most primordial definition that can be given of any human being is that (s)he is a self-questioner, forever in search of what it means universally and absolutely to be human. In questioning this statement its reality is reaffirmed: the human being is inescapably a self-questioner.

In simple terms this means that all human experience in whatever area is always some form of self-questioning, either explicitly or (mostly) implicitly. Our ultimate universal purpose as humans is to find ourselves in all we do, but we never fully realize this (otherwise we would cease to be questioners). The self is to be understood here not in the sense of what is particular, contingent, relative to me, but rather in the sense of what is universal, necessary, and absolute to all. The metaphysician is not concerned as metaphysician with the always particular *content* of this search (as the scientist is), but with the universal *structures* of what it means to be human. For instance, the *contents* of my temporality (past, present, and future) are obviously particular to me, although in decreasing degrees of particularity: to me as this individual, to me as living in this generation, to me as living in this nation, or even to me as living in this civilization. But with all humans I share the necessary *structures* (or meaning) of being temporal, of being limited by my past, of being potential (future). As we mature, we break out of the privacy of our particular situation and individual self-interests and start an unending search for what it means universally to be human in ever-widening circles.

This universal dimension should be kept in mind throughout this essay. When we speak about the self, we do not have in mind a Lockean individual who basically lives in confrontation with others, who experiences, for instance, the freedom of others primarily as a limitation to his own freedom. The truly human self is not the privatized, individualistic soul with its own views of truth, goodness, and beauty, but the unique person who struggles to realize in himself that which is universally human, true, good, and beautiful. The greatness of Shakespeare, for example, and of all great artists for that matter, does not lie in the glimpse he provides us of his private soul. Rather, he rises beyond his individual particularity, even beyond the particularity of his time, and articulates in a unique way what is universal in human love and hatred, joy and anxiety.

That we question ourselves in every situation does not mean that this self-questioning is always explicit. It usually remains implicit. This means that all human activity is reflexive, however weak this reflexive element may be (e.g., in routine activities). All our questions are self-critical; that is, we appropriate our experiences in ways that are at least implicitly questioned by us: we engage in some activity or experience half-heartedly or passionately, partially or totally, without asking ourselves explicitly how to engage ourselves.

The self-questioning human subject is the very foundation of metaphysics, which is nothing but the articulation of this eternal quest. In spite of significant differences, this foundation is present in varying degrees of explicitness in all great metaphysicians from Socrates to Heidegger. In a sense the question, "What does it mean to be human?" forms the unifying element of all metaphysics and, with that, of all philosophy. From this foundation the classical metaphysical themes are derived, especially the theme of body and soul (mind) and their relationship. Perhaps the simplest way of formulating this is to say that as self-questioner I must at the same time be and know myself (otherwise I could not question myself) and not be and know myself (otherwise I would be in no need to question myself). This fundamental experience of ambiguity lies at the bottom of the familiar dyads like soul and body, activity and passivity, intellect and sense, freedom and determinism, self and other, subject and object, universal and particular, identity and dissipation, among others.

A word of warning is in order here. What the terms just mentioned and what metaphysical concepts in general mean cannot be simply assumed, but must be derived by questioning the metaphysical starting point: the act of questioning. Nothing that is known from observation should be brought into these concepts. When the metaphysician talks, for instance, about body, he is not talking about the body that we physically *have,* which of course can never be established as an absolute necessity. Rather he is talking about what it means to be bodily or material. In this metaphysical sense body, world, matter, and similar realities cannot be known by observation, but are as unobservable as "soul" or spirit.

In this context a second warning may be sounded. Although all language is objectifying, metaphysics does not concern itself with any object but with the meaning of being a questioning subject. In general, one might say that science occupies itself with objects (including humans as objects) and hence with problems—that is, questions that through investigation lead to information (contents). Once the information is found, the problem is solved and one can proceed to another question. Metaphysics, however, is concerned not with problems but with mysteries— that is, questions that through inquiry lead to understanding. Once acquired, this understanding does not close the question, but rather renews and reopens it. What a body is, is a problem that can be solved with information from the different sciences. What it means to be bodily is a mystery that can be understood, but never exhaustively grasped, through reflection on our experience as self-questioners, which experience is never at an end.

Perhaps the dyad "activity-in-passivity" is closer to our experience as self-questioners than talk of body and soul. "Soul" is in many ways a mystifying term with a long history that has left its marks on the concept. In the present metaphysical context it would mean that we all actively search for ourselves in whatever we do, and actively make ourselves present in every experience, in varying degrees of intensity. Nothing simply happens to us while being totally passive, not even death. In some ways we have actively prepared ourselves for whatever strikes us, even if it comes unexpectedly. Nothing can simply happen to an unquestioning mind: we would not even be able to think or talk about it. We actively appropriate in some way whatever is passively suffered by us. At the same time the self-questioning subject is passive: we find ourselves in what is given. As questioners and searchers we are never completely ourselves, but also absent from ourselves and other than ourselves. An example may clarify what is meant, although it must be remembered that examples always refer to particular contents, while metaphysics is interested in structures. If I am a student I find myself in what is given, the world of academe. I suffer or undergo this world with its regulations and customs, its demands and pressures. But I cannot be purely passive: I somehow appropriate and give meaning to this world and make it mine. In this sense I actively find myself in it. In metaphysical language, being a student is the otherness that enables me to find myself. Of course, it is also possible that I cannot find myself in it, that this world remains meaningless to me, and that I suffer it because of social pressures. I am then alienated, absent from myself in this world.

Another example of this twofold structure of activity-in-passivity is a simple act of knowledge. Our knowledge of objects (also in the sciences) is not a merely passive (Lockean) registration or observation of what is simply given. There is certainly that element; we are passive or receptive with regard to the "objects" that are given. We are beings of sense (passive reception of our world and hence of ourselves). Yet knowing is at the same time an activity, an active structuring of our experience. Things appear to us according to the (self-critical) questions we ask, that is, according to our active purposes and intentions, whether they be scientific or otherwise. We actively interpret and classify what is given, create meaning in what remains otherwise absurd, bring order to what remains otherwise chaotic—in short, we make real what remains otherwise unreal. We may "humbly sit before the facts" without forgetting that facts have been made by us in the first place. In traditional language, we are beings of intellect-in-sense.

As self-questioners we are strangers to ourselves and have to go *out* of ourselves to *ex*press or *ob*jectify ourselves. I can only be "I" by becoming "me." This otherness, expressed in the terms *ex, ob, out*, provides us with the possibility of being ourselves while at the same time imposing limitation, from the rather innocuous limitations of time and space to the ultimate powerlessness and failure of being ourselves in suffering and death. Here lies the root of the metaphysical concept (that is, our most primordial experience) of body and world, of matter. Because we are ignorant of ourselves and have to go out of ourselves in order to find ourselves, we exist bodily and are of necessity material. Metaphysically, body or world is the other of myself that enables me to be myself and at the same time limits me in being myself.

The primary other in which we find ourselves in a limited or fragmented way is the human world. Hence the human being is of necessity a social or "relational" being, as has been emphasized repeatedly in various essays. People express and find themselves in a great variety of ways: in the worlds of social and political structures (from family to state to the global community of the human family), in the community of scientists, in groups of artists, and so forth. All these worlds are communal, the results of the communal efforts to create meaning out of chaos and to realize human potential. Here we have a second, more empirical or categorical meaning of universality. Above I stated that the self in searching itself tries to express, and realize in itself, what is universally human in a transcendental sense. Here it becomes clear that it does so with other selves and that the activity of creating meaning and of building the human world in art, science, economics, politics, morality, and religion is a communal or social activity. These communal worlds enable us to find ourselves, but also limit us in this effort: the universal is always realized in partial and fragmented ways. This means that people always live in a particular society, with a particular religion, morality, and so on. We are historical beings with a universal task and challenge. The human being is a self-in-otherness, or more concretely, a self-with-others. This social dimension is not something added to a more or less complete individual, as is suggested in the libertarian tradition. Rather it belongs to the very definition of a human being, to what a human being metaphysically is.

FREEDOM AND ALIENATION

The fundamental structures of activity-in-passivity can be translated into terms of freedom-in-determinism. From the metaphysical point of view, to be free means that in questioning myself I become the active author of my life and come to possess myself. At the same time, however, I am given to myself and determined: born at a particular time and into a particular class, society, civilization with a particular physical and mental makeup, and so forth. In these and other limitations I exercise my freedom and become myself. For instance, I am born male or female; my sexuality is a given. But I appropriate my sexuality and give it meaning. This is obvious especially today as we are seeking new ways of being women and men, new ways of relating between the sexes. We reinterpret and reappropriate our sexuality and in this sense are its authors, freely male and female. What from a biological point of view is completely determined is free from a metaphysical point of view.

The question is often put in terms of either-or: is the human person free or determined? This way of asking the question is misleading. A human being is both free and determined, or free in being determined. It is precisely in the many determinisms that I realize my freedom and come to possess myself. For instance, I am determined to become a lawyer (or a criminal) by my social environment and family tradition, my abilities and upbringing. But I make such determinisms actively my own and give them meaning. Or I am determined to suffer chronic depression or any other mental or emotional disturbance. But I do not undergo such sufferings in pure passivity; I actively interpret and appropriate them.

To the extent that the scientific method is based on observation, freedom is not a scientific category. For behavior cannot be observed as free, but only as brought about by observable stimuli or causes, and therefore determined. It would be very unscientific indeed to consider freedom an observable cause in competition with other observable causes. From the point of view of scientific method, all human behavior is determined, which of course does not mean that we can always find the causes or observe them. But our ignorance of observable causes does not leave open the door for freedom and certainly does not provide a basis for it. We can only speak of freedom from a first-person or participant point of view.[2]

In this light the human person is both free and determined; indeed, metaphysically freedom is primarily self-determination and self-possession. And this is always a question of degrees. The question is not, "Am I free or determined?" but rather, "To what extent am I free?" To what extent do I think my own thoughts and do not merely repeat the prevailing thoughts in my environment? To what extent do I possess my own feelings and am not merely possessed by them? To what extent do I find myself in my life-style, moral codes, religious convictions, and so on? When I say "I," to what extent is this the universal self and not merely the voice of this particular society or class, of instinct, tradition, external authority, superego, and so on? In short, to what extent am I really myself and not other? The opposite of freedom is not determinism, but alienation, not being myself, unfreedom.

To appropriate and interpret the many determinisms in my life means to act for reasons of my own. I do not merely repeat what my environment does, thinks, and feels; instead, I make it my own by understanding the reasons for it. For instance, my moral code is not simply the voice of a tyrannical superego nor is it simply based on social approval. Rather, when I am free, it is my own voice because I see the reasons for the various moral injunctions; they are my own law. From this perspective it is quite understandable that moral autonomy is the highest stage of moral development according to Kohlberg (see the essay by Clyde Steckel).

In order to understand this correctly, one must keep in mind that reasons are universal and public as opposed to whims, which are particular and private. To seek reasons for our ways of thinking and living is to seek what is universally true, to make an effort, however difficult it may be, to break away from the privacy of our views and feelings, even from the particularity of our civilization's assumptions. A simple example will clarify this. When I discuss my religious, moral, or political

---

[2]In this paragraph science is identified with an observer's third-person point of view. Admittedly, this is a narrow understanding of science, modeled after the "hard" sciences. It is not denied, however, that room for considering freedom is created if the concept of science is widened. An admirable example of this is the work of Joseph E. Rychlak, who breaks through the confines of a stimulus-response behaviorism and develops a first-person account of freedom as acting for purposes, reasons. I am free to the extent that behavior is mine, that is, done for reasons of my own, a "telosponse" rather than a mechanical response. Some of the metaphysical assertions concerning freedom in the present essay are remarkably confirmed by Rychlak's psychological studies. See, e.g., *Discovering Free Will and Personal Responsibility* (New York: Oxford University Press, 1979).

convictions, it is obviously not enough to say (although it happens only too frequently): I hold this or that because that is how I feel; or because that is what my church teaches; or because that is what everybody holds in my class, society, and culture. Instead we try to find reasons and thereby enter the arena of public discussion. Of course, it is not easy to find reasons, to discover what is universally true and good, and to distinguish reasoning from rationalizing. On the contrary, it is a never-ending process with many hurdles, failures, and constant revisions.

It is necessary to emphasize this universal dimension of human freedom against the view generally assumed by our social consciousness, which identifies freedom with choosing on the basis of individual whim, without rhyme or reason. To put it popularly, freedom is lived, if not conceptualized, as doing your own thing as long as you respect the other person's right to do his/her own thing. From the metaphysical viewpoint defended here, this popular concept and praxis of freedom constitute instead an escape from freedom and responsibility. Freedom is not doing my own thing but rather submitting to what I consider universally true and good and beautiful, that is, acting for reasons of my own.

In one sense this understanding of freedom downplays the element of choice. The clearer I see the reasons for my action, the less choice is left to me and the more free I am. For instance, if on the day before my wedding I really (and not merely legally) still have a choice between two potential partners, I am not yet free enough to give myself to any one of them. Only once I clearly see that she "is the one," and no one else, can I freely give myself in marriage. In the important decisions of life for which I can provide reasons, very often little or no choice is given between objective possibilities, whereas in more trivial matters we face alternatives (such as what to buy, where to spend a vacation).

In another sense, however, the element of choice is made much more radical in the understanding of freedom as self-determination. But this is not the (categorical) choice between two or more objective possibilities, for instance to be for or against abortion, to choose this or that career. Rather it is the (transcendental) choice between freedom and unfreedom; between acting for reasons of my own and enslaving myself to whim, impulse, instinct, or social authority; between submitting to what I see as universally human and setting up my own absolutes; between responsibility and irresponsibility. In this choice lies the root of the distinction between good and evil, between being myself and being alienated. The lived contradiction against my own universal humanity can only be expressed in a paradoxical manner: I freely choose unfreedom, I responsibly am irresponsible. It is a radical escape and abdication from self into otherness (alienation) without being able to become totally other. The ultimate and most radical alienation is self-chosen alienation. To put it in other words: in freedom as self-determination there is the ultimate choice between self-acceptance and self-rejection. Obviously this is not a choice that one makes in any particular act (a "mortal sin" as opposed to a good deed), but a choice that one lives and confirms in one's life project. Terms like apathy, self-hatred, and degeneration point to this basic contradiction between what I am and what I do.

Because I come to myself or lose myself in a historical process, my freedom is a situated freedom. The situation offers me the possibility to determine myself, but at the same time it limits me, again in various degrees depending on age, cultural development, social and political factors. The situation is given and imposed on me; I find myself or lose myself in it. Often, therefore, freedom is an answer (in yes or no) to a situation about which I can do little or nothing. It is obvious that certain situations can be severely limiting, whereas others offer more possibilities for people to determine and develop themselves.

The situation consists concretely and primarily of other people. Taking this into account, the rather formal and abstract talk of self-determination translates itself into palpable love or hatred for other people. For in creating myself I either give to and risk myself with others in a real communion, in care and compassion, or I close myself to them in a suffocating egoism that experiences the other only as limitation and obstacle to my own freedom. It may be obvious that most of our relationships are a mixture of these abstract extremes. In various degrees we usually experience the other both as an obstacle and as a challenge to our freedom; popularly speaking, most of our relations are love-hate relationships.

The ultimate determinism in which I exercise my freedom is death, not merely as an observable event at the end of life, but as the structure of mortality that runs through my whole life and affects every experience. To give meaning to my mortality is to realize the radical impossibility of being myself. Death in this sense is the clearest illustration of that basic ambiguity of human life that we called activity-in-passivity, freedom-in-determinism, soul-in-body. Death, from this metaphysical point of view, is both active and passive—actively bringing me to completion (like the final note that completes the symphony) and passively terminating me by an external fate. It is my final achievement of self, anticipated in every activity; but at the same time it is the radical powerlessness of being myself, present in all my passivity (passion, suffering). Death signals both my definitive meaning and being and my total absurdity and nothingness. These two aspects cannot be neatly divided into soul and body; they are intermingled. I attain my ultimate fulfillment as an embodied self precisely in losing myself radically. From this point of view the most radical dimension of all human activity is hope: I recognize that I am a self-questioner, that I cannot be wholly myself and establish my ultimate being and meaning on my own. Still, this recognition is suffused with the affirmation that it is meaningful to search for myself. Hope is the last cry of the human being while facing his (her) ultimate impossibility. Conversely, ultimate inhumanity is despair: feeling incapable of establishing myself on my own, of being as God is. It is the struggle in every human life between good and evil, between hope and despair, between submission to the mystery of human life and idolatry, between heaven and hell, being and nothingness.

THE EXPERIENCE OF THE MYSTERY

The above effort to describe human existence in terms of self-questioning, of activity-in-passivity, of self-presence in absence from self, of self-determination in determinisms, remains necessarily abstract and formal. It is an effort to express the unity of the human agent. But this ultimate unity is the hidden origin from which we act and the ground on which we are posited. We cannot look behind it and we have no immediate grasp of it. At the same time the unity of the subject in its unique concreteness is also the concealed aim of our restless quest. We have no clear and objective view of what it means to be fully human, to be self-identical. What the human person is can be found only in the adventure and risk of life itself, both individually and collectively. We emerge from a hidden origin (the past) and move towards a concealed destiny (the future). Essentially we are questioners and petitioners of our own meaning and being.

Thus the self as ultimate origin and goal of human life remains hidden. It is present and expresses itself in the large variety of individual actions and decisions, of collective cultures, societies, and religions. But these self-expressions are never more than a partial realization of human potential. On the individual level no one can make a final self-judgment in adequate and objective terms; one can only live out such a judgment and realize it gradually in a plurality of provisional acts.

When we begin to act as the one subject, we find ourselves in a real plurality of experiences, actions, decisions, and regions of human experience. They may have one origin in the human subject who is always more than the sum total of this plurality, but this original unity is not given. It is rather a task and a challenge to be met through a number of different dimensions of human existence. The moral dimension of a decision is not the same as its practicality and may even contradict it. My religious convictions and activities may hardly be reconcilable with my business interests. Love is not the same as sex and may be at variance with it. Above all, what I ultimately am in the center of my being is not the same as what appears in the plurality of my experiences and activities. I must live with and accept this plurality, and cannot and should not fix myself prematurely in any kind of unity, either theoretically or practically. The unity of myself as a subject is the hidden origin and future of my being. It is the mystery from which I act and towards which I want to return. This ultimate dimension or structure of human experience may properly be called the foundation of the religious experience.[3]

---

[3]The following description of the experience of the mystery is heavily indebted to the many essays of Karl Rahner on this subject. See especially "The Concept of Mystery in Catholic Theology," in *Theological Investigations,* vol. 4 (Baltimore: Helicon Press, 1966).

Religious experience, from a metaphysical point of view, is something different from and more than what we usually call the knowledge of God, as we receive it from religious instruction, doctrines, dogmas or myths, sacred books, or philosophical speculations. It is also more than observance of religious practices and worship. All these are only the expression and objectification of the more fundamental religious experience, in the same way as, for example, an essay on love is only an expression of the basic human experience of love.

In this fundamental sense religious experience is given in every human being. I am always and inescapably in touch with the holy mystery, that is, the unobjectifiable and ungraspable answer to the quest of who I am (both in knowledge and willing), whether I am explicitly aware of this or not, whether I reflect on it or not, whether I engage in God talk and religious practices or not. To make this experience of the inescapable mystery explicitly conscious, and to reflect on it is of course a difficult matter and dependent on a great many factors: psychological, sociohistorical, cultural, even political and economical.

Metaphysically, the religious experience is not primarily an experience on its own, comparable to other experiences. Throughout the day we experience many different things: in the family, at work, in meeting various people, in dealing with different situations. The religious experience is not just another experience among these. It is not primarily an experience that we have in synagogue or church, in prayers and religious practices. Rather, the religious experience is primarily a dimension or structure of every human experience. This, of course, does not mean that we are always explicitly aware of it, that we think about it consciously. Usually it remains quite hidden and implicit in our experiences and activities.

The religious experience cannot be adequately defined, because it is man's relationship to the undefinable, to the mystery. Mystery is not just another name for God, but expresses our original and most radical experience of Him. In all our experiences we make ourselves present in a limited and fragmented way, in various degrees. But we cannot experience ourselves and our world as limited unless we have some prior grasp (preconceptual) of what is infinite, unlimited: the total self-presence, the mystery. Another way of saying this is that the experience of the mystery is implied (as condition of possibility) in the experience of ourselves (subject) and our world (object) as finite. Knowledge of the mystery is implied in all that we know; love of the mystery is implied in all that we love and desire. As condition of possibility enabling us to experience ourselves as finite, the mystery is at the same time our ultimate source and aim, as mentioned above.

The infinite mystery is consequently not an object of our knowledge and choice in the same way as we can know and choose people and things. It is rather the nonobjectifiable, ever-present yet ever-receding horizon that makes every knowledge and choice of objects possible; it is presupposed to every knowledge and choice of particular objects and values. As the Medievals used to say, God is coknown and cowilled in all objective knowing and willing. The mystery is the incomprehensible preceding every comprehension. It is always present as the nameless one whenever we name finite people and things, as the undeterminable in all our determinations, the undefinable in our defining. We cannot escape from it as we can escape from particular people and things. When we try to express the inexpressible mystery we often call it God, but all such God talk can only make sense when it evokes this experience of the mystery.

From such abstract talk this, at least, may be clear: that we always live with, and in the nearness of, the mystery precisely when we deal with the nonmysterious, the finite, the objective (including ourselves as objectified). The mystery is consequently not something with which we also deal among many other things, for which we can show an interest if we wish and have the time and leisure. Its experience is ever present, implied in whatever we do and experience. The purpose of all religious instruction is to open a person up for the experience of the mystery, to make it explicit, and to maintain this openness in awe and wonder. Religious instruction should not be primarily the communication of doctrinal niceties.

From this point of view, human development is a gradual and struggling effort to come to grips with the mystery of human life, to accept or reject it. Self-acceptance is ultimately acceptance of myself in my finitude and powerlessness to be myself on my own, and therefore implies acceptance of the infinite mystery. Self-rejection is ultimately the effort to be infinite on my own terms, to domesticate and thereby abolish the mystery, to objectify the nonobjectifiable. In short, self-rejection amounts to idolatry. It is the religious dimension of the struggle between good and evil, between hope and despair. Acceptance of the mystery makes one free; its rejection entails the lived contradiction of free self-enslavement to some idol, to a manmade object, be it power, money, nation, race, sex, religion. Obviously one cannot tell from someone's acts whether that person lives in fundamental self-acceptance or self-rejection, in a basic acceptance of the mystery of human life or its radical rejection. In Christian terms, it is a choice between grace or mortal sin, heaven or hell, eternal life or eternal death. It is each person's *option fondamentale*.

Although the experience of the mystery is a fundamental and inescapable dimension of our every experience, in certain experiences this dimension comes more concretely to the fore than in others. In most everyday experiences we are in various degrees occupied or even absorbed by our work and relations with others. But in some we are more clearly confronted by the mystery of human life. In general, the more we are present to ourselves by being involved in the world, with others, the closer we are to the mystery. For instance, when we break through what seemed to be fixed, secure, and safe, the closer we come to what cannot be fixed, secured, or taken into safe possession; or when we confront a radical moral decision and all other motives for a vital decision (such as gratitude, blame, approval, success) disappear, leaving us utterly to ourselves; or in the experience of a profound communion when we are loved and/or love unconditionally; or in the experience of death, of a deep and nameless joy, of unconditional trust in another person; or in the experience of an all-pervading anxiety or desire, of total shock, of a profound peace; or in certain aesthetic experiences; or in the experience of evil, of unconscious forces. In these and many other experiences, the religious dimension of which ought to be described phenomenologically, the mystery pervades human consciousness in a more radical fashion than in the ordinary experiences of everyday life, although the mystery is also present in these.

What Christianity adds to the universal experience of the mystery is the proclamation that the mystery has communicated itself to us in absolute nearness as our absolute future in hope. It confesses that the mystery is not simply condition of possibility for experiencing ourselves as finite, but also the final aim and goal of our restless quest. In this sense Christ is the divine "Yes" to the question and petition that we *are*. This absolute nearness of the mystery in human history does not abolish it, but brings it near. Our absolute fulfillment does not lie in the abolition of the mystery and its dissolution into objective knowledge. All objective knowledge is provisional, temporary, transient, until we finally experience the mystery precisely as such. Our traditional religious discussions often seem to forget or overlook this. They are often too influenced by an ideal of knowledge that badly fits the mystery: the ideal of objective knowledge. When we say, for instance, that we will see God "face to face," this ideal is often implicitly present, if not explicitly. But Plato already realized that such knowledge is mere "opinion," the knowledge of the people in the cave, not the real knowledge of those who have seen the light. The nearness of the mystery cannot turn it into an object of our manipulative, objective knowledge. To realize this is a first prerequisite for the courage to rethink and—if need be—to revise the ancient symbols and not hold on to them as objects.

CONCLUSION

A metaphysics of hope merely states that the ultimate dimension of all human self-questioning is hope: the petition to be *and* to be human. Human life is always and everywhere a struggle and fundamental choice between hope and despair, freedom and unfreedom, humanity and inhumanity. This is true in stable and unstable times, in times of building and of destroying, of peace and war. But it may be particularly urgent to recall explicitly this metaphysical dimension of all human life in times of instability, destruction, and war such as ours is. Our civilization is profoundly threatened; its basic foundations have become questionable and are being eroded. We are not only reshaping or undermining the "mind" of Western culture; we are also capable of destroying its "body" many times over.

A metaphysics of hope cannot guarantee the survival of any civilization or religion. Perhaps we are about to see a new Renaissance in the West emerge out of the present turmoil of skepticism and individualism (in this respect our era may resemble the turbulent fourteenth century). Perhaps Western civilization as we have known it since the Renaissance has run its course and is to be replaced by something we have no knowledge of as yet (in this respect our era may be more like the last couple of centuries of the Roman Empire). We do not know. There are grounds for either possibility.

In the face of instability and destruction we are often forced to reflect on the ultimate questions of human life. Such reflection may help to uncover what is "constant," part "of nature" in all the changes that are taking place. In this sense it may transform us from skeptics into people who focus on the permanent foundations from which new possibilities of being human, and new civilizations, will emerge.

EPILOGUE

—— • ● • ——

It is hoped that readers who have worked through this text in linear fashion have experienced cumulative reinforcement of the idea introduced in the first chapter. It was there proposed that transformational knowledge, for all the limitations of its depth and perhaps precisely on account of its inherent modesty, has something to offer to reflections about the human condition in general and to our readers' thoughts about their particular selves. Derived as it is from the outlook and work of the helping professions (broadly defined to include pedagogy, guidance, counseling, healing, instructing, and other melioristic interventions), transformational knowledge accentuates the perpetual occurrence of change and the occasional need for specially designed change as one important feature of the human condition. It also holds that knowledge of changes that occur can enrich what knowledge we have about the presumably stable or structural aspects of the human condition.

With considerable flair one of the two theologians called attention to the remarkable shift that is currently taking place in the Christian understanding of humanity through new readings of the classical triad of creation, fall, and redemption. He stressed the idea that the biblical covenanting does not involve an individual contract between God and a particular soul, but a corporate alliance between the creator and a people, indeed virtually all peoples and essentially all mankind. The other theologian highlighted the meaning of people and peoplehood in biblical literature and arrived at the vision of a promised land for all in which freedom from bondage may be found precisely to the extent that the real bondage of the present is roundly acknowledged and regretted. It is interesting that both these theologians accentuate the coming dawn of freedom and see in its realization both God's plan and human destiny.

We were next confronted with the root of change and the inevitability of transformations in the chapter on "Emerging in Love." Cosmologically speaking, not only all that lives but all that exists is *in* process, nay it *is* a process; and psychologically speaking, what we know most directly and movingly about that process is revealed in the experience of love. Acting on the realization that loving and transforming are a twosome goes beyond grimly having the courage to be—it sets one free for the creativity of becoming.

Systematic, age-specific transformations are the gist of growth and development during the early years of any individual's life and are both subjectively experienced and objectively manifest. For all the structural stability that one tends to associate with the words "selfhood" and "identity," developmental psychology has made it quite clear that the self is always in transformation and that from the cradle to the grave anyone's identity is undergoing age-related redefinitions. An important lesson from the psychoanalyst's chapter on early development is the tenuousness of maturational achievements because of the continuation of primitive stirrings in the deeper strata of consciousness and the regressive pull that is so strong in some people's lives.

The chapter on early development also gave us some examples of the impact of early life experience on later relations with God, showing how vulnerable religion is to the psychological fixations and regressive potential of individual believers.

From the psychotherapist who also teaches a college course in human sexuality came the observation that a great deal of unease prevails not only in regard to sexual behavior and its moral regulation, but even in thinking and talking about sexuality. In the cacophony of voices and noises about sexuality, it is shocking to have to admit that "we literally have no Christian language for human sexuality." After surveying three major modes of talking about sexuality—the objective, the lyrical, and the normative—and finding each of these wanting in comprehensiveness, depth, or existential relevance, the author of this chapter presented us with the challenge to find or create an integrative language—one that will be theologically grounded while avoiding the doctrinaire positions of the past that, each in its own way, truncated the richness of sexuality, gender, and the embodied self.

If transformation is as basic to maturation and learning as this book holds it to be, it would behoove us to value the great cultural symbol systems of art, religion, music, literature, and science not solely for the abiding truths at which they hint. We should also appreciate the transforming psychological and social functions these symbol systems fulfill in drawing young children out of their autistic shell and carrying them beyond the pedestrian facts of commonsense reality into the life of the spirit, the blessings of culture, or the domain of values. In this functional perspective we found religion described, together with all the other symbolisms of civilization, as an illusionistic enterprise requiring a special mode of imaginative cognition that in most cases is spurred and shaped by a considerable amount of adult tutoring. Once properly practiced and continually developed, the religious imagination needs to be guided by critical awareness of its potential ability to slip into utterly subjective private whimsy or into flat-footed realism that leaves no room whatever for illusionistic (symbolic) thought.

But the humanizing and civilizing influences of culture are found side by side with the dark power of certain social processes to dehumanize persons, to alienate them from themselves, and to make them feel and act as strangers among their fellow humans. Our sociologist gave us a précis of an almost-two-centuries-old social and psychological malaise known as alienation. That deplorable condition is one result of the inevitable tensions that exist between structures of society and structures of individual personality. We were reminded of some trenchant sociological theories of alienation, but were then given a sophisticated view of selfhood as resulting from the differentiation and synthesis of an "I" and a "me" participating in a dialectic influenced by psychic and social factors. The desirable synthesis of selfhood does not always occur and indeed is thwarted on a massive scale in many modern societies. The widespread alienation to which modern people appear to be doomed may be the contemporary form in which original sin fatefully afflicts the human mood, temper, and outlook. In this respect the sociological analysis arrives at a conclusion not unlike the one Reinhold Niebuhr reached in *Moral Man and Immoral Society,* published in 1932.

Written with an overwhelmingly pastoral, therapeutic, and compassionate orientation, the chapter on the relational self in the black church brought us close to the concrete details of organized, selective oppression as experienced by black Americans. The article challenged the church-at-large to implement with equal concreteness the gospel of liberation to which it has so often only paid lip service. Though informed by sociological and psychological constructs and at times analytical in its own way, this chapter is the only one in this book frankly and boldly using the churchly word *mission.* It is the mission of the black church to liberate its people from bondage, and perhaps even more important, to teach the universal church that bondage is not to be taken as a mere pious metaphor. Instead, bondage has been and is a historical fact for millions of people from the beginnings of Christianity to the present day. Therefore, the church's liberation ethic demands concretization through acts that foster the relational selves to which people are called in freedom.

And what about morality and faith, those two essentially transformational powers that are meant to bring humankind a bit closer to its potential or destiny? Can Christian ethicists and theologians uncritically absorb the various cultural images of the human condition that history offers, including the recently articulated notions about moral development and faith development that are derived from Piagetian stage theory and Eriksonian life-cycle work? Our religion-and-personality specialist, while acknowledging the wide usefulness and the pastoral applications of developmental psychological theories, forced us to join him in questioning whether the deterministic presupposition that the defined stages are sequential, hierarchical, and universal is compatible with the Christian idea of *metanoia.* And attention was called to the tendency among developmental theorists to substitute description for normative thinking when they have to come to grips with the presumably highest stage in their series. Who or what discipline is fit to define the most advanced or highest attainable state of faith and morality? The critical chapter on developmentalism shied away from making an ex cathedra theological pronouncement, but shrewdly engaged us in thinking both theologically and psychologically about what churches might or should do to foster in their members the radical transformations that their mission requires. Christian transformation theory sees the ideal self as a redeemed self, a sanctified self, a perfected self and, even so, always only in progress.

The metaphysician forcefully reminded us that however the human condition be described or defined, the human being is a self-questioner who looks for the meanings of the universal structures of his or her own and other people's existence, such as being male or female, being temporal, being limited by one's past, and being open to the future. Leaning on Kant's critiques and the ontological searches of Hegel and Heidegger, the writer of the metaphysical chapter does not hesitate to view the self—as directly experienced and reflected in others—as a mystery, in the sense that it eludes exhaustive description and transcends definition because of its freedom. Further, the mystery of being human is embedded in the enveloping mystery of all being that the Judeo-Christian Scriptures have always described as creation, whose author has affirmed our being and all being as "good." Christianity asserts that the divine mystery has become incarnate and thus come near to us, for recognition and for providing us grounds for hope.

It is the function of an epilogue to round off a complex work, which this book certainly is by virtue of its topic as well as its multiple authors. Does the summing up also lead to conclusions? I believe it does.

In the first place, whatever the human condition may be in its abiding essence, each time and culture will articulate their own views of it, usually by criticizing previously held views. It is clear that our contributors do not subscribe to La Mettrie's man-as-machine view, to Hobbes's *homo homini lupus* model, or to any vision of persons as encapsulated, self-sufficient entities or closed little systems. Despite their respect for certain Enlightenment ideas, none of our contributors plugged for rationalism; despite their respect for scientific thought, none advocated positivism. Neither did our contributors' religious orientation lead them to espouse pop-Platonic soul-body dualism; and the word *spirit,* if used at all, was never taken in an ethereal sense.

Second, our contributors were firm about change as part of humanity's nature and destiny—some of it being orderly change that appears to follow natural and cultural rules, and some of it being mysterious and unpredictable, as if divinely inspired. They also insisted on avoiding both psychological and sociological reductionism; individuals as well as groups were granted a comparable measure of autonomy and were treated as constantly interacting. If the edge was given to the self's embeddedness *in community* and the self's essential reflections, this emphasis was mostly a pedagogical one, intending to wean some readers from the individualism that runs through much traditional religious literature.

Third, our writers implicitly, and sometimes explicitly, urged the readers to take notice not only intellectually of changes that have occurred or are progressing in relation to the human condition, but to do some work on themselves and their charges in revising their current views. This theme accounts for the admittedly sermonic quality of some chapters; it stems from the conviction, deeply held in most helping professions, that cardinal views having existential relevance and impact need periodic updating and reformulating in the course of one's life.

Fourth, in their professional capacities as well as their personal stances, the contributors to this book profoundly believe that thinking and acting should go hand in hand. A profession involves a praxis, and many of the best thoughts of any profession emerge from concrete practical engagements and from the need to address crisis situations. Could it be that what is true in this regard for professionals is only a sharp articulation of what holds for anyone?

Paul W. Pruyser

APPENDIX

Notes about the Multidisciplinary Group Process

—————————————— • ● • ——————————————

A. W. RICHARD SIPE

The process of growth and understanding experienced by the writers of these essays is not evident in the essays themselves. When we first came together, we sat around the table eyeing each other as potential threats to our expertise. We were protective of the boundaries of our disciplines, as if to say that psychiatrists and social scientists knew nothing of the human soul and clergy had no scientific grasp of the human mind and development. We jousted with words, mostly jargon, and we tried to dazzle other participants with our finesse. Our first series of discussions were strained and sometimes aimless, though we went through the motion of completing an agenda.

After the first-year seminar we went our separate ways, promising to reassemble in Collegeville for a week in each of the next four summers. Something happened during that second year. The barriers of the previous year that impeded our discussions had begun to break down; familiarity with one another grew into acceptance and respect. In exposing our own cherished perspectives on the human condition, we came to understand that none of us had a monopoly on knowledge—or truth, for that matter. All of us began to share in the endeavor to bridge the gap between faith and science. We began listening to each other as if for the first time. Whether we were clergy, scholars, or counselors, we had become colleagues.

During the third session the members of this group arrived at a point where despite their different perspectives and expertise they felt free to seek common questions and possibly common answers. One small unity was found: transformational knowledge. Members could admit that each discipline had a real interest and investment in the transformation as well as stability of the human condition. They began to see that a developmental understanding of the human condition must complement a structural view, whether one approaches the human condition theologically, sociologically, or psychologically.

The preceding essays could never have been written apart from this series of seminars sponsored by the Institute for Ecumenical and Cultural Research and the Institute for Religion and Human Development. If anything, we as participants came away with a greater understanding of the human condition from both a structural and a developmental perspective. We realized it was essential not to divorce a Christian understanding of the human being from an understanding of the social, historical, and psychological environment. Most important, we found hope—and excitement—in the prospect of reformulating some traditional perspectives on the human condition.

There are lessons to be learned here if we are to continue this ecumenical and interdisciplinary dialogue. Four elements are essential to the dynamics of fruitful discussions: (1) a physical setting that encourages the experience of sharing; (2) a mutual respect for each other and each other's discipline; (3) a shared focus that can draw together different perspectives; and (4) a frank confrontation of any obstacles that impede dialogue.

A Physical Setting. The ambience and the contemplative tradition of St. John's University and Abbey allowed us to separate ourselves from our usual cares, worries, and distractions. Being together in one spot over a period of time—and periodically coming back to it—allowed us to experience each other not only as specialists in one particular profession or discipline but also as individual personalities with different and similar values, likes and dislikes, idiosyncracies, and so forth. Moreover, we were welcomed as special guests by a cohesive group of people who know how to be hosts.

A Mutual Respect. The frustrations of the first meeting arose due to our guardedness with one another. This entailed skepticism about the value of the other participants' perspectives and an inclination to test one another's technical worth. Nonetheless, when we allowed ourselves to see that there were ways of approaching or discussing a problem other than our own, we began to grow in respect for each other's backgrounds, experiences, and learning. We were no longer in a situation where some were teachers and others students: we had all become both teachers and students, communicating to each other our insights and assimilating those of others. We agreed that we all had something to offer; each person brought something of value to our discussions.

A Shared Focus. Developing a shared focus helped to nourish the mutual respect that grew between us. We all wanted to make a new, integrated statement about the human condition, one that arose from our experience and knowledge of theology, psychiatry, human development, and counseling. Without a shared objective, one perspective would have jockeyed for primacy, thus subordinating other legitimate points of view. Friction and tension would have resulted. Instead, we had to consult with each other about the task at hand and make available to each other our own integral, though specialized, knowledge.

A Frank Confrontation. We could have had the best of accommodations, have experienced the camaraderie of colleagues, and have enjoyed the pursuit of a common goal—and all would have been to little avail if we had not been honest with each other and ourselves. Typical hindrances to an open and fruitful discussion include: language, territory, priority (agenda setting), and identity.

(1) *Language.* Every discipline develops and guards its own language by which it makes observations, explains concepts, and fosters communication between its members. Language clarifies and labels data, and so identifies a group's perspective on reality. Technical language can reveal as well as obscure. Yet if true dialogue between disciplines is to take place, participants must be open to new words and realize the limitations of familiar words in order to gain a broader understanding of reality.

(2) *Territory.* The territory staked out by a discipline for study is as closely guarded as are sovereignties: it is protectively watched for threats to boundaries. The pulpit for clergy and the consulting room for physicians are clear and easily maintained territories of privilege and expertise. Between religion and the social sciences there are large areas, intellectual and operational, open to dispute and sometimes bitterly contended. Yet if disciplines are to assist each other in understanding the human condition, territorial conceptions of knowledge must be abolished altogether and replaced by perspectival models of the disciplines.

(3) *Priorities.* Every discipline works to establish internal priorities. It determines for itself which question comes first or which course of action should be pursued for the orderly and appropriate response to human need or curiosity. But interdisciplinary work demands flexibility from all participants to seek a common agenda, which typically addresses a widespread or urgent problem.

(4) *Identity.* Each discipline works from a specific set of possible questions and observations, and thus obtains its identity. Medicine, sociology, psychology, philosophy, and theology—each has its identity in a body of primary questions and answers. Concerns about preserving this identity may make a discipline forget how to ask other interesting questions. In an open and free dialogue, specialists can reassess and clarify their primary pursuits of knowledge but also find new ventures for their respective disciplines by entertaining hitherto neglected questions.

The limitations of language, territory, priority, and identity wove in and out of our discussions over the years that the group stayed together; some of these are evident in every chapter of the book. However, it is also evident that many impediments were overcome by the participants' increasing willingness to confront themselves and the others with the dynamics that accrued during the course of our time together.

CONTRIBUTORS

Robert S. Bilheimer, Ph.D., Theologian
Executive Director, 1974-1984, Institute for Ecumenical and Cultural Research, Collegeville MN

Michael A. Cowan, Ph.D., Psychologist
Family Therapist, St. Cloud MN, and Adjunct Professor of Pastoral Theology, St. John's University, Collegeville MN

J. Alfred LeBlanc, M.D., Psychiatrist and Psychoanalyst
private practice, Bethesda MD

Bernard A. Nachbahr, Ph.D., Philosopher
Department of Philosophy, Loyola College, Baltimore MD

Paul W. Pruyser, Ph.D., Clinical Psychologist
Henry March Pfeiffer Professor Emeritus of Education and Research, The Menninger Foundation, Topeka KS

Theodore Runyon, Ph.D., Theologian
Candler School of Theology, Emory University, Atlanta GA

Jai Poong Ryu, Ph.D., Sociologist
Department of Sociology, Loyola College, Baltimore MD

A. W. Richard Sipe, M.S., Counselor
Private Practice Associates, Timonium MD, and Adjunct Professor of Pastoral Counseling, St. Mary's Seminary and University, Baltimore MD

Archie Smith, Jr., Ph.D., Pastoral Theologian
Foster Professor of Pastoral Psychology and Counseling, Pacific School of Religion, Berkeley CA

Clyde J. Steckel, Ph.D., Pastoral Theologian
Professor of Pastoral Theology and Academic Vice-President, United Theological Seminary of the Twin Cities, New Brighton MN

SUBJECT INDEX

NAME INDEX

— • —